'To succeed in life you need two things:
ignorance and confidence.'

Mark Twain

CONTENTS

DISCARDED

EVEN MORE

THINGS THAT NOBODY KNOWS

501 FURTHER MYSTERIES of LIFE, the UNIVERSE and EVERYTHING

WILLIAM HARTSTON

Atlantic Books
London

First published in hardback in Great Britain in 2015 by Atlantic Books,
an imprint of Atlantic Books Ltd.

1 2 3 4 5 6 7 8 9

A CIP catalogue record for this book is available from the British Library.

Trade paperback ISBN: 978-1-78239-610-9
E-book ISBN: 978-1-78239-611-6
Paperback ISBN: 978-1-78239-612-3

Printed in Great Britain
Design: carrdesignstudio.com
Illustrations: © Nathan Burton

Atlantic Books
An Imprint of Atlantic Books Ltd
Ormond House
26–27 Boswell Street
London
WC1N 3JZ

www.atlantic-books.co.uk

INTRODUCTION

'Real knowledge is to know the extent
of one's ignorance.'

Confucius (6th–5th century BC)

I have always found it much more enlightening listening to experts talking about what they don't know rather than what they do know. Only when we start peering over the boundaries of human knowledge do things begin to grow really interesting.

Every year, an estimated 1.5 million papers appear in academic journals. Each one of these pushes the boundaries of our knowledge a little further forwards. Just as important, it points the way into the unknown, giving us ideas for where our explorations should go next. The majority of the 501 unanswered questions in this book are about those areas where 'further research is needed', as the writers of those papers love to put it. Even if that is only a way of asking for their research grant to be renewed, it may also serve as a bright signpost into the unknown.

When I wrote the previous *Things That Nobody Knows* book in 2011, some readers were apparently disappointed that I did not give answers to the 501 questions posed. They both missed the point and clearly didn't read the title carefully: if I, or anyone else, were able to give the answers, the questions wouldn't have been in the book. These aren't the things that *most* people don't know; they are the things that *nobody* knows.

So here are another 501 unanswered questions. I hope you will find that my discussion of each of them is nonetheless enlightening, intriguing and in some cases even amusing.

William Hartston
Cambridge, 2015

AESOP

1. Was Aesop a fable?

The collection of stories known as Aesop's Fables dates back to around the sixth century BC, but whether Aesop himself was fact or fiction is still an open question. Herodotus, in the fifth century BC, and Aristotle in the fourth century BC both wrote of Aesop being a slave in Samos. Plutarch, some 300 years later, wrote of Aesop visiting Delphi on a diplomatic mission, annoying the locals and being thrown from cliffs to his death. Later still, probably around the first century AD, a work entitled *The Aesop Romance* appeared, putting together and further embellishing tales of Aesop's life.

Great doubt, however, has been cast on the accuracy of these tales, and in some cases the chronology simply does not add up. In 1965 the Aesop scholar Ben Edwin Perry concluded that much of what had been written about Aesop 'must be reckoned as literary fiction'. So the question of whether Aesop himself was a fable is still open.

'Ignorance is the softest pillow on which a man can rest his head.'

Michel de Montaigne

ALCHEMY

2. Who was Fulcanelli?

In the 1920s a Frenchman who called himself Fulcanelli gained the reputation in Paris of being the last of the great alchemists. His writing style and knowledge of Latin, Greek and several modern languages marked him out as a well-educated man and references in his writings to a wife suggest that he was married, yet no evidence has been found of his education or marriage. He disappeared in 1926, after which tales of alleged sightings have only added to the mystery surrounding his true identity.

Fulcanelli is said to have met with the Russian/French spy Jacques Bergier in 1937 to warn him of the dangers of atomic explosives, which he said alchemists had known of for centuries. He is also said to have told a pupil, Eugène Canseliet, the secret of transmuting lead into gold, and there is an account of Canseliet demonstrating the method successfully by turning 100 grams of lead into gold at the gasworks of Sarcelles in the north of Paris.

Canseliet was also responsible for ensuring the publication of Fulcanelli's great work, *Le Mystère des cathédrales*, which his master had left with him before he disappeared. It has been suggested that Fulcanelli was in fact Canseliet himself, which would of course have involved a deception of great ingenuity to stage the disappearance of a man who didn't exist.

Canseliet insisted that Fulcanelli survived the Second World War and that the two men had their last meeting in 1953, when Fulcanelli would have been in his eighties but was said to look about thirty years younger. Canseliet died in 1982 and, if one is to believe the tales about

Fulcanelli, the secrets of the Philosopher's Stone and eternal youth vanished with him.

SEE ALSO FRANCE 201; LONGEVITY 280; PHYSICS 372

ALCOHOL

3. Why does alcohol make women less fertile?

In 1998 a paper was published in the *British Medical Journal* with the title 'Does moderate alcohol consumption affect fertility?' Based on a study of 430 Danish couples who were trying to conceive their first child, it concluded, after correlating their conception rates with their drinking behaviour, that: 'A woman's alcohol intake is associated with decreased fecundability even among women with a weekly alcohol intake corresponding to five or fewer drinks.'

Previous research studies had shown lower conception rates among women who drank more than five units of alcohol a week, but most of them had not detected any such effects for moderate drinking. Another surprise was that: 'Among men no dose–response association was found after control for confounders including women's alcohol intake.' In other words, previous studies reporting low conception rates among male drinkers may have occurred because men who drink a lot may be more likely to have partners who drink a lot and whose conception rates suffer as a result.

Since then, many further studies have failed to reach agreement on whether low alcohol intake can decrease chances of conception. Alcohol has been associated with effects on the production of oestrogen and other hormones in women, but the mechanism by which this occurs is not properly understood.

A further complication was added in 2014 when a study in the USA reported that stress may diminish a woman's fertility. Measurements of the levels of an enzyme associated with stress showed that women with higher levels were twice as likely to be infertile. Since people may have a greater tendency to drink when they are feeling stressed, this finding raises the possibility that the alcohol effect reported in earlier studies may, at least in part, be explained by stress.

See also ATILLA 31; BIOLOGY 58; CANNABIS 87; WINE 494

ANATOMY

4. Why do we have pubic hair?

In the course of human evolution, we have shed a great deal of our bodily hair. With much of our heat loss occurring through the head, it makes sense to have retained hair there to perform a warming function, but armpit and pubic hair need a different explanation. Here are a few theories:

(i) Pubic hair has a similar warming or protective effect for our reproductive organs.

This is hardly convincing. The hair is not very well located to perform either of those functions in regions where it might be useful.

(ii) Hair reduces friction when love-making.

This is also unconvincing when one considers the amount of time people spend making love.

(iii) Hair acts as a protective barrier to prevent dirt and unwanted organisms from entering the vagina or penis.

This appears a more likely explanation, by analogy with the hairs in our ears and nostrils and on our eyelashes and eyebrows, but while pubic hair may perform a similar function for women, it would only have a limited effect in that respect in men. Indeed, a consideration of the relative amount of protection one might think necessary for the vaginal and penile openings, pubic hair might by now be expected to have survived only in women.

(iv) Pubic hair plays a role in mate selection through its ability to enhance bodily smells.

There is some evidence that smells created by secretions from glands near our genitals help us select sexual partners in a manner that is most likely to be evolutionarily successful. These apocrine glands secrete a fluid which only develops an odour when it meets bacteria on the surface of the skin. Our pubic hair is perfectly placed to absorb these fluids, thereby increasing the smell. Whether this theory, and our pubic hair, can survive the ever-increasing use of deodorants, however, is open to question.

5. How did the corpus callosum evolve?

The two halves of our brains are joined by a thick bundle of nerve fibres known as the corpus callosum, which provides the pathways through which the two hemispheres communicate with one another. However, not all animals with two cerebral hemispheres have a corpus callosum. In fact, every species of mammal that develops a placenta during pregnancy has a corpus callosum while non-placental mammals, including all marsupials, do not have one.

In 1863 the zoologist T. H. Huxley wrote: 'the appearance of the corpus callosum in the placental mammals is the greatest and most sudden modification exhibited by the brain in the whole series of vertebrated animals...' Over 150 years later, we still have no idea how the corpus callosum evolved or of any connection between having a placenta and having a corpus callosum.

Having a brain divided into two halves makes little sense unless something joins them, and in the non-placental animals, that function is served by more primitive structures called commissures. How the primitive corpus callosum evolved with the commissures already in place is a mystery.

6. Does the human appendix serve any useful purpose?

Until recently, the appendix was seen as some sort of vestigial organ which may have served some useful purpose in our evolutionary past, but now had no function other than to give people appendicitis. Surgeons would remove the appendix at the first signs of the disease, and sometimes it would be removed as a prophylactic measure when other stomach surgery was being performed.

In the last few years, however, the view has grown that the appendix may have a useful function after all. First, it was found to be a reservoir of useful bacteria that may play a part in the role white blood cells perform in our immune system, and then a comparison of human appendices with those of other animals suggested that there may be more to these organs than had been thought. A study in 2013 reported a hitherto unsuspected degree of evolution in the appendix, suggesting that it had evolved thirty times in its long history to perform varying functions in different animals according to their diets.

Quite what the human appendix does is still unclear, but it is looking more likely that it does have a useful function after all.

7. Why are the left sides of people's faces more expressive than the right sides?

A curious result that has been confirmed in numerous studies since the 1970s is that people find the left sides of other people's faces more expressive, more attractive and generally more fun than the right sides.

It has been conjectured that this may have something to do with the right hemisphere of the brain being more involved with emotions and also controlling the muscles on the left side of the face, but how this would work in shaping human preferences for left or right side is quite unclear and further complicated by the problems caused by mirrors transposing left and right. How can we find the left sides of our faces more expressive when we see them in a mirror, when the image is then on the same side as the right side of anyone we look at?

The closely related question of left–right preferences by painters and their portrait subjects is discussed later (→ ART 25).

See also BRAINS 78, CHINA 103, EARS 162, HUMAN EVOLUTION 237, LEGS 269

ANCIENT CITIES

Our knowledge of the ancient world is infuriatingly incomplete, with remains of many lost cities leaving few if any clues as to who were the people who built them or how they were constructed. Here are just a few such mysteries.

8. Who built the ancient Mexican city of Teotihuacan?

More than a thousand years before the Aztecs arrived in Mexico, the great city of Teotihuacan became one of the world's largest cities. It had an estimated population between 100,000 and 250,000, and its structures included the Pyramid of the Sun, which was one of the largest buildings in the western world.

We do not know who built it; we do not know what name they called it; but archaeological investigations have dated its beginnings to around 100 BC and believe that it reached its zenith between AD 250 and 650. When the Aztecs discovered the ruins of the city, they called it Teotihuacan, meaning 'place where the gods were born', as they believed it to be the place where the world was created.

For a long time, it was thought that the Toltec people built Teotihuacan, but the Toltec civilization did not become powerful until hundreds of years after the city was built, so this seems unlikely. The Totonac, who were another pre-Columbian, pre-Aztec people in Mexico, have also been suggested, and even claimed themselves to have built Teotihuacan, but whether their history goes back that far is also doubtful. When the city collapsed in the seventh or eighth century, so much of it was destroyed that modern archaeologists have been left with few clues as to its origins.

9. Why did Teotihuacan collapse?

Teotihuacan was by any standards, but particularly by those of the first millennium, a huge city, covering a vast area including massive pyramids, temples, canals and canoe traffic. It thrived for at least 500 years, but around AD 550 many of its major buildings were sacked and burnt to the ground, and the city appears to have been completely abandoned in the seventh or eighth century.

With no evidence of a war or of a successfully invading force taking the city over, it has been suggested that the collapse was caused by an internal uprising against the most powerful classes in the city, but again there is no evidence of any other group seizing power. Climate change, droughts and ecological disaster have also been suggested, but without enough supporting evidence to be convincing. With several other sudden collapses of cities and entire civilizations in the region, Teotihuacan serves as a reminder of how little we know about Central and South America in the era before the Aztecs.

10. Who built the city of Nan Madol and how did they do it?

On Pohnpei island in Micronesia in the Pacific Ocean lies the ruined city of Nan Madol. Built within a lagoon, it consists of a number of artificial islands linked by a series of canals, which have led to its being described as the 'Venice of the Pacific', but its origins are unknown.

According to local legend, Nan Madol was constructed by twin sorcerers Olisihpa and Olosohpa, who used a flying dragon to lift the stones used in its construction. Archaeological investigations have failed to support that view, with carbon dating indicating that Nan Madol's construction began around 1200, though the region may have been occupied since 250 BC.

The mortuary sector alone contains over fifty islets on which high walls surround the tombs. On the royal mortuary islet of Nandauwas, the walls are 5.5–7.5 metres (18–25 ft) high, raising the question of where the stones came from to enable all this construction and how they were moved there. A number of possible quarry sites on Pohnpei have been identified, but the exact origin of the stones has not been determined, nor has their method of transportation ever been explained.

11. How did the Incas build Puma Punku?

Like Teotihuacan in Mexico (→ 8 and 9), the Inca city of Puma Punku (or Pumapunku) in Bolivia was identified by a legend as the place the world began, and its age, together with the extraordinary precision of its construction, show why. At its heart, Puma Punku consists of a massive clay mound, decorated with polished metal plaques and brightly coloured fabrics and ceramics, and surrounded by massive stone blocks chiselled to fit together with astonishing accuracy.

Radiocarbon dating shows that the stonework was constructed around the seventh century, but chemical samples from the stones indicate that they came from a quarry 10 kilometres away. The largest of these stone blocks is 7.8 metres long, 5.1 metres wide, 1 metre thick, and weighs about 131 tonnes. The blocks are also said to be cut with such precision that they fit together in a way that would not allow even a razor blade to be inserted between them. The standards of engineering needed both to transport the blocks and particularly to carve them with the necessary precision must have been far in advance of those known to have been achieved by the Incas hundreds of years later.

See also BRAZIL 82; INCAS 247

ANCIENT HISTORY

12. Who built thousands of giant stone wheel-like structures in the Middle East?

In 1927 RAF pilot Percy Maitland was on a routine mail delivery flight in the Middle East when he spotted beneath him hundreds of wheel-like patterns up to 70 metres in diameter made of stone. When he asked local

Bedouin tribesmen about them, he reports that their reaction was fearful and all they would say was that they were 'the works of old men'.

Stretching from Syria to Saudi Arabia, they are only visible from the air and are now known to number well into the thousands. They depict a number of designs, the most common of which is a circle with spokes radiating from the centre, but the direction of the spokes seems to follow no clear pattern. Several conjectures have been made of their purpose, but none are more than guesses. They are thought to date back around 2,000 years, but who made them and why is totally unknown.

13. How did ancient Minorcans build the Taulas?

The Taulas is the name given to thirty-five huge stone megaliths on the island of Minorca. Their appearance is remarkably like the similar structures at Stonehenge in England, but rather than being together at one place, as they are at Stonehenge, they are scattered at various locations throughout the island. Each Taula (which takes its name from a Catalan word meaning 'table') consists of one or two stones over 3 metres high, with a stone of similar size placed horizontally across the top.

They are thought to have been constructed by the Talayot people, who are believed to have lived in Minorca for around 2,000 years until the Romans arrived in 123 BC, but their reasons for building them and the means by which they transported and lifted the huge monoliths are an even greater mystery than that of Stonehenge. The positions of the stones at the English site at least seem to be connected with the motion of the Sun, which indicates a purpose connected with astronomy or astrology, but the Minorcan stones offer nothing more than a weak hint in that many of them appear to be set in horseshoe patterns facing south.

One theory is that the Taulas were used to predict solar eclipses; another suggestion is that they formed part of a healing ritual; but we know so little of the Talayot people and their beliefs that evidence for such ideas is scanty.

See also ANCIENT CITIES 8–11; ANCIENT ROME 14; CHINA 99–103; EGYPT 168; INCAS 247; MAYANS 293; MESOPOTAMIA 305; MUMMIES 322; PREHISTORY 380–3; TURKEY 457

ANCIENT ROME

14. What happened to Spartacus?

We all know, even if only from the 1960 film starring Kirk Douglas, that Spartacus was a slave and gladiator who plotted an escape from his captors and led an uprising of his fellow slaves against the might of the Roman empire. Taken by surprise by Spartacus' forces, and hampered by the fact that many of their legions were taking part in other military operations, a number of Roman army camps were overrun, which enabled the slave army to grow to around 70,000 men in the years around 70 BC.

Spartacus' forces were finally defeated by the legions of Pompey and some Roman historians said that Spartacus was slain in the final battle, but his body was never found. Six thousand survivors were captured and crucified along the Appian Way, but Spartacus was not among them. Had he been captured or his body found, the Romans would no doubt have wished to make a spectacle of him, so precisely what happened to him is a mystery.

Another problem concerns the intentions of Spartacus in his battles against the Romans. His aim had always been to fight his way to freedom and lead his followers across the Alps and back to their homelands, but when that objective was in sight, he turned his forces back towards Rome and the final hopeless battle. Some of his men may not have joined this final march, but escaped over the Alps. There is a slim possibility that Spartacus did the same.

See also ENGLISH HISTORY 177; ITALY 258; NAMES 334

ANIMALS

15. Is the number of animal species on Earth increasing or decreasing?

Environmentalists and ecologists frequently warn us of the potentially negative effects of human activity on biodiversity. Hunting and deforestation reduce animal numbers, constantly driving more species to the verge of extinction. Yet while this is going on, new species are constantly being discovered, and we have no idea whether they have existed unnoticed for centuries or are recently evolved.

Around 1.3 million species have been named and catalogued, and each year another 15,000 or so are added to the list. Attempts to estimate the total number of species on Earth have varied between about 3 million and 100 million. In 2011 a paper was published using a new and apparently logical method, which came up with an answer of 8.7 million plus or minus 1.3 million. All estimates are based largely on the number of species that have already been identified and the rate at which new ones are being discovered. That, however, may be more a measure of human activity and interests than the true biodiversity that exists.

Research on flies and fleas and periwinkles and urchins and many other creatures has shown that animals evolve into new species to cope with environmental changes. Even changes wrought by human intervention may be creating as many new species as we destroy. Frankly, we have no idea.

16. Are there more species on land or in the oceans?

One of the problems of estimating species numbers is our relative lack of knowledge of life in the oceans, particularly at great depths. The research mentioned in the previous item estimated the number of species on Earth as 6.5 million on land and 2.2 million in the oceans, but those figures were based on what we know now. Yet 71 per cent of the planet is covered by seas and oceans, with only 29 per cent land. So why should we believe that there are three times as many species on land as in the water?

Perhaps because we live on the land ourselves, our researches have concentrated on that 29 per cent of the planet, for reasons of both convenience and anthropic self-interest.

17. How should a species be defined?

Before we can even try to answer the previous two questions, we need to come up with a good working definition of what a species is, and that is not as easy as it may seem. When Charles Darwin wrote *On the Origin of Species* in 1859, he spent some time trying to explain to the reader what he and others meant by the word 'species'. The nearest he came to a definition was this: 'I look at the term species, as one arbitrarily given for the sake of convenience to a set of individuals closely resembling each other.'

The words 'arbitrarily' and 'for the sake of convenience', however, are hardly what one is looking for in a rigorous scientific definition. When such a serious definition has been attempted, the scientific literature reveals over twenty versions, each different from the others in some small but significant way. Most such definitions are based on the idea of a population that can interbreed and produce fertile offspring. That introduces the immediate problem of how one expands the idea to include organisms that reproduce asexually, but even if we restrict our attention to sexual reproduction, problems emerge.

What about animals that can mate with each other, in the laboratory or in captivity, for example, but do not do so in the wild? What about three varieties of an animal, A, B and C, distinguishable by sight, of which members of A mate with members of B, and B with C, but A does not, or cannot, mate with C? Should we consider them all the same species?

Darwin himself questioned whether our concept of a species is something that exists in nature, or whether the boundaries between one species and another are too blurred for the word to have a precise meaning. Even now, scientists and philosophers struggle with the same problem. When we cannot even agree whether Neanderthals and *Homo sapiens* were the same species, the task of enumerating all the species on Earth is impossible.

18. Do animals suffer from depression?

In recent years, there have been reports of cats, rats and even goats showing signs of depression. Vets have increasingly been prescribing antidepressants for dogs, and in 2014 the Home Office in the UK was reported to be funding research into whether laboratory monkeys get depressed. The question of whether animals do, or even can, suffer from depression is not so easy to answer.

The problem is that the diagnosis of depression in humans depends on identifying symptoms that are subjective. Animals cannot directly communicate how they feel and the question of whether they can be said to have emotions at all is open. From that point of view, we would have to conclude that we cannot say whether animals suffer from depression.

On the other hand, research has associated certain physical symptoms, such as low serotonin levels in dogs and a shrinking hippocampus in rats, with apparently depressive animal behaviour. This may suggest that a diagnosis of depression for such animals is more than just anthropomorphism. Quite apart from the communication problem, however, we do not understand enough about depression in humans to draw clear conclusions from such evidence about depression in animals (→ PSYCHOLOGY 389).

19. Is there any species of animal in which homosexuality does not exist?

Ever since Darwin, the issue of homosexuality in animals has been contentious. The very idea of it seemed to run against the principles of evolution. It seemed even less compatible with the religious concept of intelligent design, and anyone who suggested that homosexuality might exist in the animal world ran the risk of being howled down by both homophobic and religious communities.

In 1999, however, the Canadian biologist Bruce Bagemihl blew the lid off the gay animal taboo by publishing his book *Biological Exuberance: Animal Homosexuality and Natural Diversity*, which gave a detailed analysis of just how widespread same-sex encounters are in the animal kingdom. Darwinists rationalized that a baby creature looked after by two lesbians could lead to better childcare, while having a gay uncle could also be of positive survival value.

Bagemihl's research indicated that homosexual behaviour had been identified in almost 1,500 species, from apes to worms, and was well documented in some 500 of them. In particular, lesbian albatrosses, gay giraffes and bisexual bonobos have attracted much attention. According to a recent estimate, homosexuality has been observed in around 10 per cent of all known species.

Twenty years ago, animals were generally considered to act by instinct, and instinct made them want to have sex in order to propagate their species. Having sex for fun was out of the question. Now, however, the question is not whether any animal can be considered truly homosexual, but whether some members of every species display such tendencies.

See also under names of individual animals: ANTS, BABOONS, BEARS, BEES, ETC.

ANTS

20. Do ants have personalities?

For social insects, ants can be very cruel to one another. There are over 15,000 known species of ant worldwide which vary considerably in aggression. Some species even live by making slaves of other species. Even within a single species, it has long been accepted that different colonies may display different 'personalities'. Some colonies seem naturally aggressive; others show a marked tendency to run away when threatened. The question of whether individual ants have personalities, however, has only recently begun to be addressed.

Research at the Johannes Gutenberg University in Mainz in 2011 reported that a single colony of ants may display a wide range of aggression in its individuals. Ants with high aggression were employed in fighting other colonies, while less aggressive ants were assigned to brood care. Further evidence for ant personalities was claimed by research at the University of Arizona in 2014, where individual ants of the same species were seen to show different behavioural traits when foraging for food.

It is an open question, however, whether such individual differences are merely the result of learnt behaviour or evidence of truly innate personality differences.

21. Which weighs more: all the people on Earth or all the ants?

In their book *Journey to the Ants* (1994), Wilson and Hölldobler assert that the weight of all the ants on Earth is equal to that of all the humans, but it is far from clear whether this is correct.

As of 2015, there are around 7.2 billion people on Earth with an average weight of about 62 kilograms. That gives a total weight of just over 446 billion kilograms for all the people. The weight of an average ant is estimated to be about 2 milligrams, so for the ants to equal the weight of all the humans, there would need to be 223,000 trillion of them. Nobody really has much idea of the true figure for the number of ants in the world, but estimates range from 100 trillion to 10,000 trillion. Even taking the higher figure, the ants would be well behind the humans in weight.

It has also been estimated, however, that there are twenty-seven times as many termites as ants in the world, and termites are generally bigger than ants, so if this is right, there is good reason to believe that all the termites weigh more than all of us.

See also BEES 47; PANGOLINS 354

ART

22. Who was Vermeer's *Girl with a Pearl Earring*?

Thanks to Tracy Chevalier's 1999 historical novel *Girl with a Pearl Earring* and the 2003 film of the same title starring Scarlett Johansson, Vermeer's painting of that name has become one of the world's best-known works of art, but nobody knows who the girl depicted in the painting was.

The work, originally entitled *Girl with a Turban*, is thought to have been painted around 1665–7, and one suggestion is that she could be Vermeer's eldest daughter Maria, who was eleven or twelve at the time. Apart from her being roughly the right age, however, there is no real evidence that she was the sitter.

Another suggestion is that she may have been Magdalena, the only daughter of Vermeer's patron Pieter van Ruijven. The only supporting evidence for that idea is that van Ruijven once owned the painting. In any case, if the girl really is either Maria or Magdalena, it would raise the question of why Vermeer painted her against a totally dark background. Some identification of either the person or the location might have been expected in the picture.

23. What is going on in Velázquez's painting *Las Meninas*?

Velásquez's 1656 painting *Las Meninas* ('The Ladies-in-Waiting') is one of the most enigmatic in the history of art. Velásquez himself is seen in the painting, working on a large canvas, but we cannot see what he is painting, as only the back of the canvas faces us. Behind Velásquez is a mirror in which we can clearly see King Philip IV and Queen Mariana of

Spain, but it is unclear whether the mirror reflects Velásquez's painting or is showing us the king and queen standing outside the painting and watching the scene as Velásquez paints someone or something else.

The other figures in the painting only add to the mystery. At the centre stands the five-year-old infanta Margaret Theresa, who is attended by two ladies-in-waiting, who are the Meninas of the title. On her right are two dwarfs, one of whom is nudging a large dog with his foot. Behind them, the infanta's chaperone may be seen talking to a bodyguard, who is the only figure in the painting who cannot be identified. Right at the back of the painting is the queen's chamberlain, Don José Nieto Velásquez, who is caught in a pose on a staircase with one foot on a higher step than the other. It is impossible to judge whether he is coming into the room or leaving it. It is also unknown whether this Velásquez was related to the painter or not.

Some say that Velásquez is painting the infanta, who at the time was the only child of the king and queen, and the function of the other characters in the painting was to keep the young child entertained while she sat for the painting. Meanwhile, her parents are watching, as seen in the mirror. Several of the characters, however, are seen looking out of the canvas directly at the viewer. Some have taken this to suggest that the whole painting depicts the viewpoint of the king and queen as they watch Velásquez painting their daughter. The fact that one of those looking directly out of the picture at us is Velásquez himself adds further mystery to the question of who is looking at whom. Perhaps the fundamental uncertainty is conveyed by the idea of looking at a painting and seeing the painter looking back at us.

No two art critics or historians seem to agree on their interpretation of this picture. All they agree on is that it is a masterpiece.

24. Did Thomas Gainsborough use skimmed milk in his *Study of a Cow*?

In the 1770s Thomas Gainsborough experimented with unusual innovative techniques to improve the pictorial quality of his drawings on paper. According to the 1772 Royal Academy exhibition catalogue, his drawings were 'in imitation of oil painting'. Gainsborough himself, in 1773, revealed 'my secret of making those studies' when using chalk for his drawing, telling how he would dip his paper in skimmed milk to adhere the white chalk to it, thereby building up layers of chalk and colour. Finally, he would complete the work with varnish or, as he put it, 'float it all over with Gum'.

The collection at Tate Britain includes Gainsborough's *Study of a Cow in a Landscape*, which it dates to 1758–9. This is a pencil drawing on paper which, according to the Tate's own description of the work, 'has been coated with a layer of fixative which has subsequently discoloured'. They go on to say: 'Gainsborough recommended "skim'd milk" for fixing chalk, but whether he used the same substance for fixing pencil is not known.'

Using skimmed milk to fix a drawing of a cow would have been somehow appropriate, but whether Gainsborough would have let such a thing influence him is unlikely.

25. Why do most portrait sitters incline their heads to the right?

Several studies of portraits have identified a significant bias in the way the face of the sitter is inclined. One comprehensive study of nearly 1,500 portraits painted in Europe over the last 500 years found that roughly 60 per cent showed the sitter favouring the left side of their face. Male portraits showed this tendency 56 per cent of the time, portraits of women 68 per cent. Later studies confirmed this finding, extending it back to the fourteenth century and American paintings. Paintings depicting the Crucifixion were found to display the left side of Christ's face more prominently an astounding 90 per cent of the time. A recent study showed that the same is true of selfie photographs: the left side of the face is preferred.

Why this should be so is not at all clear. One theory links it to the differences in function between the two sides of the brain. Emotions are said to be controlled by the right brain, which also controls the muscles in the left side of the face. This would tie in with other research reporting that the left sides of our faces are seen as more sensitive and generally pleasing. On the other hand, other studies have shown that when we look at other people's faces, we pay more attention to their right sides, which is odd if we think the left side is more sensitive and pleasing.

Such lateral preferences are often most simply explained by the fact that a large majority of people are right-handed, but the portrait results still seem to be true for left-handed painters. The main exception seems to be self-portraits, but as these were generally painted with the use of a mirror, even that may confirm the general finding.

The ambidextrous Leonardo da Vinci was one of the few painters who showed no left or right preference in his portraits, though it should be noted that the Mona Lisa, who is the subject of his most famous portrait, is indeed inclining the left side of her face towards the artist. And so is Vermeer's *Girl with a Pearl Earring* (→ 22).

See also AUSTEN 33; AZTECS 38; BIBLE 53; CODES 107; HITLER 232; HUMAN EVOLUTION 238; LEONARDO 273; MUSIC 330–1; OPERA 348

ASPARAGUS

26. Does asparagus make our urine smell?

The science of post-asparagus urine sniffing goes back to 1731 when the Scottish mathematician and doctor John Arbuthnot wrote that 'asparagus affects the urine with a foetid smell'. Marcel Proust said that asparagus 'transforms my chamber-pot into a flask of perfume', while Benjamin Franklin, in a letter to the Royal Academy of Brussels in 1781, wrote that 'A few stems of asparagus eaten shall give our urine a disagreeable odour'.

For almost 200 years, asparagus retained this reputation, until in the 1950s some research papers appeared suggesting that the effect of asparagus on urine was not universal – it was detectable in some people but not others. In 1980 a classic experiment was conducted in Israel in which subjects were asked to sniff not only their own urine but that of other subjects who may or may not have eaten asparagus.

The conclusion was that people differ not in the production of smelly post-asparagus urine but in the ability to detect the smell: 'Those who could smell the odour in their own urine could all smell it in the urine of anyone who had eaten asparagus, whether or not that person was able to smell it himself.' They also reported that 10 per cent of their subjects could detect the smell even at very low concentrations, which suggested that some people were hypersensitive to the odour.

In the 1980s research generally seemed to support the view that we all produced the smell, but only some of us could detect it, and chemists even identified a number of sulphurous compounds, including methanethiol, in post-asparagus urine that could be producing it. A study in 2011, however, reported that three out of thirty-seven subjects produced urine after eating asparagus in which the characteristic smell could not be detected by any of the other subjects.

Researchers seem to be coming round to the view that the ability to produce the smell and the ability to detect it are two distinct traits, probably genetically based. According to another report in 2011, 'excreting may be a simple one-gene character, with the allele for excreting dominant, but more work needs to be done'. The same report also concluded that 'There is no family data on the smelling/non-smelling trait... so more work needs to be done on this trait as well'.

ASTRONOMY

27. How do stars form in galaxies?

In the immediate aftermath of the Big Bang, the universe consisted of radiation and subatomic particles. Out of that were formed the stars, star clusters and galaxies we know today, but how that happened is a matter of intense dispute. Did the small particles clump together into bigger and bigger celestial bodies, or did the early universe consist of even huger bodies than we know today, which later split into galaxies?

On the one hand, everything is being brought together by the gravitational pull of every particle on every other particle; on the other hand, the energy of the expansion of the early universe is flinging everything apart. Our knowledge of what must have happened in the earliest moments after the Big Bang led astronomers to produce the idea of dark matter and dark energy, without which everything would indeed have fallen apart. The gravitational forces exerted by the mass we can detect is far too little to hold it all together.

The latest hope for progress on this question lies in the study of some recently discovered dwarf galaxies in the Milky Way which have appeared in regions thought to be free of dark energy. These may provide a clue to where stars come from and how they form.

28. Why do space probes change speed?

When space probes are sent on long missions, their routes are often calculated to take them via the regions of planets or moons in order to use the gravitational fields of those bodies to add to their momentum. Gravity accelerates their speed in the region of the body before they are catapulted out into space again.

For over twenty years, precise monitoring of such craft has revealed something known as the 'fly-by anomaly', which causes an unexpected variation in the craft's speed. In 1990 and 1992, when the Galileo space probe flew over Earth, its speed increased by a small but totally unexpected four millimetres per second on both occasions. In 1998 the spacecraft NEAR was measured to be going at thirteen millimetres per second faster than it ought to have been, and similar anomalies were found for Cassini in 1999 (whose speed was two millimetres per second less than expected), and for the Messenger and Rosetta probes in 2005.

In all these cases, the deviation from the expected speed was tiny, but it remains unexplained. Various theories have been put forward, including solar radiation, the influence of tides, magnetic fields, dark matter and a hypothetical gravitomagnetic field, but none of these has attracted great support, so the mystery remains.

29. Why is Betelgeuse shrinking?

Over the past twenty years, astronomical observations have shown that the star Betelgeuse seems to be getting smaller. Between 1993 and 2009 it was reported to have lost 15 per cent of its size, and nobody is sure why. Actually nobody is even sure whether these figures can be trusted or are just an illusion, but recent measurements from the Hubble Space Telescope seem to confirm that it is smaller than it used to be.

Betelgeuse, in the constellation Orion, is one of the brightest stars in our sky. It is a red supergiant 600 light years away; it is about 135,000 times as bright as our Sun, with a diameter about 700 times that of the Sun, and it is believed to be near the end of its life. Soon – which in astronomical terms means probably within a million years, and perhaps as soon as a thousand – it will explode into a massive supernova. In our skies, it will be as bright as the full moon, and it is possible that its decrease in size is part of its process of dying. It could also be due to a number of other factors:

(i)   Red supergiants do not have a true surface. They are just a core surrounded by massive balls of gas, so we may be measuring something happening in the atmosphere of Betelgeuse rather than the star itself.

(ii) Betelgeuse is rotating but it is not spherical; it may have just turned and be presenting a smaller surface towards us.

(iii) There is evidence that such stars undergo an oscillation in their apparent size. Two such pulsations have already been identified for Betelgeuse. We may have just caught it in another slimming period which will be followed by one in which it regains its former size.

(iv) The whole thing may be an illusion caused by temperature differences in different parts of Betelgeuse's atmosphere.

A decent supernova has not been widely seen on Earth since 1054, and an explosion of Betelgeuse promises to be even brighter than that one. Those who hanker after great astronomical events would be delighted to hear that Betelgeuse's weight loss is a real sign of its impending death, but the truth is we just don't know.

30. What, if anything, was the Star of Bethlehem?

Now when Jesus was born in Bethlehem of Judaea in the days
of Herod the king, behold, there came wise men from the east to
Jerusalem, Saying, Where is he that is born King of the Jews? for we
have seen his star in the east, and are come to worship him.
Matthew 2:1–2 (King James Bible)

Was there really such a star, or is Matthew's tale just a piece of religious romanticism?

The birth of Christ is now dated at around 4 BC. It cannot have been later, for that was the date Herod the Great died and Herod is clearly identified as king at the time of the birth. So what was going on in the sky at that time? Anyone in search of astronomical verification of the star has a surprising number of candidates to choose from.

The only genuine star among those candidates is found in the records of Chinese astronomers which identify a new star being born in the constellation of Aquila in 4 BC. A new star, or nova, can be bright when it first appears, then fade, so it might have drawn the attention of the wise men. Whether one tiny new star could have been seen as sufficiently important to draw them to Jerusalem, however, seems unlikely.

A more visually striking candidate is not a star at all but a comet. In 5 BC a bright comet appeared in the constellation of Capricorn, which was again recorded by the Chinese. This would have appeared in the southern sky with its tail pointing upwards. This could be taken as a south-pointing signpost, and Bethlehem was due south of Jerusalem, so following the 'star' might have taken the wise men to the right place. One problem with this theory, however, is that comets tended to be associated with disasters or other destructive events.

A third idea rejects the star or comet hypotheses and suggests that the event was a triple conjunction of Jupiter and Saturn, which would have brought the Sun, the Earth and those two planets into close alignment in the sky on three closely spaced occasions. The appearance of two bright planets together in the sky would have made quite an impact on people who believed in astrological portents.

Finally, the Greek astronomer George Banos published a paper in 1979 suggesting that the 'star' was in fact the planet Uranus, which the

Magi had discovered some 1,800 years before William Herschel did so.

See also BIG BANG 54–6; BLACK HOLES 70–1; COSMOLOGY 117–26; ENERGY 172–4; MARS 285–6; MILKY WAY 315–17; OUTER SPACE 350; SOLAR SYSTEM 441–4; UNIVERSE 463–7; VENUS 479–80

ATILLA

31. How did Atilla die?

The Huns were a nomadic people who lived in eastern Europe and central Asia between the first and fifth centuries AD. Little is known about them until the fifth century when, under the leadership of Atilla, they became an unlikely threat to the Roman empire, both in the east and the west. His campaigns stretched from Persia to Constantinople to Roman Gaul and to Italy itself, all of which he attempted and failed to conquer. In 453, at the estimated age of forty-seven, Atilla died, though the cause of his death has never been clear.

The only contemporary account was by a chronicler named Priscus, who said that Atilla suffered a severe nosebleed at a banquet held to celebrate his marriage and choked to death in an alcoholic stupor. A later analysis of this story from a more modern medical viewpoint suggested that the nosebleed might have been a symptom of internal bleeding caused by a condition called oesophageal varices, which can be caused by heavy drinking. However, the Roman chronicler Marcellinus Comes, writing some eighty years later, reported that Atilla was stabbed by his wife.

For over 1,500 years, historians had only these two versions to choose from and most went for Priscus' account, despite the fact that other accounts of Atilla's life portrayed him as a man of simple tastes who did not drink excessively. Comes' account was generally viewed simply as a means of blackening Atilla's name.

In 2005, however, a new theory emerged in a book by the American philologist Michael A. Babcock called *The Night Atilla Died*. In his view, Atilla had made enough enemies during his rise to power and subsequent conquests for an assassination to be a distinct possibility. Indeed, there is evidence of a failed plot to have him killed a year or two earlier. A painstaking reconstruction of the politics of the time led Babcock to believe that Priscus' account was just a cover story for an assassination plotted by Emperor Marcian, ruler of the Eastern Roman empire in the 450s.

According to legend, after Atilla's death his body was placed in a triple coffin of gold, silver and iron, which was buried under a riverbed. The burial party were all killed when they returned, so that nobody would be able to find the body. Until it is found, however, there seems no hope of advancing our knowledge of how he died.

32. What language did the Huns speak?

Under Atilla, the Huns conquered much of Asia and a good deal of Europe to form a huge empire, yet we do not know what language they spoke. It is not even known if they had a script for writing their language, and the little we do know has come through the writings of others. All we have to go on are a few unidentified inscriptions on pots which may or may not have been part of the Hunnic language, and three words which are the only ones generally agreed to be Hunnic: *medos*, a drink possibly similar to mead; *kamos*, a drink made from barley; and *strava*, a word for a funeral feast. These words, together with the names of various Huns, have fuelled a long debate about the origins of the language, but there is no agreement on which other languages it may be related to, if any.

AUSTEN

33. What did Jane Austen look like?

Only two paintings of Jane Austen exist that were painted in her lifetime: both were by her sister Cassandra, and one is a back view. The other, an unfinished portrait, was painted in 1817, the year of Jane Austen's death, and depicts her looking pale and rather sickly. Her family reportedly declared the painting a bad likeness, and fifty years after her death her nephew James Edward Austen-Leigh commissioned an artist to paint a more flattering portrait of her.

His own account of his aunt, in his 1872 *Memoir of Jane Austen*, described her as 'very attractive' and went on to say:

> *Her figure was rather tall and slender, her step light and firm,
> and her whole appearance expressive of health and animation. In
> complexion she was a clear brunette with a rich colour; she had full
> round cheeks, with mouth and nose small and well-formed, bright
> hazel eyes, and brown hair forming natural curls round her face.*

In 2014 the forensic artist Melissa Dring was commissioned to produce a waxwork of Jane Austen based on that description. Austen lovers generally approved of the result, which was definitely more cheerful than Cassandra's portrait, but whether it looked more like her or was just an idealized chocolate-box type of image is open to debate.

34. What did Jane Austen die of?

In the last year of her life, Jane Austen suffered from increasing ill health. She described her illness as 'bile' and a form of rheumatism, but she found herself having difficulty walking or finding the energy to work. She died on 18 July 1817 at the age of forty-one.

For many years, her death was attributed to a chronic disorder of the adrenal glands now known as Addison's disease, but recently a number of alternative diagnoses have been made. One suggestion is Hodgkin's lymphoma, a type of cancer affecting the white blood cells. Another idea is bovine tuberculosis, which is now associated with drinking unpasteurized milk. And finally there is Brill–Zinsser disease, a recurrent form of typhus which she is known to have had as a child.

Unsurprisingly, there is little enthusiasm for the idea of exhuming Jane Austen's body and trying to settle the matter.

AUSTRALIA

35. When did the first Aboriginal people reach Australia?

Until about 12,000 years ago, Australia, New Guinea and Tasmania were joined by a land bridge and together formed a continent which has been called Sahul. The earliest colonization of Australia is thought to have been by settlers crossing this land bridge from New Guinea. These settlers would have been the ancestors of the Aboriginals, but when they first reached Australia has been hotly debated.

The traditional view, supported by carbon dating of various artefacts, puts their arrival at 40–45,000 years ago. Carbon dating, however, is considered an unreliable method in general for dating items more than 40,000 years old, so the first Aboriginals would be stretching it to its limits and the true answer could be further back in history.

More recently, thermoluminescence has been increasingly used for dating ancient objects. Like carbon dating, it is based on measurements of radioactivity, but it is not linked to the decay of an isotope of carbon, so is not subject to the same limitations.

A few sites in northern Australia have been dated by thermoluminescence to around 50,000 years ago, but recent finds in western Australia have been dated to 70,000 years ago, while reef deposits in Queensland have suggested that humans may have been there up to 100,000 years ago. The most extreme suggestion came in 1998 when data from a rock shelter in northern Australia were published suggesting that artefacts had been found in levels of sand that had been dated by thermoluminescence to between 116,000 and 176,000 years ago.

Until we have more confidence in the results of thermoluminescence as a dating method, or some more accurate method is developed, the debate will continue.

See also BIRDS 69; DOLPHINS 156; HUMAN EVOLUTION 240; KANGAROOS 265; MICE 313; PLATYPUS 374

AUTISM

36. Can vaccines cause autism?

In the 1990s huge debates erupted on the question of whether certain vaccinations that were routinely being given to children increased the chance of those children developing autism. In the USA the prime suspect was thimerosal, a preservative containing mercury that was often added to extend the shelf life of various vaccines. In the UK the argument centred on MMR vaccines against measles, mumps and rubella, which were thought by some to have an effect on the brain development of children.

Many studies followed on both sides of the argument, but the majority of medical opinion seems to support the view that vaccines do not cause autism and the entire scare resulted from the fact that the first symptoms of autism tend to occur in children around the same time as vaccines are administered. Nevertheless, in 1999 the American Academy of Pediatrics and vaccine manufacturers reached an agreement that thimerosal should be reduced or eliminated in all childhood vaccines for children aged six or younger.

Since then, further studies have been published showing that the rates of autism among children receiving thimerosal-containing vaccines are no worse than among children given thimerosal-free vaccines. Despite this, however, several courts in various countries have awarded damages to children for alleged vaccine-induced autism. In 2012 an Italian court ruled that a child's autism had been caused by the MMR vaccine; in 2014 a court in Milan awarded compensation to a child who was adjudged 'more likely than not' to have suffered brain damage and autism because of the neurotoxic mercury and aluminium in a vaccine that contained thimerosal.

Doctors and politicians may be convinced that vaccines do not cause autism, but the legal profession is clearly not so sure.

AVOCADOS

37. How did avocados survive the extinction of the giant sloth?

In order to reproduce successfully, plants need a method to disperse their seeds. Just dropping the seeds on the ground leaves them all competing for the same nutriment in a limited space. Sometimes the seeds are carried by the wind; sometimes they are carried by birds or insects which eat the succulent part of the plant, then excrete the seeds elsewhere. Avocados evolved in the age of giant fauna when huge creatures roamed the land – animals such as the rhinoceros-like *Toxodon*, *Glyptodon*, which was an armadillo the size of a family car, the gomphotheres, which were early four-tusked giant elephants, and *Megatherium*, the giant ground sloth as tall as a giraffe and weighing four tons.

In Mexico the ground sloth is thought to have been particularly effective in spreading avocado stones. Its mouth and digestive tract had no problems coping with a whole avocado, and when it had digested the soft fleshy part, it would excrete the stone. Around 13,000 years ago, however, giant sloths and the other megafauna died out, after which there were no animals capable of swallowing a whole avocado.

The Mexicans are known to have cultivated avocado trees from as long ago as 5,000 BC, but that still leaves a gap of 8,000 years since the giant sloths had become extinct. How the avocado survived during that period is a mystery.

AZTECS

38. Was Aztlan, the legendary original home of the Aztecs, a real place?

According to legend, Aztlan was the ancestral home of the Aztec people from which they emigrated to Mexico. According to traditional sources, the Aztec ancestors dwelled in the place of the seven caves called Chicomoztoc, where each cave corresponded to one of the Nahuatl tribes which would later reach the Valley of Mexico, but whether this is all an old myth or Aztlan really existed is unknown.

Some say Aztlan was in northern Mexico, but another idea is that it was in the southern United States. No real evidence has been found of its existence, though a cave painting was recently discovered in Utah that appears to be of an Aztec god. All that would show, however, is that early Aztecs visited Utah, though there is also claimed to be some similarity between the language of the Ute tribe of Native Americans and the Nahuatl language of the Aztecs.

39. Did the Aztecs use wheels for transport?

Although several examples have been found of Aztec toys with wheels on them, there is a curious lack of evidence that the Aztecs ever used wheels for transportation. It has been speculated that they used logs to move large stones when they built their pyramids, but even that is not clear.

There is a theory that the early Aztecs lived in regions that were mountainous or on an island in the middle of a lake. In the former case, carrying things may have been simpler than using a wheeled vehicle, while in the latter, most transportation would have been done by boat, so wheeled vehicles might have been seen as unnecessary. All the same, there must have been times when throwing something on the back of a cart would have been easier than carrying it.

See also ANCIENT CITIES 8–9; CHOCOLATE 105

BABOONS

40. Do baboons eavesdrop?

Baboons make a good deal of noise while having sex. The males grunt loudly and the females emit what have been described as 'long operatic calls'. And in 2007 an academic paper appeared claiming that other male baboons eavesdrop on them while they are doing it.

The experiment reported in the paper involved a group of free-ranging chacma baboons in Botswana. High-ranking male baboons were seen to dominate females and stay with them for up to a week. During that period, the experimenters played the sounds of male grunting and female copulatory squealing through separate loudspeakers. When the speakers were far enough apart, the effect was similar to the sounds associated with a baboon couple breaking up. However, it was not the couples that were being studied but the lower-ranking males.

These seemed to ignore the male grunt and concentrate their attention on the female squeals. Deducing that the female had been left by her lover, the male, who was previously a hopeful bystander, would then rush to approach her and, with luck, would mate with her himself. By eavesdropping, the low-status males were provided with a chance to mate.

It is unclear whether this behaviour can properly be described as eavesdropping or whether the males are simply excited by the sounds of sex. If we do call it eavesdropping, it raises the question of whether female baboons eavesdrop too.

BEARS

41. Why do bears pee in the woods?

American brown bears are known to mark their territory by leaving their scent on trees, either by rubbing against them or by urination. In 2013 research was published showing that, in one region of Canada at least, tree-marking behaviour varied according to food availability (specifically according to the amount of pink salmon in a nearby river). Interestingly, males marked more trees with their scent at times of low food availability, while females marked more trees when food availability was high.

Another research paper in the same year, however, reported that the criteria used by a bear in determining which trees to mark are primarily location, species and size. Bears, they found, will mark trees in often-visited areas and will select the largest trees and those of rarer species.

There appears to be more going through a bear's mind when it chooses which tree to rub against or pee on than one might have imagined.

42. Why do female grizzly bears have six nipples?

Male bears, like male humans, have two nipples, but the nipple count on female bears varies according to the species. Female polar bears generally have four nipples, though five or even six have been seen. Female black bears, grizzly bears and Kodiak bears all have six nipples.

In the case of Kodiak bears, this makes sense, as six is a normal litter size for newborn Kodiak bear cubs. Black bears tend to have two or three cubs, though a litter of six has been recorded. Grizzly bears, however, have six nipples and the most common number of cubs in a litter is two or three, though litters of four have been seen. Six nipples therefore seems surplus to requirements.

See also POLAR BEARS 377–8

BEES

43. Can bees count?

Since 1995 a growing amount of research has suggested that bees may be able to count but get into difficulties with numbers greater than four. In that year an experiment was performed in Germany in which bees were trained to find food left for them in a tunnel. As a clue to remembering where they had found the food, a series of 'landmarks' were placed in the tunnel with the feeder positioned between the third and fourth landmarks.

After learning where the food was, the bees would fly past the third landmark and then slow down and start looking for it. Even when the landmarks were placed closer together or further apart, the bees would start looking for the food between the third and fourth landmark. Some bees were seen to fly the same distance before hunting, but the majority seemed to be counting landmarks. When the number of landmarks was increased to five, however, the bees became confused.

In 2008 a similar result was reached by researchers in Australia, who then went on to give the bees a more demanding counting task. This involved the use of a Y-shaped tunnel at the start of which there was a sign at the bottom of the Y, and then two more signs where it branched into two paths. The signs all contained a number of dots and the bee would only find its food reward if it chose the branch with the same number of dots as had been displayed at the start of its flight.

The bees quickly mastered this task, and even when the shape, colour and pattern of the dots were altered, they still chose the path displaying the same number of dots as the starting sign. Again the bees showed the ability to distinguish between three and four dots, but distinguishing between four and five, or even four and six, was beyond them.

Whether the bees are doing something analogous to what we think of as counting is open to question, but the current conclusion seems to be that if bees can count, they can only count up to four.

44. Do bees always dance as well as they can?

Ever since 1967, when Karl von Frisch published his findings in which he decoded the 'waggle dance' of bees, there has been much research on this strange means of communication. By repeatedly running along a figure-of-eight pattern, the bee appears to communicate the quality of a recently discovered food source as well as its direction and how far away it is. Recent research, however, has cast doubt on both the degree of accuracy of the information imparted by the dance and the ability of other bees to follow it.

One interesting finding concerns the direction of the food source. This has been shown to contain an apparent inbuilt error, which grows larger when the food source is closer. One suggestion is that the dancing bee is not trying to convey accurately where the food is but just to give a vague idea in order to get other bees in the colony to forage in the same area in the hope of finding further sources of food. An Australian study published in 2014 suggested that the inbuilt imprecision in the dance may spread followers over a roughly constant area as distance increases and direction becomes more accurate. But are the dancing bees deliberately giving vague information in order to spread their colony members over a wide area, or is inaccuracy of information an inbuilt defect of the dance language itself? After analysing all the studies done on the topic, Kaitlyn Preece and Madeleine Beekman concluded: 'the bees dance as best they can.'

Until we know how much information is conveyed, how much is picked up, and what other means the bees have of communicating to one another the location of food sources, we cannot be sure they are dancing to the best of their abilities.

45. Why do bumblebees spend so long having sex?

In 2009 a study on the mating habits of bumblebees reported that when a male copulated with a queen, the average mating time was thirty minutes and most matings lasted between twenty and forty minutes. When a queen was only allowed to continue mating for between two and five minutes, however, there was only a 7.2 per cent chance on average that she would accept another mating. However, 'Incompletely mated queens... did not show significant difference from fully mated queens in production of new queens and males.' In other words, the longer mating times were found to convey no advantage. As the researchers put it: 'This study shows that colony development was not affected by short copulation duration.' So from an evolutionary perspective, we may well ask why they spend so long over it.

46. How does a single bee find its way home?

There has been a good deal of research on the navigational abilities of bees, but some of the results are contradictory. When a young bee leaves its hive for the first time, it makes a series of figure-of-eight flights of increasing size as though surveying its surroundings and getting its bearings. How it codifies the information it obtains, however, is far from clear.

In 2004 the results of a study into the homing behaviour of leaf-cutter bees was published showing that manipulations of devices forming geometrical figures surrounding a bee's nest could affect its ability to find its way home. 'Manipulations of the edges provided by the boundaries of the device... strongly impaired the homing performance.' Manipulating edges near their hive confused them more than changes to edges further away. 'These results suggest that bees learn the distances of the various edges from the goal.'

A paper in 1995, however, had suggested that, for honeybees, distances were something the bees were likely to ignore. In their paper 'Can honeybees count landmarks?' Chittka and Geiger reported how they trained some bees along a row of four identical tent-shaped landmarks leading from their hive to a feeder. After the training sessions were completed, the number and distance apart of the landmarks were changed. In subsequent trials, most of the bees were seen to fly greater distances when the number of landmarks was decreased and shorter distances when they were increased. Only a significant minority of bees were observed to be flying the correct distances. Similar results have been found for a bee's ability to find its way back to a hive when the landscape is altered.

47. Why are bees so sociable?

There is more to being social than just living together as a group. True sociality, known as 'eusociality', is defined by three features:

(i) co-operative brood care rather than each creature caring for its own offspring;

(ii) an overlapping of generations so that the group may be sustained, with offspring assisting parents; and

(iii) a division of both labour and reproduction with not every individual reproducing equally in the group.

Almost all species in which eusociality has been found are ants, bees, wasps or termites. Bees are especially interesting because different species may show all or none of the above features, or anything in between.

Honeybees, in particular, are eusocial, but how this characteristic evolved is unclear. Analysis of the genomes of different species of bees has shown that eusocial behaviour depends on more than a hundred genes, and it has evolved at least eleven times. The problem is that the eusocial lifestyle involves a large number of individuals being sterile, and sterility is not generally an asset in passing on genes.

In his *On the Origin of Species*, Darwin described the existence of sterile worker castes in social insects as 'the one special difficulty, which at first appeared to me insuperable and actually fatal to my whole theory'. He did find ways of getting round the problem, but there is still no general agreement on how eusociality evolved and how solitary bees developed into eusocial bees.

BIBLE

48. Did the biblical cities of Sodom and Gomorrah exist?

The Book of Genesis tells of the cities of Sodom and Gomorrah being destroyed by fire and brimstone by a wrathful God, and the Qur'an also tells of miracles there, but the question of whether Sodom and Gomorrah were real places is still a matter of debate.

The Greek geographer and historian Strabo, who died around AD 24, wrote of 'thirteen inhabited cities in that region of which Sodom was the metropolis', but no archaeological evidence has been found to support that opinion. A number of excavations around the Dead Sea have found signs of ancient cities, and there have even been claims of signs of fire and sulphur, but nothing very convincing.

The account of fire and brimstone has been linked to a suggestion that the Dead Sea was devastated by an earthquake between 2100 and 1900 BC, which is plausible as the Jordan Rift Valley fault line runs through the region. Another suggestion, however, has been based on an analysis of a cuneiform tablet in the British Museum, thought to have been produced by an Assyrian scribe around 700 BC, which depicts a celestial body heading for Earth. Is this evidence that Sodom and Gomorrah were destroyed by an asteroid impact? Well, probably not, but we cannot rule it out.

49. Was the biblical King David a real person?

As the second king of Israel, David appears as a leading character in the Old Testament, yet there is little historical evidence of his existence. Perhaps this ought not to surprise us: most modern chronologies of the Old Testament story place King David around the tenth century BC, which would place him somewhere towards the end of the Bronze Age. This is not a period from which many documents have survived.

Until the 1990s it could have been fairly claimed that no evidence at all existed outside biblical sources of the existence of King David. In 1993, however, excavations at a site believed to be the ancient city of Dan revealed a victory stone including the letters 'dwd', which are thought to refer to the House of David. The stone has been dated to around 850–835 BC and another victory stone from the same period also contains references to a name that may be that of David.

In 1995 a stone structure was discovered in Jerusalem which it was claimed might have been David's palace, or possibly the Fortress of Zion which David was said to have captured, but the dating of the structure is in great doubt. In December 2014, however, the journal *Near Eastern Archaeology* published preliminary results of an excavation by a team from Mississippi State University indicating signs of a state already being formed in a region east of Gaza in the tenth century BC. If confirmed, this may show that the biblical account of King David has its foundations in fact, but there is still no evidence of how accurately the king himself was portrayed.

50. Who wrote the Book of Esther?

Much doubt exists over the authorship of many parts of the Bible, both Old and New Testaments, but the puzzle over the Book of Esther is greater than most. The book itself gives no hint as to its author and tells the tale of a Jewish girl who becomes queen of Persia and saves her people from genocide. Other than the Song of Songs, which is also of unknown authorship, it is the only book in the Bible which contains no explicit mention of God. There is also not a single act of worship. To add to the mystery, there is also an ancient tradition that the Book of Esther is displayed on a scroll which only has one roller on the left-hand side rather than the customary two, one on each side.

The Babylonian Talmud attributes the writing of Esther to the men of the Great Synagogue, but whoever the author was, he (or she) must have been Jewish with a detailed knowledge of Persian customs and culture. According to the Roman historian Josephus, it was written by Mordecai, who features in the book as the cousin and adoptive father of Esther. Whether Mordecai would have heaped praise upon himself the way the book does, however, gives rise to considerable doubt. The other main candidate for authorship is Ezra.

There is also the question of why this highly unusual book was selected to be included in the official canon of the Old Testament. Perhaps if we knew who wrote it, we would be in a better position to understand that selection.

51. Why did Nebuchadnezzar II go mad for seven years?

Nebuchadnezzar II was a Chaldean king of Babylon who reigned for over forty years until his death in 562 BC. The construction of the Hanging Gardens of Babylon has been ascribed to him, but he is best known through his portrayal in the Book of Daniel in which he is punished by God for his boasting by being driven mad and forced to live like an animal in the wild for seven years.

St Jerome was of the opinion that Nebuchadnezzar was suffering from hypochondriacal monomania, an extreme form of illness anxiety, but more modern writers have made different diagnoses. These include clinical lycanthropy, which involves a belief that one is turning into a wolf, and porphyria, which was the form of madness that was later to afflict King George III of Britain. A form of dementia associated with advanced cases of syphilis has also been suggested, but that is difficult to reconcile with Daniel's account of Nebuchadnezzar regaining his reason after seven years.

Another suggestion is that the biblical story mixes facts from the lives of two Babylonian kings, Nebuchadnezzar II and Nabonidus. A fragment of the Dead Sea Scrolls tells of Nabonidus being similarly smitten by God with a fever for seven years, and there is also an account of Nabonidus spending a long time in the desert. Details of this fever, however, are even more scanty than those of Nebuchadnezzar's lycanthropic madness.

52. Who wrote the Epistle of Mathetes to Diognetus?

In the early years of the Christian church, a group of writers emerged who used information and logical argument to defend the church against its critics and persecutors. These were called 'apologists' and the anonymous author of the Epistle of Mathetes to Diognetus has been called the first apologist.

The one thing we know about its author is that he wasn't called Mathetes, which is a word simply meaning 'disciple'. The identity of its intended recipient is also unclear. There was a tutor of the emperor Marcus Aurelius who was called Diognetus, but it is thought very unlikely that he would have been the person the epistle was directed at.

The epistle itself was found in a thirteenth-century manuscript collection but it was destroyed in a fire in 1870. Fortunately a printed version existed, dating back to 1592, so the text, apart from a couple of lines which were presumably illegible in the original, has been preserved. Written in Greek, it deals with the state of the world at the time of Christ, and the need for His coming, with one chapter on 'Why the son was sent so late'. The names 'Jesus' and 'Christ', however, are never used, with the writer preferring to call him simply 'the son'.

The language and style in which it was written have led to its being dated at some time in the second century, possibly as early as AD 130, which could mean that the writer was a contemporary of one or more of the gospel writers. Whoever he was, he describes himself as 'a disciple of Apostles', but no further clues as to who he was have ever been found.

53. How many wise men did Matthew think visited the baby Jesus?

Now when Jesus was born in Bethlehem of Judaea in the days of Herod the king, behold, there came wise men from the east to Jerusalem. Matthew 2:1

Matthew did not, please note, identify the number of the wise men, nor say that they were kings. The tradition of referring to the 'three wise men' came later and derived solely from Matthew's identification of three gifts: gold, frankincense and myrrh. The identification of the three as Caspar, Balthazar and Melchior, the kings of India, Arabia and Persia, dates only from around AD 500. Referring to them as kings may have its origin in Psalm 72, which predicted: 'all kings shall fall down before him.'

But whether they were kings or not, how many of them did Matthew think there were? One might well think that if there had only been three, he would have specified the number. By saying 'wise men from the east', he gives the impression of a rather larger group. Some early references in the eastern Christian churches referred to twelve Magi, which ties in with the feeling that three would have been too few for Matthew's account.

In Botticelli's 1475 painting *Visit of the Magi*, his sons were the models for the three visitors, so that number must have already been traditional. It was, however, only in 1857 that the number became irrevocably part of the Christmas story, for that was when the Episcopal bishop John Henry Hopkins (1820–91) of Vermont penned the carol known as 'We Three Kings' and that is the way they have been seen ever since – even if they weren't kings, and there were more than three of them.

See also ASTRONOMY 30; CAMELS 83; JESUS 259–63; LITERATURE 276

BIG BANG

54. What happened in the first 10^{-37} of a second after the Big Bang?

Most astronomers now agree that the universe began about 13.8 billion years ago with a huge burst of energy known as the Big Bang. This agreement is comparatively recent. Until about fifty years ago, the debate was over whether we live in a steady state universe or an expanding universe. Indeed, the term 'Big Bang' was coined in 1949 by the astronomer Fred Hoyle to mock those who suggested that the universe had grown from almost nothing.

Increasingly, however, evidence supported the expanding universe theory, and once it was seen that galaxies are moving further and further apart, it became possible to trace the expansion backwards to a point 13.8 billion years ago when it all began. Einstein had taught us the equivalence of energy and matter, and vast experiments, such as those taking place at the Large Hadron Collider at CERN in Switzerland, have increased our knowledge of how the massive explosion of energy at the Big Bang might have led to the creation of the universe as it is now.

Measurements of the cosmic microwave background (CMB), which is a sort of echo of the explosion of the Big Bang, and gravitational waves, whose existence is predicted by some models of what happened immediately following the Big Bang, have led to increasingly refined pictures of the very first moments of the universe.

It must have started with almost inconceivably high temperatures, pressure and energy density forcing rapid expansion and cooling. According to the model now most generally agreed, after about 10^{-37} of a second (that's a decimal point followed by 37 zeros and a 1), a phase known as cosmic inflation began when the universe grew exponentially. Elementary particles such as quarks and gluons began to appear, with the first protons and neutrons appearing at about a millionth of a second after the Big Bang. Electrons and positrons arrived after about one second, after which it took only about another 400,000 years before atoms formed.

But what was going on in that first 10^{-37} of a second before even the elementary particles had come into existence? And that question leads to the next one...

55. What was the nature of the energy that filled the universe at the time of the Big Bang?

When we run time backwards to the moment of the Big Bang, the big question is what happens when we get there. We can talk about the massive expansion that must have taken place when the universe was a tiny fraction of a second old, but when we take it back to time zero, we reach a single point of infinite density and infinite temperature where the laws of physics fall apart. Mathematicians know such an imponderable as a singularity, much like what you get when you try to divide something by zero.

Talking about what happened before the Big Bang makes no sense because we have to get through that singularity to get to a 'before', and all the maths suggests that time itself began at the moment of the bang, so there was no 'before' anyway.

There is no doubt that it all started in the burst of a massive amount of energy, but we have no way of knowing where that energy came from and what its nature was. All we can say is that some unknown form of energy made the young universe inflate at a rate that was faster than the speed of light. That is highly unsatisfactory, of course, but it's the best we can do at present.

56. What is the origin of the matter–antimatter imbalance?

The world of physics, which is the physical world as we understand it, is made up of matter and antimatter. Particles of antimatter have the same mass as their corresponding matter particles but the opposite electric charge. A positively charged positron, for example, is the antimatter equivalent of a negatively charged electron. When corresponding matter and antimatter particles come into contact with each other, the result is mutual annihilation, leaving only pure energy behind.

The same thing in reverse, starting with the energy of the Big Bang, ought to have resulted in an equal number of particles of matter and antimatter popping into existence, then immediately destroying each other and turning back into energy. Yet wherever we look, there seems to be a vast excess of matter over antimatter. From the tiniest life forms to huge galaxies, everything seems to be made out of matter. Even detecting a few particles of antimatter is a huge achievement.

At some moment very shortly after the Big Bang, something must have happened to result in a small excess of matter over antimatter. There is then enough matter to annihilate all the antimatter, with a bit of matter left over to grow into the universe as we know it. But the laws of physics are supposed to be symmetric: if the number of antimatter particles declined, the number of matter particles should have declined too.

Apart from being annihilated by their corresponding partners, particles can disappear through decay, and it is supposed that something must have caused more antimatter to decay than matter. But what that something was is unknown.

See also BLACK HOLES 71; COSMOLOGY 119, 122–4, 126

BIOLOGY

57. Do STAP cells exist?

In 2014 a debate erupted over the existence of a type of cell that would have answered biologists' dreams. Stimulus-Triggered Acquisition of Pluripotency, or STAP for short, was the name given to cells that, like stem cells, had the propensity to develop into any type of cell its organism required. The theory was that if the right stimulus could be found, a developed cell could be turned back into a type of stem cell that could develop into whatever was needed.

If this could be done, it could pave the way towards techniques for regeneration of lost limbs or other body parts, which explains the massive interest aroused by a paper in *Nature* in January 2014 announcing the development of STAP cells in Japan. Over the next few months, huge resources were poured into STAP cell research and a patent was even taken out for the process to produce them.

Then it all began to fall apart, beginning with some deep criticism of the original paper and ending with its retraction after a number of experiments had failed to reproduce its findings. One of its authors has since resigned; another has committed suicide.

None of this, however, proves that STAP cells cannot exist, just that the method claimed for their production has been shown to be wrong.

58. Why are some people so much more prone to drug or alcohol addiction than others?

There can hardly be any aspect of human behaviour that has been so intensively studied yet remains so poorly understood as addiction. Behaviour that starts as simple pleasure-seeking turns into a pathological malfunctioning of the brain's reward system to such an extent that drug-craving overrules the normal decision-making function. Even though the addict knows it is disastrous for him, he cannot give up the habit.

We know that drug dependence is connected to the release of dopamine and other chemicals in the brain which result in a positive emotional state. We know that continued use of drugs results in an increase in synaptic connections between the brain's neurons that strengthen the perceived need for the drug, though we do not know how this happens. We know that some people seem much more prone to addiction than others, though we cannot say why. We know that some addicts seem able to recover completely, while others are prone to a relapse, even long after all withdrawal symptoms have disappeared. In short, we are still some way from understanding the biological basis of addiction and why some people become addicts and others do not.

59. How do our circadian clocks keep time?

Most of us live most of our lives in a cycle in which the Sun rises every morning and sets every evening, leading to a regular rhythm of days of 24 hours in length. Our bodies are geared to that schedule, with our waking and sleeping hours more or less matching it. When something such as jet lag badly disrupts our sleep and waking schedule, our bodies react to it. What keeps us more or less in sync with the Earth's rotation is our circadian clock, which is our bodies' internal time-keeping.

The word 'circadian' comes from the Latin *circa diem*, meaning 'about a day', which is a brilliantly accurate approximation. For our body clocks work to a day length of about 24.5 hours. Why this is about half an hour longer than the real day is unclear. A mouse's body clock, by contrast, is only about 23.5 hours long. One can only speculate on why humans have evolved to feel comfortable about staying up late, while mice want to go to sleep earlier.

In practice, what happens is that our body clocks reset every morning when we wake up. Their operation, however, is not run by the cycle of light and dark. Even if we live in total darkness, or in artificial light providing an apparent day length different from 24 hours, the body clock still maintains its 24.5-hour cycle.

We now know the genes that control the body clock, but we don't know how the circadian clock itself keeps time or how the cells of the body all agree what time it is.

60. How many different proteins make up a human being?

If the human genome is the blueprint for building a human body, then proteins are the building blocks. Between them come the amino acids of which there are about twenty. Proteins are strings of amino acids of various lengths. Since amino acids can be strung together in arbitrary order and the longest known protein is close to 27,000 amino acids long, the number of potential proteins is enormous.

In 2014 two teams in the USA and Germany independently produced drafts for maps of the human proteome – the protein equivalent of the genome. The American team identified proteins encoded by 17,294 genes out of the 19,629 genes that had been predicted to encode proteins. They also found 193 new proteins that came from regions of the genome that had not been thought to code for proteins, so the 19,629 figure cannot be seen as an upper limit. The German team reported a similar result with around 400 unexpected proteins. They referred to 'potentially 20,000 protein-coding genes'.

Research on a large number of human genomes has identified around a million different proteins, while the total number in all terrestrial organisms has been estimated at over 10 million. However, with the most recent results suggesting that gene-counting may be giving a false picture, those figures are no more than an educated guess.

61. How do prions replicate?

First discovered in 1982, prions are quite unlike any other biological structures. Consisting mostly of proteins, they appear to behave like viruses, yet they are not alive, have no DNA or RNA, and therefore cannot reproduce more of their own kind. The do replicate, however, in a manner that can cause degeneration of brain tissue and death, as we have discovered in scrapie in sheep, BSE in cows and CJD in humans, all of which are prion-based diseases.

Prions come in two types: cellular prion proteins, which are normal and harmless, and infectious prions (their name comes from the opening and closing letters of **PR**oteinaceous infect**ION**). Normal prions are thought to have a role in protecting cells, primarily in the nervous system, but infectious prions have the capacity to refold into the infectious form. One factor that makes prion diseases so effective is the body's failure to recognize them as abnormal and thus its inability to produce an immune response.

The big question about their ability to replicate is how the abnormal prion recruits normal prion protein and causes it to convert to the abnormal form.

62. What triggers puberty?

To some extent, we know what triggers puberty in both boys and girls. The hypothalamus in the brain secretes a hormone GnRH (gonadotropin-releasing hormone), which stimulates the pituitary gland to emit luteinizing hormone and follicle-stimulating hormone. These prompt the sex organs to release oestrogen in females and testosterone in males, which lead to the usual signs of puberty in the body.

These signs usually start to appear in girls aged between eight and fourteen and boys aged between nine and fifteen. When they occur in a girl below the age of eight or a boy under nine, it is called 'precocious puberty', and it is such cases that suggest we still have much to learn about what really triggers puberty. In around 50 per cent of cases of precocious puberty in boys and 10 per cent in girls, a physiological or genetic cause can be identified to explain why it happened early, but in the remaining 50 per cent of boys and 90 per cent of girls, no cause can be found. Such cases are known as 'idiopathic precocious puberty', and 'idiopathic' in this expression just means we don't know what triggered it at all.

63. How do some loriciferans live without oxygen?

Until the twenty-first century, every multicellular life form known to man needed oxygen to survive. Even the molluscs known as giant tube worms found in the Pacific at depths of several miles were found to live by hydrothermal vents from which they obtained dissolved oxygen. From 2000 onwards, however, a team of researchers from Italy conducted expeditions to search for life in mud samples deep under the Mediterranean Sea.

Expecting to find only bacteria and viruses, they were surprised to discover signs of multicellular creatures, some of which were found to be still alive. Given the name Loricifera, from two Latin words meaning 'armour-bearing', these strange shelled creatures less than a millimetre long live in the spaces between marine gravel and have now been confirmed as the first multicellular life forms that live in environments totally free of oxygen. Besides a shell, they have a head, a mouth and a digestive system and are thought to live on primitive oxygen-free micro-organisms called hydrogenosomes.

Whether this discovery of loriciferans is the forerunner of similar findings in the oxygen-free deep sea is a matter of speculation, as is the question of whether such creatures could exist on other planets with no oxygen in their atmospheres.

BIRDS

64. Are birds the only creatures alive today that descended from dinosaurs?

The idea that birds descended from dinosaurs dates back to an 1870 treatise by Thomas Henry Huxley in which he pointed out similarities between the skeletal structure of birds and those of some dinosaur fossils. It was the discovery of an archaeopteryx in Germany in 1861 that had led Huxley to his idea, and over the next century further fossil discoveries supported it. Fused clavicles were identified as prehistoric wishbones; flexible wrist joints had much in common with birds' wing joints; and the three-toed feet of some dinosaurs were seen as precursors of birds' feet. Finally, in 1996, came the discovery in China of dinosaur fossils with feathers.

This settled the matter for most, leaving only a few still doubting the dinosaur ancestry of birds, but what is more open to question is whether birds are their only living descendants. What about crocodiles and other reptiles, which at least look more like our common image of dinosaurs than birds do?

Crocodiles are thought to have evolved around 200 million years ago in the Mesozoic era, which was a long time before dinosaurs became extinct, but the term 'dinosaur' (meaning 'terrible lizard') was never intended to apply to all prehistoric animals. Dinosaurs had four legs, an upright gait and lived on the land. Prehistoric crocodiles spent too long in the water and walked with their bodies too close to the ground to be considered dinosaurs. In fact, it is thought that crocodiles and dinosaurs had a common ancestor around 250 million years ago called the archosaur from which both groups evolved independently.

When the vast majority of dinosaurs became extinct, probably after an asteroid impact around 66 million years ago, the survivors included some avian dinosaurs and some species of small dinosaur that later evolved into birds. Turtles, snakes, lizards and about half the species of crocodiles also survived, presumably, in some cases, thanks to their living in the water, but also because of their small size and adaptable metabolisms.

Whether other animals alive today are direct descendants of small dinosaurs that survived the asteroid impact is an open question, though no fossil records have yet been found to allow such a link to be traced back for any modern species.

65. Are crows impatient?

Patience demands self-control and restraint, and until 2011 those aspects of behaviour were thought to be found exclusively in primates. In that year, however, research was published with evidence that crows and ravens could be patient too. The experiments involved giving the birds items of food and training them to wait before they were offered the opportunity to exchange the food for something they liked more.

The design was simple. The bird was placed in an enclosure and given the initial foodstuff. The superior food was in full view outside the enclosure. After a period of time had elapsed, a bell was rung and the bird was offered the chance to exchange the food it had for the one it preferred. It was denied the better food if it had already eaten the first piece, or if it tried to exchange before the bell was rung. The researchers found that crows and ravens could learn to wait for up to 5 minutes 20 seconds, restraining themselves from eating the food they had been given to preserve the chance of exchanging it for something better.

In 2014, however, this view of corvine patience was modified by another paper reporting a refinement of the result. What the new research revealed was that crows can wait for a superior foodstuff but not for a larger portion of the same food. They are patient enough to wait for quality but not for quantity.

In his *Devil's Dictionary* Ambrose Bierce defined patience as: 'A minor form of despair, disguised as a virtue.' For crows and ravens, it is clearly something more complicated.

66. Do female birds prefer intelligent males?

Research on a number of species of birds has shown that females prefer to mate with more intelligent males. Female songbirds choose males with more complex songs, and complexity of song is a sign of superior brain development. Female crossbills choose males who have shown the greatest prowess at foraging. Female bower birds go for males with the snazziest displays in their nests. Both female zebra finches and female bower birds have been shown to go for the males that perform best at problem-solving tasks.

With the exception of the crossbills, however, none of the females in the above studies saw the male performing a task that could be directly linked to intelligence. If we could ask the birds whether they preferred more intelligent males, we cannot tell if they would say 'yes'.

There is also the possibility that the male birds have simply learned how to attract females. If the girls like a pretty nest, or a nicely warbled song, the brighter males will give it to them. The females need not think of their chosen males as 'intelligent', merely as good home decorators or singers. An increasing number of studies seem to show that intelligent male birds achieve more copulations, but it may be a Machiavellian form of intelligence that is designed just to give the girls what they want.

In any case, intelligence may not be the best thing for males to have in all species of bird. Female African widow birds choose males with the longest tails, and long tails in widow birds have never been associated with a high level of intelligence.

'Learning, *n*. The king of ignorance distinguishing the studious.'

Ambrose Bierce

67. Why do birds return to their nesting grounds in the summer?

Many species of birds escape winter climates by migrating, often over considerable distances. That makes sense. Energy demands increase in cold weather and food becomes scarce. How birds decide where to migrate to, and, even more, why they travel all the way back are puzzling questions.

A recent study on Eurasian spoonbills, for example, showed that the most popular places to spend winter were the most southerly of their common migration sites, which are found in Mauritius and Senegal. Those countries, however, surprisingly turned out to be among the places that had the lowest survival rates for the birds. The spoonbills that set up their winter homes in southern France or Spain tended to do better.

Equally, research on the migratory patterns of birds in North America has raised the question of why they bother to fly all the way back home to their original nesting grounds in the spring. The longer the return flight, the greater the energy expenditure and the greater the danger, so one might expect birds from the far north to move home, stopping at the first hospitable location they fly over in spring. In general, however, that does not happen and the birds fly all the way to the original home again.

68. Why do female boobies cheat on their mates?

How do female birds in basically monogamous relationships choose which males to be unfaithful with? According to the 'good genes' hypothesis, a female who is paired with a low-quality male might be expected to be less faithful (or have more 'extrapair copulations', as the researchers put it) than females with high-quality mates. Research on blue-footed booby seabirds, however, provided no more than very weak support for that idea.

Females with younger mates were found to be more likely to indulge in courtship behaviour with other males, but their choice of which males to copulate with following courtship was not found to be predicted by the age, size, condition or previous breeding success of the male. The female birds with the most attractive partners were found to be more likely to indulge in extrapair copulation with males whose blue feet had the strongest tinge of green. Unattractive females, however, were found to indulge in fewer extrapair copulations than attractive ones, suggesting that male choice may also have some effect on observed female behaviour.

The researchers concluded that 'EP [extrapair] interactions involve more complexity than originally envisioned'.

69. Do male songbirds try harder when singing at more attractive females?

In most songbird species of the northern hemisphere, only the males sing. In Australia and New Zealand, however, both males and females tend to sing. The ability of males and females to sing duets has been given as a reason for stronger pair-bonding in antipodean birds compared with the one-sided role of song in the north, where only the males use song to attract mates.

Research has shown that females are more attracted to longer and more complex songs, which may indicate superior fitness or control of greater territorial space in the singer. Male birds, however, have been shown to sing longer and more complex songs when there are rivals in the vicinity.

The question of whether male birds try harder in the presence of an attractive female was addressed in some research at the University of Wyoming. After placing male finches together with various females, they recorded and analysed the songs they sang and reported that both the quantity and the quality of the songs they performed to different females varied. Interestingly, they also found that songs performed at the start of each interaction were significantly more attractive than those they sang later. Whether this shows that they try harder with more attractive females, especially at the start of a potential relationship, is an open question.

See also EVOLUTION 180, 183; MUSIC 329; PANGOLINS 354; PLATYPUSES 375; SLEEP 423

BLACK HOLES

70. What happens to the information in black holes?

The traditional view of black holes was that anything swallowed up by them was lost for ever. Their huge mass all scrunched into an infinitesimal space had such a gravitational pull that even light itself could not escape. With nothing ever coming out, the information about anything that went in was irretrievably lost to the outside observer.

In 1975, however, Stephen Hawking showed that the laws of quantum physics meant that black holes would leak radiation which eventually, even though it might take trillions of years, would lead to the evaporation of the black hole itself.

The question then arose about what this Hawking radiation could tell us about the inside of the black hole. Does the radiation that comes out of a black hole depend on what went into it? If so, then the information contained in matter forming the black hole cannot be said to have been lost at all.

Scientific views have been split on the answer to that question ever since. The real problem was that general relativity insisted that the information that went into a black hole could never come out, while quantum theory said that the future of the hole, including the radiation that emerged from it, would depend on its past history, which would mean that the information it contained was not lost at all.

Even Hawking changed his mind about it, and new theories to reconcile the Black Hole Information Paradox appear every few years to sway the views of top physicists. But they are still completely split on the matter.

71. Can black holes turn into white holes?

In 2014 a radical new theory was proposed to resolve some of the problems posed by black holes. Just as black holes are regions that sucked material in which could never escape, the new proposal was that the exact opposite may also exist: a white hole that spews out massive amounts of matter in a Big Bang all of its own. Just as a black hole had a way in but no way out, a white hole would have a way out but no way back.

Based on the theory of loop quantum gravity, which maintains that the universe is composed of fundamental particles in the form of vibrating loops, the new theory predicts that a black hole will, under its own ever-increasing gravity, be crushed smaller and smaller until it reaches the size of these fundamental loops. It will then be unable to diminish in size and become subject to a force known as 'quantum bounce', which sends everything into reverse and all the energy and material that went into the black hole are flung out again.

The existence of white holes is still only a theoretical possibility as none have yet been observed. One suggestion is that they may have occurred but been mistaken for supernovas. Another is that they have not been observed because the white hole that a black hole turns into will be in a parallel universe.

See also COSMOLOGY 123; QUASARS 390–1; UNIVERSE 466

BONES

72. Why don't human males have penis bones?

- Humans and hyenas are the only carnivorous mammals that don't have one.

- Humans and spider monkeys are the only primates that don't have one.
- The walrus has a bigger one than any other animal.

We are talking, of course, about the baculum or penis bone, and the reason human males are missing it is lost in our evolutionary history.

The main advantage of having a penis bone is that it allows a male to have quick and frequent sex. Instead of having to wait for increased blood pressure to make the penis erect, creatures with a baculum can just push it from inside them into the penis and they are ready for action. One theory about its absence in humans suggests that our ancestor males were very good at sticking close to their chosen female, keeping her free from molestation from rival males while also ensuring that she was close whenever he wanted her. Result: the male could wait for an erection to occur in the knowledge that the female would still be there when he was ready.

Another suggestion links the bone's absence to the short length of primate penises relative to other mammals. Shorter penises led to shorter bones until, in humans, it eventually disappeared. Why almost all other primates have one, however, is unexplained.

Finally, there is the suggestion that the baculum was the 'rib' from which God created Eve out of Adam. This is advocated in a letter published in the *American Journal of Medical Genetics* in 2001, though the point of the letter may have been to suggest that the lack of a human penis bone was the origin of the story, rather than that the loss of the baculum dates back to the Garden of Eden.

73. Why do human bones become brittle in space?

One of the problems faced by astronauts on the International Space Station is a loss of bone mass. This begins within days of arriving in space and becomes severe between the second and fifth months. Long stays have resulted in loss of as much as 20 per cent of bone mass.

Increase in the amount of calcium found in the blood of astronauts confirms that the loss of bone mass is due to calcium in the bones being broken down and released into the bloodstream. This is known as 'disuse osteoporosis' and leaves bones weak and brittle. It is presumably caused by near-weightlessness in the microgravity of space, which leaves the bones free from their usual task of supporting the weight of the body.

NASA says that the mechanism causing this loss of calcium is unknown. One suggestion is that microgravity may cause bone to break down much faster than it takes to build up, but 'the exact trigger for this rate change has not been found'.

See also BIRDS 64; CAMELS 83; CANNIBALISM 88; CATS 91; DINOSAURS 137; ENGLISH HISTORY 176; HUMAN EVOLUTION 234, 239, 243; POLAR BEARS 378; SHIPS 421; SLOTHS 430-1; TYRANNOSAURUSES 461; WALRUSES 486

BRAINS

74. How do we recognize faces?

Our ability to recognize the faces of other people, even if we have not seen them for a long time, is one of the most remarkable feats of the human brain. The evidence suggests that we can remember up to 10,000 faces, and experiments have shown that we can generally recognize people even if we have not seen them for ten years or more.

The temporal lobe of the brain, the right fusiform gyrus, the anterior temporal cortex, the inferior occipital gyri, the superior temporal sulcus and the amygdala are all brain regions that have been associated with face recognition by various researchers, and studies of prosopagnosia, or face blindness, have shown that damage to the fusiform area can lead to inability to recognize faces.

With age and sex and emotions as well as identity being read from people's faces, our brains are processing a very large amount of data at a glance. How we can do all this so quickly is one of the most remarkable of our abilities and we really don't understand how we do it.

75. How does the brain put together information from the various senses?

We all know about the five senses of sight, hearing, touch, smell and taste, and some would add other senses such as balance, pain, temperature, body position and motion. However many senses you count, though, they were, until recently, seen as independent means of receiving information about the world, and the brain's task was to build up a complete picture from the various sensory inputs. We can perceive what something looks like, sounds like, feels like, smells like and tastes like; put them all together and we have the complete picture. Recent research, however, has shown that it's not so simple.

Both psychological studies and research on the brain itself have shown that the senses are not independent at all. One sense can influence others in surprising ways. Perhaps the clearest demonstrations of this have been given by the Oxford psychologist Charles Spence, who has produced astonishing results on how our sense of taste can be tricked by the other senses. Strawberries taste sweeter and better when served on white plates than on black. White wallpaper makes red wine taste worse. Different sounds can bring out different flavours in food. Away from the dining table, it has also been shown that what we think we hear can be changed by what we think we see.

Such findings have been supported by brain scans which have identified individual neurons that react to information perceived by more than one sense simultaneously. This ability seems not to exist at birth but to begin to develop at a very early stage of development. The brain doesn't just put information together, but by letting the senses overlap it somehow develops a wiring that lets them function together in a dynamic way automatically. But if senses can overlap and change one another, how this helps us draw up an accurate and consistent picture of what we perceive is quite unclear.

76. How is information coded in the brain?

There are many unanswered questions about the way the brain functions, but one of the most basic is the question of how information is encoded and transmitted from one brain region to another. Our brains are seen as massively complex networks involving connections between neurons, but how one neuron communicates with another is unclear. Measurement of fluctuation voltages at the membranes of neurons has suggested two basic components: the average rate of the pulses of the fluctuation and the timings of individual pulses.

After half a century of argument about which of these components was more important, a team in Germany suggested in 2010 that both pulses and timings could operate simultaneously. Then, in 2014, another German team proposed that resonance may also play a part, with different networks of cells having different frequencies which enable them to communicate with one another or inhibit the activity of other cells.

None of this gets us significantly closer to understanding what information looks like in the brain, or how one neuron knows what another is telling it, but at least we may be getting closer to understanding the mechanisms by which they communicate.

77. How does the brain pay attention to something?

In 1999 the psychologists Daniel Simons and Christopher Chabris conducted an extraordinary experiment on human attentiveness. Subjects were shown a film of six people practising on a basketball court. Three wore white and three wore black, and each team had its own ball which they passed to team-mates while wandering around the court. The subjects were asked to watch the film and count how many passes took place between members of the white team. Many came up with the correct answer of fifteen passes, but very few, when asked if they had seen anything unusual happening in the film, noticed that a man in a gorilla suit had walked right across the court, stopping in the middle to face the camera and beat his chest. In various trials the number spotting the gorilla varied from none at all to around 20 per cent.

The 'inattentional blindness' shown in this experiment is as clear a demonstration as one could wish for of the way our brains can miss something, however glaring, when they are looking for something else. On the other hand, it is important for our self-preservation that we pay attention to unexpected sounds and sights that could signal a threat. But how do our brains decide what is worth paying attention to?

This may be linked to other things we don't understand, such as free will and consciousness. All that is clear is that our brains can choose what to pay attention to and what to ignore before we are conscious of having had any influence on such decisions.

78. Why did our brains divide into two hemispheres?

All mammals and even fish have brains divided into two almost identical parts which constantly communicate with each other. This confirms that the evolution of the split brain occurred very early in our development, but what advantage it conferred is a matter of pure speculation.

Since the left side of the brain controls the right side of the body, and vice versa, it is generally assumed that the split brain must have something to do with lateral specialization, but why it should be an advantage for the two halves to be physically so strongly separated and joined only by a thick tube of fibres is unknown.

In 2000 an experiment was performed on unborn chicks to try to determine the advantages of a lateralized brain. One group of unhatched chicks was incubated in the dark, while another was exposed to light in a manner that had been previously shown to lead to brain lateralization in a number of visual tasks. When they hatched, the chicks were tested on two tasks at the same time, one involving pecking at seeds, the other detecting predators. It was found that the lateralized chicks performed the tasks better. This supported the theory that two half-brains are better than a single brain at the parallel processing required when doing two things at the same time.

To go from that single result to a theory of the evolution of the brain, however, is a large step for chick-kind, let alone humankind.

79. What goes on in the brain during hypnosis?

When a person is in a hypnotic trance, they may perform actions that they would not normally do, and when they come out of the trance, they are liable to have no memory of what they did. So what is going on in the brain to make this happen?

Most hard data on the question come from electroencephalographs measuring the brain waves of people under hypnosis. Some studies have revealed an increase in lower-frequency waves and a drop in higher-frequency, which is a pattern similar to sleeping and dreaming. Other studies have reported a lower level of activity in the left hemisphere of the cerebral cortex, accompanied by increased activity in the right hemisphere. This is in line with the idea that associates the left brain with conscious logic and deduction and the right brain with the subconscious mind and creativity; hypnosis is thus seen as subduing the subject's conscious inhibitions.

How someone enters a hypnotic state, however, remains unexplained. There is general agreement that the hypnotist does no more than relax and guide the subject to induce hypnosis, but how the subject then turns off the conscious mind without falling asleep is quite unknown. There is clearly a difference between the hypnotic state and the dream state, but it is unclear physiologically what that difference is.

80. Is morality hard-wired into the brain?

Eating, staying alive, having sex and caring for our children are basic instinctive desires that we are born with. Our brains are necessarily hard-wired for these things as essential to the survival of our species. From ancient philosophers to modern neurologists, however, people have long argued over whether the same applies to moral judgements and our views on the differences between what is 'good' and what is 'evil'. Are the rules of morality something that we acquire from our education and culture, or are they inbuilt in our brains?

Two dilemmas are often cited as arguments to support the hard-wired morality argument:

(i) You are a railway man standing by the side of a track on which a train is speeding out of control. If you do nothing, it will stay on the same track and run straight into a group of five people. You can avoid this by flicking a lever which will send it onto another track where it will kill only one person. What do you do?

(ii) A doctor is in charge of a ward where five people will die if they don't receive transplants immediately. A healthy stranger walks into the ward. If the doctor kills the stranger, he can harvest his organs and save all five patients. Should he do so?

The vast majority of people say that it is morally correct to flick the lever in the first case, but not to kill the stranger in the second, yet in both cases one person is sacrificed to save five. The fact that such a moral judgement appears to be universal has been claimed to support the idea that morality itself is universal and we are born with it.

On the other hand, one could say that flicking a switch is a very different type of decision to make than cold-bloodedly killing someone, and it is no surprise that different cultures reach the same moral conclusions by a rational rather than hard-wired process.

81. Why does the cerebellum have so many neurons?

The cerebellum (which gets its name from a Latin word meaning 'little brain') contains about half the total number of neurons in the human brain, yet it is only a tenth of the total size of the brain. Situated at the bottom of the brain, beneath the cerebral hemispheres, it used to be considered mainly as the motor centre of the brain, with an important role in maintaining balance and co-ordinating movements and motor learning. It was also known to play a part in certain cognitive functions such as language, which might also, at least for spoken language, be said to involve motor skills. In all these cases, the cerebellum does not initiate the movement but seems to be essential in carrying it out.

Recent research comparing a number of primate species has suggested that a fast expansion of the size of the cerebellum occurred when apes and monkeys diverged. It has even been suggested that a large cerebellum lies at the centre of human cognitive abilities. Its large number of neurons and vast number of connections suggest that the cerebellum plays a vital part in the brain's function, but we still have very little knowledge of what it does and how it does it. As anthropology professor Robert Barton of Durham University wrote in October 2014: 'Nobody really knows what all these neurons are for, but they must be doing something important.'

BRAZIL

82. Did Percy Fawcett find the lost city of Z?

In 1925 Colonel Percy Harrison Fawcett disappeared during an expedition to find a city he called 'Z' in the uncharted jungles of Brazil. After studying ancient legends and other records, he was convinced there was an ancient city in the Mato Grosso region which was possibly the fabled El Dorado. The last that was heard of him was a letter to his wife on 29 May 1925 saying that he was setting off into unexplored territory with his son Jack and one of Jack's old friends. They were never seen again. Many rumours followed about what had happened to him: that he had been killed by tribesmen; that he had been killed by animals; that he had become chief of a cannibal tribe. But no evidence of him or his remains was ever confirmed.

The lost city of Z, which Fawcett was seeking, had been described in 1753 by a Portuguese slave trader who gave a detailed description of the city but omitted to reveal its location. In January 2010, however, the journal *Antiquity* reported the identification, using Google Earth, of more than 200 massive earthworks in the upper Amazon basin near Brazil's border with Bolivia.

So Percy Fawcett might have been right after all, and he might even have found his lost city. He has, after all, been cited as a possible inspiration for the character of Indiana Jones.

'Not ignorance, but ignorance of ignorance is the death of knowledge.'

Alfred North Whitehead

CAMELS

83. Did Abraham have camels?

And he entreated Abram well for her sake: and he had sheep, and oxen, and he asses, and menservants, and maidservants, and she asses, and camels. Genesis 12, 16

There are twenty-two mentions of camels in the Book of Genesis, and they led to a huge dispute between archaeologists and theologians in 2014. At the heart of it were excavations of copper mines between the Red Sea and the Dead Sea which had revealed some camel bones.

The bones, said the archaeologists, appear abruptly in the strata of the mines and thus give a clear indication of when domesticated camels arrived in the region. Radiocarbon dating, they claim, has allowed them to pinpoint that moment, which they say was around the ninth century BC.

According to the traditional Bible chronology, however, Abraham lived around 2000 BC, which was more than a millennium too early for the camels. The archaeologists say their findings show that a camel-based economy only became established after the rise of Egyptian power in the region, which was too late even for King Solomon and King David to have had camels.

In reply, theologians have questioned the reliability of radiocarbon dating, which has made mistakes in the past.

CANCER

84. How do blind mole rats resist cancer?

The blind mole rat lives underground, digs with its teeth, has skin over its eyes, survives with very little oxygen and no light, and has never been known to have a cancerous tumour. Even when treated with carcinogenic chemicals, it shows total resistance to cancer, which is one reason the sequencing of its genome in 2014 was seen as a possible step forward in understanding the disease.

The genetic adaptation that enables the blind mole rat to cope with very low oxygen levels is thought to be responsible for its highly effective defence against cancer. Whether this has applications in human cancer treatment has yet to be discovered, but the publication of the mole rat's genome will certainly lift the animal's status in medical research.

85. Why do some moles become cancerous?

Moving from blind mole rats to moles on the skin...

We used to call moles 'beauty spots' until their beauty became tarnished with the link to skin cancer. A mole, or nevus, is a benign (non-cancerous) pigmented skin tumour. Most moles never cause any problems, but sometimes they become cancerous, and it is not known why this occurs.

A number of factors have been identified that increase the chances of moles turning into cancerous melanomas. One risk factor is excessive exposure to sunlight, particularly in one's youth. The ultraviolet light from the Sun or from tanning beds, particularly UVB rays, can damage the DNA in skin cells and cancers can be caused by DNA changes. People with many moles seem more likely to develop cancers than people with only a few. A large, flat and often irregular type of mole called 'dysplastic' (or 'atypical') is known to be more likely to become cancerous.

Yet in all of these cases, we cannot tell whether a particular benign mole is going to develop into a melanoma until it happens.

86. How does physical activity affect cancer risk?

A study published in December 2011 estimated that about 1 per cent of cancers in the UK are linked to people doing less physical activity than is recommended in the government guidelines. Cases of bowel cancer in particular were seen to be significantly less frequent among people who indulged in most physical activity, as were cases of breast cancer in women.

Inactive lifestyles have been linked to many health problems, including stroke and heart disease, diabetes, osteoporosis and a range of problems associated with weight gain. Regular physical activity is claimed to have a protective effect against cancer, over and above its effect on bodyweight, but without better knowledge of the causes of cancer, we cannot be sure of such things. As statisticians often remind us, correlation does not imply causation. If inactive people are more likely to develop cancers, it could even be that proneness to cancer is a cause of an inactive lifestyle, rather than the other way round.

Physical activity has an effect on levels of insulin, some hormones and our hormone-like prostaglandins, all of which may have a role in fighting cancer, but that is a speculative explanation of how cancer and physical activity may be linked – if indeed they are connected at all.

See also AUSTEN 34; CHEMICALS 95; HENRY VIII 230; LONGEVITY 280; MEDICINE 295

CANNABIS

87. Does cannabis have a direct effect on men's sperm production?

An extensive study in 2014 reported that taking cannabis was the only factor found to have a negative effect on men's sperm production. Alcohol, smoking, obesity and even wearing tight underwear were found to have no effect on sperm quality, but taking cannabis was reported to double the chances of men under the age of thirty producing abnormal sperm.

However, the researchers admit that it is not known how or even whether cannabis has a direct effect on sperm production, or whether the correlation is caused by an association with another unknown factor. Also, the study was based on analysis of sperm samples from men who had attended fertility clinics, which may not be representative. Poor sperm quality is one of many possible reasons for attending a fertility clinic. One might say that the study showed that cannabis-taking had a beneficial effect on the other possible reasons for their attendance at the clinics.

See also MEDICINE 299

'We are all born ignorant but one must work hard to remain stupid.'

Benjamin Franklin

CANNIBALISM

88. Did the cannibal cavemen of Spain eat members of their own clan?

Most, if not all, accounts of cannibalism among early humans have either been associated with ritual killing and eating of selected body parts of enemies, or were thought to have taken place at times of famine. In 2010, however, bones were found in a cave in Spain which were claimed as evidence that cannibalism was just another meal to our ancestors 800,000 years ago.

Marks on the bones of around a dozen humans were seen as evidence that their flesh had been removed; decapitation and marks on the skulls suggested that their brains had been eaten; and smashed bones were taken as evidence that their marrow had been consumed.

The fact that the bones were found mixed up with those of bison, deer, sheep and other animals suggested that the human flesh was seen as nothing special among *Homo antecessor*, who are thought to be Europe's earliest humans. Furthermore, the region was thought to have been rich in food and water and to have had a mild climate, all of which would argue against cannibalism being a last resort in time of famine.

DNA studies of the bones in 2013 revealed that they were all from one family and included three men, three women, three teenagers and three children aged two to nine. Their relationship to the people who ate them, however, is not known, and there is some argument about how often human flesh was on the menu and whether people ate their friends as well as enemies.

See also BRAZIL 82; DISEASE 144–5

CARROLL

89. Why was Lewis Carroll so generous to Mr Dymes?

There has long been a mystery concerning the relationship between Lewis Carroll, author of *Alice in Wonderland,* and a Mr Dymes, whom he is believed to have met on holiday. Dymes had a large family and Carroll records having dinner with Mrs Dymes and taking his daughters to the theatre. He wrote an acrostic poem for Ruth Dymes and is known to have helped some of Dymes's older daughters get work.

In 2006 details of Carroll's bank account were found at a bank in Oxford. They reveal substantial payments to Mr Dymes between 1883 and 1885, a period during which Carroll himself was in constant financial difficulties. Not only did Carroll give or lend money to Dymes on various occasions (which was never repaid), but he even paid off Dymes's landlord when he was threatening to seize his furniture.

Carroll's own letters and correspondence suggest that he didn't like Dymes much, but saw him as a dull character always moaning about his misfortunes. He did not even seem to have strong feelings towards any of Dymes's family.

Carroll's giving Dymes money that he could ill afford can only be explained by his being a very generous man without much financial good sense, or by his having something to hide which he was paying Dymes not to reveal.

CATS

90. Why do cats sit in circles?

Towards the end of 2014, a sudden spate of pictures of cats sitting inside circles began appearing in the popular press and the Internet. Somebody had started the craze by noticing that if you make a circular shape on the floor of a room or on the ground outside with a piece of string, or electrical wire, or masking tape, or indeed almost anything, any cat in the vicinity will be liable to wander over, step into the circle, settle down and refuse to move. And it doesn't even have to be a circle: as many of the pictures showed, a square, a pentagon or almost any closed shape would do.

A range of possible explanations have been advanced to account for this newly discovered aspect of feline behaviour:

- The cat may be defending the territory marked out by the newly created boundary.
- The cat may see the boundary as a sort of wall offering it greater security.
- The cat may assume that the person who created the circle must have done so for a reason, so the circle must be important.
- The cat may like the feeling of being enclosed that the circle gives it.
- The cat may just be investigating something new in its environment.
- The cat may be attracted not by the circle but by the smell of whatever was used to create the boundary.

In short, nobody really has any idea why cats like to sit in circles.

91. Why do cats purr?

As all cat owners know, their pets purr when they are contented. But cats also purr when they are in pain or when they are nervous, so what is this purring all about?

One theory is that a cat's purr evolved as medically beneficial. A purr is a sound made at a frequency of between 250 and 150 Hertz, which has also been found to be the frequency of vibrations that help muscles and bones grow or repair themselves when damaged. Purring may thus have begun as a beneficial therapeutic process and then turned into a general expression of well-being and contentment.

Another theory is that purring is a form of communication. Cats have been shown to purr at similar frequencies to the crying of human babies when they want food, and it has been suggested that cats purr when they are hungry too. Or the purring of baby cats may be a way for the blind newborn kittens to locate and communicate with their mothers.

Or perhaps cats just purr because they like purring. We really don't know.

92. What happened to Peter the Great's Russian blue cat?

The earliest known example of the Russian blue breed of cat was a pet of the Russian tsar Peter the Great. His name was Vaska, a diminutive of the name Vassily, and he is said to have been looked after by the tsar's daughter Elizabeth.

Lenin used to tell the tale of Vaska the cat, living in the palace of the tsar and stealing food from the kitchen. The palace cook used to make appeals to the cat to refrain from its immoral banditry. The cat listened but went on eating.

Lenin cited this as an example of the futility of making moral appeals to the exploitative classes, but neither he nor anyone else seems to have told what eventually happened to Vaska.

See also ANIMALS 18; WALRUSES 486

CHAPLIN

93. When and where was Charlie Chaplin born?

Biographies of Charlie Chaplin all seem to agree that he was born in London on 16 April 1889. Chaplin himself confirmed that date, and until 2012 there seemed no reason to doubt it. In that year, however, newly declassified files from Britain's MI5 revealed considerable uncertainty about the star's origins.

In the 1950s MI5 had been asked by the FBI to investigate Chaplin, whom they suspected of having communist sympathies. Even J. Edgar Hoover himself was said to have denounced Chaplin in private as being 'one of Hollywood's parlour Bolsheviks'. What must have seemed a routine enquiry from the FBI, however, became a mystery when MI5 could find no record of Chaplin's birth. Their conclusion was: 'It would seem that Chaplin was either not born in this country or that his name at birth was other than those mentioned.' MI5 also found no evidence to support a theory that Chaplin was really a Frenchman named Israel Thornstein. The 1891 UK census does, however, record the two-year-old Charles Chaplin as living in London with his mother and elder brother.

At around the same time as the declassification of the MI5 files, another clue emerged in the form of a letter found in a locked drawer of a bureau that had belonged to Chaplin. Written by an Englishman named Jack Hill in the early 1970s, it told Chaplin that he had been born 'in a caravan belonging to the Gypsy Queen, who was my auntie', in a Roma community in Smethwick, near Birmingham, England. Chaplin's mother's maiden name was Hill.

CHEESE

94. Does Roquefort cheese have sex?

Until 2012 nobody had ever suggested that Roquefort cheese might be having sex, but in that year a paper appeared reporting a study in France suggesting that it could indeed be happening. 'Sex in cheese: Evidence for sexuality in the fungus Penicillium roqueforti' (by Jeanne Ropars and others) begins by saying that: 'Although most eukaryotes reproduce sexually at some moment of their life cycle, as much as a fifth of fungal species were thought to reproduce exclusively asexually', but goes on to say: 'recent studies have revealed the occurrence of sex in some of these supposedly asexual species.' Their study of reproduction in the Roquefort fungus 'revealed the existence of individuals of both mating types, even in the very same cheese', and they concluded that: '*P. roqueforti* underwent more or less recent sex events.' So the Roquefort fungus might be having sex after all.

See also USA 473

'Education is a progressive discovery
of our own ignorance.'

Will Durant

CHEMICALS

95. Is dimethyl sulfoxide good for you?

For more than fifty years, arguments have raged over the use of dimethyl sulfoxide (DMSO) as a medicine. Its supporters see it as a modern panacea with an unending list of potential applications, particularly in the realm of pain-killing, but ranging from the treatment of headaches to cancer. Others, however, including the US Food and Drug Administration (FDA), have severe doubts about both its efficacy and its safety. In fact the FDA has approved its use only for the relief of symptoms of interstitial cystitis and as a preservative for transplant organs.

A by-product of the wood industry, DMSO has been used as an industrial solvent since 1953. Over 40,000 articles in scientific journals have been written on its chemistry and over 10,000 on its potential medical applications. Two factors, however, interfered with research. One was its ready availability for industrial applications, which led to a good deal of unsupervised use; the other was that even when absorbed through the skin, it made people's breath smell of garlic. That made double-blind studies difficult to conduct, as researchers could always tell who had taken DMSO and who had not. The smell may also have put off drug companies from studying DMSO, as it was seen as difficult to market.

In 1965 a woman in Ireland died of an allergic reaction after taking DMSO and some other drugs. Although the precise cause of death was never established, clinical trials of DMSO were stopped and suspicion against the drug has persisted ever since.

Meanwhile, DMSO has continued to be produced and sold in private clinics, with good results claimed for its effect as a fast-working analgesic and as a slower-working treatment for chronic pain. But the garlic-smelling breath is still seen as a problem.

See also BIOLOGY 58; CANCER 84; CHOCOLATE 105; DISEASE 146; INTELLIGENCE 250; JUPITER 264; POLAR BEARS 378; SMELL 436; TERMITES 452

CHEWING GUM

96. Did General Santa Anna invent chewing gum?

General Antonio Lopez de Santa Anna (1794–1876) is best known for his success in leading the Mexican forces at the Battle of the Alamo in 1836 and for his subsequent periods in office as president of Mexico, but, according to some accounts, another of his greatest achievements may have been generally overlooked: the invention of chewing gum.

After being overthrown as president of Mexico in 1855, Santa Anna fled to Cuba where he lived in exile, trying to raise money to fund an army to take over Mexico City. In 1869 he visited Staten Island, New York, where he was hoping to sell the idea of using chicle, a sticky gum from trees, as a rubber substitute.

Like other similar gums, chicle was often chewed by Mexicans for its high sugar content, but Santa Anna never saw that as a potentially lucrative application. When in Staten Island, however, he met an inventor named Thomas Adams whom he hoped would join him in his rubber project. Adams bought a ton of chicle from him but was unable to produce a workable rubber from it.

Adams's son Horatio, however, saw its chewability and gave 200 balls of it to a drugstore owner who sold them at two a penny. The Adams family went on to create Adams Clove Gum, Chiclets and other chewing gums, the first of their type in the USA. Adams may have been the real inventor of chewing gum, but he would never have done it without the hero of the Alamo.

CHICKENS

97. Why do chickens count from left to right?

Research has shown that when people think of numbers, they arrange them on a mental number line (MNL) with lower numbers on the left and higher numbers on the right. A wonderfully designed experiment, the results of which were published in 2015, showed that three-day-old chickens do the same thing.

The chicks were first placed in an enclosure with a centrally placed panel on which a number of spots were visible. When one of the chicks walked round the panel, it was rewarded with food. After some time, the chicks got the hang of it and learnt to associate walking round the panel with receiving a reward.

When this had been reliably learnt, the experiment moved on to its second stage in which the single panel was now replaced by two panels, one on the left and the other on the right, at equal distances and angles from the chicks. The two panels had equal numbers of spots on them, but it was not the same number as had been there during training. The researchers held their breath and waited to see which panel was preferred by the chicks.

Remarkably, they found that when the number of spots was lower than had been there during training, about 70 per cent of chicks went to the left panel, but when it was higher, 70 per cent chose the right. The experiment was performed with varying numbers of spots, both during the initial training and the subsequent experiment, but the chicks always went left for lower numbers than had appeared in training and right for higher ones.

The fact that chickens and humans share this left–right bias in our number lines suggests that it may be something that occurred very early in our joint evolution. Why chickens think of numbers from left to right is an even bigger problem than the same question for humans.

See also FOOTBALL 199; GORILLAS 220; PANGOLINS 356

CHIMPANZEES

98. Is aggression in chimpanzees the result of human influence?

Chimpanzees and humans have often been described as the only species that wage war on their own kind. Other creatures, such as various spiders and certain insects, may kill their own kind when competing for sex or food, but humans and chimps get involved in a form of intergroup conflict that has been likened to primitive warfare. Bonobos, on the other hand, which are even more closely related to humans, are remarkably peaceful.

Ever since the anthropologist Jane Goodall reported on warlike chimpanzee behaviour in the 1970s, there has been a debate about whether this aggression is caused by human intervention or is innate and natural behaviour. In 2014 the journal *Nature* published a paper based on an extensive survey of 152 lethal attacks by chimpanzees on their own kind in eighteen chimpanzee and four bonobo communities over the past fifty years. The conclusion was that 'lethal aggression directed toward members of other groups is part of the natural behavioural repertoire of chimpanzees' and human intervention plays no part.

That finding, however, was immediately challenged by other anthropologists, particularly on its lack of a clear definition of 'human influence' and the statistical methods used to establish the root causes of chimpanzee aggression.

Interestingly, however, the study reported that, much as in human warfare, 92 per cent of the attackers and 73 per cent of the victims in the killings were male, and 66 per cent of them were the result of attacks on one community by another. Perhaps we have more in common with chimpanzees than we thought, and perhaps what we should really be studying is what makes bonobos so peaceful.

See also EBOLA 167; INTELLIGENCE 254; WALRUSES 486

CHINA

99. Where did the Tarim mummies come from?

Early in the twentieth century, various European explorers reported finding desiccated bodies at the eastern end of the Tarim Basin (now Xinjiang) in China. Many were tall or red-haired, indicating an origin more European than Chinese. The earliest mummies have been dated to around 1800 BC, and both their physiology and the textiles they wore support the theory that they had a European origin.

Pliny the Elder, in his *Natural History*, written around AD 77–9, mentioned a report from a Ceylonese ambassador to the Roman emperor Claudius of people in north-west China who 'exceeded the ordinary human height, had flaxen hair, and blue eyes, and made an uncouth sort of noise by way of talking'.

Until the discovery of the 'Tarim mummies', Pliny's description was viewed as fanciful, but recent DNA analyses have confirmed that they probably did have a European rather than Asian origin. How they got there and precisely where they came from, however, has never been revealed.

100. Who built the Longyou caves?

In 1992 a villager in Longyou County in China made an extraordinary discovery while pumping water from a cave. What he found was the first of a series of massive caves, with a floor of over 2,000 square metres and a height at its tallest point of over 30 metres. He went on to discover four more such caves and now twenty-four of them are known, all with wall carvings of horses, fishes and birds, which confirm that they were man-made. They are thought to date back to between 500 and 200 BC, and their scale is awesome. According to one estimate, almost 1 million cubic metres of rock must have been removed to build them.

Yet their origin is a complete mystery, with nothing known of who constructed them or why they were built. To add to that mystery, no reference to them has ever been found in historical records.

101. How did the hanging coffins of Sichuan get there?

From around AD 1000 to 1600, the Bo people of Sichuan in south-west China practised an extraordinary form of burial which involved placing bodies in coffins made of hollowed-out tree trunks that were then hung on limestone cliffs at heights between 10 and 130 metres above the ground. Over 300 such coffins are known in Sichuan, but the reasons behind the ritual and the methods used have long been a matter for speculation.

Presumably the location of the coffins was intended to protect the bodies, possibly from wild animals, or perhaps as part of a religious ritual to smooth their passage to an afterlife. The Bo people are known, from historical records, to have believed that coffins set high up were propitious, and the higher they were, the more propitious. But how did they get the coffins to such inaccessible places?

One idea is that they may have built earth ramps to allow the coffins to be lifted high, but that would have involved an immense amount of labour for each coffin, as the ramp would presumably be destroyed after each burial to keep the body safe. Another suggestion involves the building of timber scaffolds supported by stakes in the rocks, but no stake holes have ever been found that would support such a theory.

The idea that has attracted the most support is that the coffins were lowered on ropes from the cliff tops, and some signs that such ropes were used have recently been discovered, but that would not explain why some coffins are relatively close to the ground.

There is a similar mystery about the hanging coffins of the Guyue people on the cliffs of Dragon-Tiger mountain in Jiangxi. These include coffins big enough for ten bodies and they are hung in such inaccessible spots that some say they can only have been placed there with the aid of the immortals in heaven.

102. What is inside the tomb of China's first emperor?

China's first emperor, Qin Shi Huang, died on 10 September 210 BC and was buried in the most elaborate tomb complex ever known, a series of caverns the size of a city built in a hillside and guarded by an army of terracotta soldiers. So far, around 2,000 such soldiers have been uncovered, but there may be many more. Terracotta concubines are also thought likely to have been made to accompany the late emperor into the afterlife.

As for the central tomb, which is thought to contain a palace and the body of Qin Shi Huang, nobody has been inside for over 2,000 years and nobody is likely to in the near future. One problem is a reluctance of the Chinese government to disturb their first emperor, but there are also concerns about current excavation methods and the likelihood that these would damage the findings. When the terracotta soldiers were first exposed to air, their paint crumbled, and there is a natural fear that something similar would happen if the tomb were broken into.

There is also a little problem about mercury. According to ancient writing, the tomb is encircled with rivers of liquid mercury, which the ancient Chinese believed could bestow immortality. While he was alive, the emperor even took pills containing mercury, believing it would give him immortality. The resulting mercury poisoning is probably why he died at the age of thirty-nine. Soil samples from the area of the tomb have revealed very high levels of mercury contamination, which would make excavations very dangerous. So for the time being, the emperor may rest in peace.

103. How did the ancient Chinese get Neanderthal ears?

How do you recognize a Neanderthal? Well one way, until very recently, was to look in its ears. Neanderthal ears display an arrangement of the semicircular canals of their temporal labyrinth which is thought to have been a remnant from a primitive balance system. This arrangement was found in nearly all examinations of Neanderthal skulls and was thought to be unique to them.

In 2014, however, a re-examination of a 100,000-year-old skull that had been found in China thirty-five years earlier revealed the same arrangement. This came as a great surprise, as Neanderthals were thought to have lived only in Europe. The finding is thought to support the view that Neanderthals did not die out completely around 40,000 years ago, but interbred with other more modern human species. That would explain how a man in China acquired the gene responsible for Neanderthal ears.

See also EVOLUTION 183; INVENTIONS 255; SEX DIFFERENCES 411; USA 473

CHOCOLATE

104. Does chocolate consumption predict Nobel Prize winners?

In 2012 the *New England Journal of Medicine* published a paper showing a strong correlation between the number of Nobel Prizes a country has won and the amount of chocolate eaten per capita in that country. While accepting that correlation does not imply causation, Dr Franz Messerli, the author of the paper, said: 'since chocolate consumption has been documented to improve cognitive function, it seems most likely that in a dose-dependent way, chocolate intake provides the abundant fertile ground needed for the sprouting of Nobel laureates.' According to his calculation, a country's Nobel Prize score rises by one for each 0.4 kilogram rise in the average chocolate consumption rate per person per year.

Later research, however, raised some doubts about these conclusions. According to a paper in the *Journal of Nutrition* in 2013, the improvements in cognitive function mentioned above referred to benefits derived from cocoa flavanols, but national consumption rates of other flavanol-rich nutriments, such as tea and wine, do not show any correlation with Nobel Prize awards.

105. Is chocolate an aphrodisiac?

Belief in the aphrodisiac properties of chocolate date back to the days of the Mayans and Aztecs, with reports that the Aztec ruler Montezuma liked to drink fifty cups of chocolate elixir before visiting his harem. More recently, Casanova declared chocolate to be the world's second-best aphrodisiac, beaten only by champagne.

In the scientific age, chocolate's supposed aphrodisiac properties have been linked to its phenylethylamine (PEA) content, which is a chemical that has been shown not only to be present in the brains of people who are in love but also to release the same hormone as having sex. Chocolate has also been shown to produce natural opiates in the brain, which may have a general feel-good effect, while other chemicals in chocolate may have similar effects to marijuana in boosting dopamine production.

The only thing wrong with all this is that the levels of these chemicals in chocolate seem far too low to have any significant effect. Not only does the PEA from chocolate not remain long enough in our systems to have the desired effect, but according to the National Institute of Mental Health in the USA, an average person would have to eat 25 pounds of chocolate to perceive a marijuana-like effect.

See also SNAILS 438

CHRISTIANITY

106. Did Origen castrate himself?

One of the most prolific writers and theologians of the early Christian church was Origen, whose 6,000 works had a great influence on the development of Christianity itself. A profoundly devout man, he has been described as the first Christian theologian, but the question of whether he castrated himself has never been resolved.

According to the Roman historian Eusebius, who lived shortly after Origen, he so strongly believed in the doctrine of self-denial that he took the words of Matthew 19:12 literally:

> *For there are some eunuchs, which were so born from their mother's womb: and there are some eunuchs, which were made eunuchs of men: and there be eunuchs, which have made themselves eunuchs for the kingdom of heaven's sake.*

Origen, Eusebius said, was one of the last group and that story was believed throughout the Middle Ages and until the nineteenth century. More recent historians, however, have suggested that the self-castration was malicious gossip by Origen's enemies, and that Origen himself had expressed strong views against a literal interpretation of Matthew's words given above.

See also ART 25; ASTRONOMY 30; BIBLE 52–3; JESUS CHRIST 259–63

CODES

107. What does the Shugborough inscription mean?

In the grounds of Shugborough Hall in Staffordshire, England, lies the Shepherd's Monument enclosed in a stone arch. The monument shows a reversed copy, in relief, of Poussin's painting *The Shepherds of Arcadia*, and below the carving are ten letters: D and M, placed low down and well separated, and above and between them, O U O S V A V V.

Charles Dickens and Charles Darwin are among those who were fascinated by the inscription and tried to work out what it might mean, but neither they, nor anyone else, has explained it. Theories include the initial letters of a new translation of various biblical phrases; a dedication of the monument to the late wife of the owner of the hall; a love message; a coded treasure map; and a coded anagrammatic sign-off by the stonemason.

In 2014 a spokesman for Shugborough Hall was quoted as saying: 'We get five or six people a week who believe they have solved the code so we are a bit wary of them now.'

108. What are the symbols on the Phaistos Disc?

The Phaistos Disc is a piece of clay found in 1908 on the site of the Minoan palace of Phaistos on Crete. It is thought to date back to around 1700 BC. Made of fired clay, it is a disc about fifteen centimetres in diameter with a spiral of symbols on both sides. The hieroglyphic symbols seem to have been made by pressing seals into the soft clay. There are 242 such symbols featuring forty-five different signs.

The number and distribution of the signs is tantalizing: there are enough of them to offer hope to someone trying to break their code, but not enough to give a realistic prospect of success when the context of their message is not known. The fact that different occurrences of the same sign are identical has led to the disc being described as one of the earliest known examples of movable type printing. Some scholars, however, think the whole thing is a hoax.

109. What is the secret of the Beale Ciphers?

In 1885 a pamphlet was published containing three coded texts said to relate to treasure buried by a man named Thomas J. Beale around 1820. The texts were alleged to have been found in a box given by Beale to a local innkeeper, who opened the box twenty-three years later; then, many years later still, passed it on to a friend before he died. In the meantime, Beale had disappeared, leaving the unnamed friend with the three coded messages. The first was said to give details of where the treasure was buried; the second contained a description of the treasure itself; the third lists the names of the owners of the treasure and their next of kin.

The friend is said to have spent the next twenty years trying to decode the texts, but managing to do so only in the case of the second, which described a treasure of over 35,000 troy ounces of gold, worth around $65 million at today's prices. There was also around $1 million worth of silver and various jewels. The code used to encrypt the second message, however, did not work for the first or the third.

A computer analysis of the coded messages in the late 1960s convinced one specialist that they were probably legitimate coded versions of an intelligible text, though later cryptographers have given their opinions that they are unlikely to be encoded versions of anything in English. Some of the language in the decoded second message has also been thought unlikely to date back to the 1820s as it is supposed to. Attempts to confirm the existence of Thomas J. Beale have not been successful.

There is, however, a Cheyenne legend dating back to around 1820 relating to gold and silver being taken from the west and buried in mountains in the east, which may help explain why so many treasure-hunters have been arrested for trespassing in Bedford County, Virginia, where some say Beale buried his treasure.

COFFEE

110. Can you tell whether coffee is roasted just by the sounds of its cracking?

The art of perfect coffee-roasting is said to be a skill acquired by using all five of one's senses. The colour of the bean, its smell, its taste, the cracking sound it makes during the roasting and its texture all provide information to the roaster. But can a perfect roast be achieved on the basis of sound alone?

That was the question addressed by Preston S. Wilson in his paper 'Coffee roasting acoustics' in 2014. After recording and analysing the sounds emitted by coffee beans during the roasting process, he identified three factors that might lead to an automated roasting process based on sound alone. The 'first crack' sounds emitted near the end of roasting are louder than 'second crack' sounds emitted later. First crack also emits more low-frequency energy than second crack. Thirdly, 'the rate of cracks appearing in the second crack chorus is higher than the rate in the first crack chorus'. All of these factors may be measured independently of other roasting noises.

Whether the results correlate with the excellence of the roast, however, has not been determined. Wilson also suggests that: 'Future work should include analysis of all the various types of green coffee beans of interest and different roasting processes and machines.'

See also DISEASE 143

COMETS

111. Why did comet P/2013 P5 have six comet-like tails?

On 27 August 2013 astronomers working in Hawaii announced the discovery of a puzzling body in the asteroid belt. Asteroids usually appear as a point of light, but this one was strangely fuzzy, so they used the Hubble Space Telescope to take a closer look. When the Hubble image arrived on 10 September, they became even more puzzled. Amazingly, it had six comet-like tails, and when Hubble looked again on 23 September, its appearance had changed even more, looking as though it had completely swung around.

Because of the tails, P/2013 P5 was classified as a comet, despite the fact that it was thought to be an asteroid, which is mainly rock, rather than a comet, which is mainly ice. Its tails are thought to consist of dust from its surface smudged out behind it by the pressure of solar radiation, with the multiple tails caused by different ejections of dust. It is also possible that the whole body is breaking up, possibly as a result of an increase in its rotational speed. But nothing like a six-tailed comet/asteroid has ever been seen before, so until further evidence of its progress is available, its tails remain a mystery.

112. Why is comet 67P/Churyumov–Gerasimenko singing?

When the Rosetta spacecraft succeeded in sending its robotic lander Philae down to the surface of comet 67P/Churyumov-Gerasimenko in November 2014, it made a strange discovery: the comet was singing. The 'song' takes the form of oscillations in the magnetic field around the comet, emitted at 40–50 millihertz. The frequencies would need to be multiplied by about 10,000 to be audible to the human ear, but they have been clearly identified by monitoring equipment on Rosetta.

The oscillations are thought to be caused by ionization of particles released by the comet, but such a thing has never been detected before and the physical process behind it is completely unknown.

113. What is the origin of the long-period comets?

Around 4.6 billion years ago, the Solar System is thought to have begun to form with the collapse of a vast molecular cloud. Most of this collapsing mass formed the Sun, with the planets forming from much of the leftovers. This still left a great deal of 'crumbs' (comparatively speaking) which are now thought to account for the comets.

These are much smaller bodies than the planets, with very eccentric orbits round the Sun, and they come in two types: short-period and long-period. The short-period comets take less than 200 Earth years to orbit the Sun and originate in the Kuiper Belt, which is a disc-shaped region of space, past the orbit of Neptune and about 30–100 astronomical units (AU) from the Sun. An AU is defined as the average distance between the Earth and the Sun, so 30–100 AU is a huge distance. The Kuiper Belt is named after the Dutch-American astronomer Gerard Kuiper, who predicted its existence in 1951, though his prediction was not confirmed until 1992. There are thought to be around 70,000 small, icy bodies in the Kuiper Belt, some of which become comets when they are flung by the gravitational force of other stars towards the inner Solar System.

The long-period comets are far more mysterious. These are thought to have orbital periods of between 200 and several million years, and they do not come from a reasonably flat disc like the Kuiper Belt, but have been seen to enter our skies from all directions. In 1950 calculations by the Dutch astronomer Jan H. Oort led to his prediction that these comets originated in a spherical cloud of up to a trillion rocks on the very fringe of the Solar System, surrounding the rest of it at a distance of perhaps 100,000 AU from the Sun, which is about half the distance to the nearest star.

The only problem with this is that no direct confirmation or observation of the Oort Cloud has ever been made. Evidence for its existence is based entirely on calculations of the motion of comets. So the generally held theory on the origin of long-period comets is still unconfirmed.

See also ASTRONOMY 30; COSMOLOGY 121; GEOLOGY 212; NAMES 336; SOLAR SYSTEM 442

COMPUTERS

114. Will computers ever be able to understand natural human speech?

Science-fiction films for decades have featured scenes in which a human carries on a conversation with a robot or the ship's computer. Progress on voice synthesizers and voice-recognition programs have made such a scenario appear ever more plausible, and rather stilted versions of such conversations have become possible, but there are huge problems to overcome before computers can be said to understand natural language.

The basic problem is that computers rely on logic and humans don't. Language, as we use it, is not just an application of a dictionary and the rules of grammar. Language is full of ambiguity and illogicalities such that effective linguistic communication depends on the shared culture of the speaker and listener. Asking a human 'Do you have the time?' may invite the answer 'Half past four', but a computer would be more likely to tell you that it had some time at its disposal and ask how much you needed. Even if you asked, more precisely, 'Can you tell me the time?', it would probably just say 'Yes'.

Of course, it is easy enough to program a machine to deal with specific questions such as these, but language is full of such imprecise sayings.

Understanding what someone really means demands a knowledge of the real world that is wide enough to cut through the imprecision of language. Giving a computer such knowledge seems unlikely to be achieved in the foreseeable future.

115. Will machine intelligence ever be impossible for humans to comprehend?

Computers can now play chess better than almost all humans, and it seems inevitable that 'almost all' will soon become 'all'. They can make more accurate predictions of the weather and are well on the way to making more reliable medical diagnoses. All of these achievements, however, are due to human programming combined with phenomenal calculating speed. We understand what they are doing because we told them how to do it, but their speed and accuracy in carrying out our instructions have led to better results than we can hope for on our own.

What would happen, though, if computers could write their own programs? There seems no inherent reason why we could not program a computer to increase its own efficiency by analysing its own program and improving it. Perhaps it could then move on to producing the design specifications for a better computer. Then the improved computer could produce an even better one, leading eventually to a self-programming machine whose program is beyond human understanding.

Whether a machine can move outside its own operating system to design a better one, however, is a highly speculative question which may depend on the next one.

116. Are there any limits to machine intelligence?

Since the 1950s scientists and science-fiction writers have written about the 'technological singularity' that could lead to the sort of machine-dominated world depicted in films such as the Terminator and Matrix series. Computers in such a world will have moved so far beyond human intelligence that they can not only perform at a level that we can no longer comprehend, but make their own decisions about what they do and therefore pose a threat to the human race.

In 2014 Stephen Hawking wrote about the prospect of developing true artificial intelligence (AI) to the extent that it not only surpassed human intelligence but became responsible for its own design: 'Success in creating AI would be the biggest event in human history. Unfortunately, it might also be the last, unless we learn how to avoid the risks.'

Quite what those risks might be, however, depends on the answer to the above question.

See also INTELLIGENCE 252; MILKY WAY 315–16; SCIENCE 403; SEX DIFFERENCES 411; SHAKESPEARE 415

COSMOLOGY

117. Where do cosmic rays come from?

Every second billions of high-energy tiny particles moving at almost the speed of light bombard the Earth's atmosphere. These are called cosmic rays, though they are not rays at all but mostly the protons from hydrogen or helium atoms. Unlike the rest of the energy we receive from space, however, they do not come from the Sun. If they did, their concentration would presumably vary throughout the day as light and heat from the Sun do, but the energy from cosmic rays hitting the Earth seems constant throughout time and place.

Most cosmic rays are thought to come from outside our galaxy and may be the result of the massive explosions of supernovas. Some cosmic ray bursts have been linked to specific supernovas, but it is by no means clear that they all have such origins. The main problem is that the electrical charges of the particles make them susceptible to having their direction altered as they travel through space, and this makes it impossible to work out where they came from.

118. Why have we found so few dwarf galaxies?

By most standards dwarf galaxies are pretty huge. They include several billion stars and may be hundreds or even thousands of light years across, but compared with the 200–400 billion stars in the 100,000 light years of the Milky Way, they are real dwarfs – and the Milky Way isn't even a large galaxy. So far, just under thirty dwarf galaxies have been found in orbit around the Milky Way, but according to some estimates, there ought to be far more.

Galaxies in general are thought to have been formed in the early universe mostly by the interaction between gas clouds and dark matter. The trouble is that computer simulations of this theoretical galaxy formation predict around 500 dwarf galaxies forming around the Milky Way. One possibility is that the predicted dwarf galaxies are all there, but we cannot see them as they contain so much dark matter. Another theory is that larger galaxies have been eating up smaller ones in a way that we don't understand.

119. What is the origin of cosmic magnetic fields?

Throughout the known universe, magnetic fields are everywhere. Planets, stars, galaxies and the gas between stars all have a very small magnetic field. The generation of such fields requires huge amounts of electrically charged material or the motion of such masses of material, but whether the formation of galaxies was responsible for the creation of these fields or the magnetic fields played a vital part in the formation of the galaxies is unclear.

In 2015 it was shown that an instability in electromagnetic plasmas can create such a magnetic field, which ties in with the idea of the universe consisting mainly of plasma after its massive expansion following the Big Bang. That seems the best theory yet of how cosmic magnetic fields were formed.

120. What caused the blast of energy that hit the Earth in AD 770?

A good deal of evidence from widely spaced places on the globe points to the Earth's having been hit by a massive blast of radiation around AD 770. In Japan, examination of the carbon-14 in tree rings formed between 774 and 775 shows a 1.2 per cent increase over that year compared with the usual figure of 0.05 per cent. Such an increase, Japanese researchers say, can only have been caused by extremely high-energy cosmic rays hitting the Earth. Similar rises in carbon-14 have been found in trees in both America and Europe, while the cosmic ray theory is also supported by examination of Antarctic ice cores from 775. What might have caused this blast, however, is a matter of great dispute.

One theory suggests that it was a very energetic solar flare, but if that was the case, it would have been highly visible on Earth, yet there is no historical record of such a thing being observed. Another suggestion is that it was a supernova, but that would have left remnants that would be visible today, and no such remnants have been found.

The latest idea is a short gamma-ray burst caused by the collision of two neutron stars several thousand light years away. Such gamma-ray bursts, however, are thought to be very rare. They have been detected in other galaxies, but too little is known about them (see the next question) to test the theory that one may have hit the Earth in AD 775.

121. What causes gamma-ray bursts?

Gamma rays are a form of electromagnetic radiation of extremely high energy. They were first detected in 1900 and massively powerful gamma-ray bursts (GRBs) were first discovered in space in 1967 by US satellites that had been designed to detect secret tests of nuclear weapons. It has been estimated that a typical GRB releases as much energy in a few seconds as our Sun will in its 10-billion-year lifetime. Bursts can last from a few milliseconds to several minutes, and they are the brightest electromagnetic events in the known universe. All known GRBs have occurred outside our galaxy, sometimes billions of light years away. They are thought to consist of a narrow beam of intense radiation released during the collapse of a star or a cosmic collision.

It has been suggested that long-burst GRBs are released during a supernova when a star of high mass collapses to form a neutron star or a black hole, while short-burst GRBs may be the result of a collision or merger of binary neutron stars. Collisions between comets and neutron stars have also been suggested as a possible cause. Unfortunately for science, GRBs are very rare, with only a few taking place in any galaxy over a million-year period, so we really have too little evidence to determine their causes. This may be fortunate for us, as it has been estimated that a GRB pointing directly at Earth could result in a mass extinction of all life on our planet.

122. Do gravitational waves exist?

In 1916 Einstein predicted the existence of gravitational waves as a consequence of his theory of general relativity. He saw them as ripples in the space–time continuum transporting energy as gravitational radiation. In the century since then, however, neither gravitational radiation nor gravitational waves have been directly observed, though there is a good deal of indirect evidence for them.

One of the problems is that the ripples of gravitational waves, if they exist, are predicted to be very small, but in 2014 astronomers in the USA announced that they had identified a 'direct image of gravitational waves across the primordial sky'. Within months, however, doubts began to be expressed about this claim to have detected gravitational ripples caused by the Big Bang.

Further papers towards the end of 2014 and at the beginning of 2015 raised further doubts, so it seems fair to say that we still do not know whether Einstein's gravitational waves exist.

123. Is Roger Penrose's cosmic censorship hypothesis correct?

What happened before the Big Bang? What goes on inside a black hole? Questions such as these, and even whether it makes sense to ask such questions, raise almost philosophical problems for physicists. The problem behind them is connected with the idea of a singularity, where mathematics breaks down and the laws of physics no longer hold.

Tracing the universe back to its start or predicting the future of a huge collapsing star both run into the problem of a huge mass occupying an ever-decreasing volume. The density keeps increasing to a point when we find ourselves dividing by zero, which is mathematically impossible. In the case of the Big Bang, the problem is neatly side-stepped by saying that it marked the beginning of time itself, so asking what happened 'before' makes no sense. In the case of black holes, the question is again sometimes side-stepped by saying that information cannot ever escape from a black hole, so has effectively ceased to exist (→ BLACK HOLES 71).

Is it possible, however, for singularities to exist which do let us see what is going on? In 1969 the theoretical physicist Roger Penrose proposed some sort of cosmic censorship hypothesis – 'some sort of' because even Penrose did not seek to define precisely what he meant by the term. His idea was that there may be some sort of meta-law of physics guaranteeing that any singularity must be accompanied by an 'event horizon', like the outer reaches of a black hole, beyond which nothing can be known. Singularities would then become no-go areas for the usual laws of physics and the problems associated with them would be defined out of existence.

It's a nice idea, but nearly fifty years after Penrose raised the question, his cosmic censorship hypothesis has not only been neither proved nor disproved, but there is not even agreement on how it should be formulated.

124. When did cosmic acceleration begin?

Until comparatively recently, we had a nice simple picture of the universe: it had all started with a massive explosion of energy at the Big Bang, which flung everything outwards creating its own space and thus giving an expanding universe. The gravitational attraction of everything in the universe, however, would be bound to slow down that process, eventually bringing things closer together either to a steady state or to a 'Big Crunch', when everything would go back to the singularity whence it came.

In the 1990s, however, measurements of the motion of distant galaxies revealed that the rate of expansion of the universe was not decreasing but speeding up. We have already encountered the concept of dark matter – intangible and invisible, yet exerting gravitational pull by its mass; to this was now added dark energy, the name given to the all-pervading force that seemed to be behind the acceleration of the universe.

But if dark energy is pushing everything apart with more force than gravity can keep it together, how long has this been going on? Dark energy, or whatever is causing the unexpected acceleration, is seen as a property of space itself, so its density throughout space is thought to be constant. The density of matter, however, has been decreasing as it gets further spread out. Presumably, at some stage in the expansion of the universe, the total inward gravitational pull was greater than the outward force of dark matter, and only the outward energy of the Big Bang was stopping a Big Crunch. It was also the inward gravitational pull that allowed matter to be drawn together and stars and galaxies to form.

The question of when the effect of dark energy became greater than the effect of gravity may hold the key to our understanding of how the early universe formed and how it will eventually end.

125. Is there life on Gliese 581g?

In 2010 the discovery was announced of a planet orbiting the red dwarf star Gliese 581. The planet's distance from its star was only about one seventh of the distance between Earth and the Sun, but Gliese 581 is much weaker than the Sun. As a result calculations showed that Gliese 581g (as the planet was named) was in the range within which life and habitability might be possible.

With other information about Gliese 581 and its planets, such as their atmosphere and geology, also not ruling out the possibility of life, Gliese 581g was hailed as the first potentially habitable extra-solar planet to have been found. Since it is twenty light years away, and any probe launched from Earth would take about half a million years or more to reach it, it is unlikely that we will have an answer soon.

There is also a small further problem that later observations have cast doubt on whether Gliese 581g exists at all.

126. Can wormholes exist?

Wormholes are one of Albert Einstein's greatest contributions to the world of science fiction. When a sci-fi film-maker wants his starship commander to travel unimaginable distances at speeds faster than light, or flit between different time periods, or even travel to another universe, the solution is simple: take a short-cut through a wormhole. But are such things conceivable?

The idea of wormholes, which were given that name by the US physicist John Wheeler in 1957, stemmed from Einstein's equations of general relativity. These equations were found to have mathematically valid solutions that would permit short-cuts across the space–time continuum. No evidence of the existence of wormholes has ever been found, but that has not stopped some notable physicists from entertaining the concept. Even Stephen Hawking has suggested that travel through wormholes might not be impossible.

One mathematically justified idea is that wormholes might lead through black holes into parallel universes. Trying to travel through them, however, would presumably be fatal. Another idea for traversable wormholes involves their being stabilized by something called 'exotic matter' which has negative energy. Again, such exotic matter has not been found, but is not ruled out by the laws of physics. A third idea is the 'quantum foam' hypothesis, which is based on subatomic particles that formed the fabric of the universe at the moment of the Big Bang. These could have created tiny wormholes which, with the expansion of the universe, could now be big enough to travel through.

So the laws of physics do not absolutely rule out the existence of wormholes, but there is absolutely no reason to rule them in either.

See also ASTRONOMY 27–30; MILKY WAY 315–17; OUTER SPACE 350; SOLAR SYSTEM 441–4

COSTA RICA

127. What were the Costa Rican spheres for?

When the jungles of Costa Rica were being cleared in the 1930s to make room for banana plantations, workmen discovered a large number of stone spheres. Some of the stones were destroyed by the workers who thought they might contain gold, but around 300 remain, varying in size from a few centimetres to over two metres in diameter. The largest of them weigh up to two tons.

Known locally as 'Las Bolas', the stones are thought to have been made by the Precolumbian Diquis culture, which became extinct around 1530. The oldest of the stones may date back to AD 600. How the Diquis made them and what their function was supposed to be is completely unknown.

See also SLOTHS 432

CRICKETS

128. Is the courtship of crickets affected by traffic noise?

Many animals use mating calls to attract partners and a number of studies have shown that traffic noise and other human-generated sounds can disrupt this process. In 2014 a paper was published on research conducted to see if such an effect occurred in tree crickets in the USA.

After recording some road noise, the researchers played it back to see what effect it had on the production of sound by male crickets and the reception of the sound by females. Since acoustic signals by males are of low amplitude and easily masked by traffic noise, the playbacks were expected to lead to changes in their behaviour.

Surprisingly, they found that male tree crickets did not change the characteristics of their signals when the traffic noise was played, though they called less frequently. The behaviour of female crickets in response to the calls was not changed at all. The researchers suggest that: 'Because tree crickets often communicate in environments with many species of calling insects, tree crickets may be adapted to tolerate novel sources of acoustic interference.' In view of the unexpected result, however, it is clear that more research is needed.

CRIME

129. Did Frank Morris and his companions escape from Alcatraz in 1962?

The 1979 film *Escape From Alcatraz*, starring Clint Eastwood, was based on a genuine incident that happened in 1962. Alcatraz prison in San Francisco Bay was, at the time, widely seen as escape-proof. Almost all who had tried to escape were shot by guards or recaptured quickly. Only one is known to have reached the mainland and he was arrested almost as soon as he reached San Francisco.

On the night of 11 June 1962, however, a well-planned escape attempt was made by three men, Frank Morris and the brothers John and Clarence Anglin. After leaving dummy heads made of soap, toilet paper and hair in their beds to fool the guards, they crawled through holes dug with spoons in their cell walls, reached the roof through ventilation shafts, scaled a fence, made a raft out of raincoats and paddled away.

There is no evidence that they survived the strong currents to reach land and no confirmation that any of them were seen again. The FBI closed the case in 1979 after a seventeen-year investigation, concluding that the prisoners had drowned. But no bodies were ever found.

See also DEATH 131; GOLD 219; NAZIS 339; WORDS 497

CROCODILES

130. Does fruit benefit from being eaten by crocodiles?

Research published in 2013 produced two surprising revelations: first, that crocodiles eat fruit; and second, that this might be good for the fruit.

Until recently, crocodiles were assumed to be solely carnivorous and unable to digest vegetable proteins, but out of eighteen species of crocodile under observation, thirteen had been seen eating fruit. The interesting question of whether this might also benefit the fruit hinged on whether being eaten by crocodiles was an effective mode of seed dispersal.

Ingested seeds were often found to be retained in the crocodiles' stomachs for lengthy periods, regurgitated, or passed through the digestive tract and excreted. Despite not knowing what effect these processes had on the viability or the ultimate fate of the seeds, the researchers concluded that it was likely that crocodiles are effective agents of seed dispersal.

See also AVOCADOS 37; BIRDS 64; TYRANNOSAURUSES 461

DEATH

131. Does the death penalty have a deterrent effect?

This question has been the subject of dozens, perhaps hundreds, of studies by criminologists and statisticians, but huge variance in their conclusions ensures that the debate continues.

One argument often advocated by those claiming that there is no deterrent effect is the fact that US states with the death penalty have significantly higher murder rates than those without. Critics, however, would argue that the high murder rates are precisely why those states have chosen to keep the death penalty. Without it there would, they claim, be even more murders.

Some studies have even identified – or so they claim – precisely how many murders each execution prevents. The fact that their answers range from three to forty-two, however, suggests that they are at best based on imprecise methods.

In the UK the rates for unlawful killings have more than doubled since abolition of capital punishment in 1964, but whether this may be attributed even in part to that abolition is debatable, as the nature of society in general and crime in particular has changed dramatically over that period. Drug-related gun crime, for example, has greatly increased, as have stabbings and virtually motiveless killings in street fights. Domestic murders have decreased, possibly because divorce has become so much easier.

Statistics, it seems, will never answer this question, but without reliable information on the influence of the death penalty on the intentions of potential murderers, that is the only way we have of trying to find an answer.

132. Did Sigurd Eysteinsson really die after being bitten by a severed head?

Sigurd Eysteinsson, also known as Sigurd the Mighty, was the second Viking Lord of Orkney and a leader in the ninth-century Viking conquest of northern Scotland. According to the Orkneyinga saga, written by an unknown Icelandic author around 1230, the cause of his death was a bite from a dead man's head.

The saga recounts how Sigurd challenged a native ruler, Mael Brigte the Bucktoothed, to a battle with forces of forty men on each side. Sigurd treacherously brought eighty men, and after winning the battle beheaded Mael Brigte and strapped the head to his saddle to take it back as a trophy. On the ride back, however, his leg was scratched by Mael Brigte's buck-tooth. The wound became infected and killed him.

It's a great story and seems to have been generally accepted as true, but the Norse sagas are such a mix of historic truth, legend and romanticism that we shall probably never know.

133. Was King Harold shot in the eye with an arrow at the Battle of Hastings?

As everyone knows from the Bayeux Tapestry (which isn't a tapestry anyway, but an embroidery), King Harold II of England died at the Battle of Hastings in 1066 from an arrow shot into his eye. Or did he? Recently, increasing doubts have been expressed about this long-held view.

First, there is the matter of other accounts of Harold's death, the earliest of which was written long before the tapestry appeared. In the *Gesta Normannorum Ducum* ('Deeds of the Norman Kings') by William of Jumièges, which was written around 1070, Harold is said to have fallen 'covered with deadly wounds', but there is no mention of an arrow in his eye.

Second, there is evidence from the tapestry itself on which investigations have raised all sorts of questions concerning the horseman with an arrow in his eye. The words 'HAROLD REX INTERFECTUS EST' ('King Harold is killed') are inscribed above it, but they may refer to another character in the picture, particularly the soldier falling to the ground next to an axe. Also, it has been suggested that the 'arrow' was in fact a mistake in restoration of the embroidery, having originally been no more than a dotted line of stitch marks.

Towards the end of 2014, an even more surprising account was found in a twelfth-century document in the British Museum which claimed that Harold survived the battle and died quietly of old age some forty years later after living out his life in obscurity.

134. How did King Edward II die?

After a massively contentious and unsuccessful twenty-year reign, Edward II was forced to abdicate in 1327 by forces led by his wife, Isabella of France, whom he had married when she was twelve, and her lover Roger Mortimer. The king was imprisoned first at Kenilworth Castle, then moved to Berkeley Castle in Gloucestershire. On 23 September his son was informed that his father had died and he took the throne as Edward III. Over the next fifteen years very different accounts of how he died emerged.

Until 1330 such stories followed the official account that the king had died of natural causes, but after that date the suggestion that he had been murdered became common. Around 1340 accounts began to appear that the mode of murder had been by a piece of metal pushed up his anus through a horn to destroy his entrails while leaving no mark on the outside of his body. Early such accounts said the metal was a rod of copper, but this soon changed into a red-hot iron poker. Such a suggestion may have been made to draw attention to the king's long-term homosexual relationship with Piers Gaveston.

Most modern historians discount the red-hot iron story as a myth, but accept that he was murdered in September 1327. Recently, however, increasing attention has been given to evidence purporting to show that Edward II was still alive in 1330. There had certainly been attempts made to rescue him from his imprisonments, and it could be argued that if such a rescue had succeeded, it might have been in the interests of both his supporters and his enemies to pretend he was dead.

135. What happened to Antoine de Saint-Exupéry?

Antoine Marie Jean-Baptiste Roger, comte de Saint-Exupéry (1900–44) was an aviator, writer, poet and French aristocrat best known for his fantasy *The Little Prince*, which has been translated into 250 languages and is said by some to have been outsold, as a work of fiction, only by Tolkien's *Lord of the Rings*.

At the outbreak of the Second World War, Saint-Exupéry was flying planes on airmail routes in Europe and signed up for the French Air Force. When France capitulated to Germany, he travelled to the USA on a mission to persuade the Americans to join the war against the Nazis. During that period he wrote *The Little Prince*, but returned to join the Free French Air Force in North Africa, despite officially being well over the age limit for pilots.

Flying from Corsica on a reconnaissance mission in July 1944, he disappeared over the Mediterranean, vanishing without trace. In September 1998 an identity bracelet with the names of Saint-Exupéry, his wife and his publisher was found near Riou island, south of Marseilles. That, however, was a long way from his flight path and its authenticity was therefore disputed.

In May 2000 a diver found remains from a Lockheed P-38 Lightning spread over a large area again south of Marseilles. The remains were later confirmed to have come from the plane Saint-Exupéry was flying. None of the remnants bore any signs indicating that the plane had been shot down. Why it crashed and how it came to be found so far from its flight path remain open questions.

See also GUILLOTINES 224; SHEEP 417; SOCRATES 440

DINOSAURS

136. Why did some dinosaurs have such extravagant horns or crests on their heads?

Many large dinosaurs such as *Triceratops* had huge horns, crests or neck frills, but what was the function of these impressive structures? There have been many suggestions:

- They may have served to attract mates.
- They may have helped individuals to identify themselves to members of their own species.
- They may have served as weapons when fighting rivals.
- They may have acted as resonance chambers to increase the power of the creature's roar.
- They may have served a protective function.
- They may have had a thermostatic function to help control the creature's body temperature.

We just don't know.

137. How did dinosaurs mate?

How did tyrannosauruses and other large dinosaurs have sex? In 2012 and 2013 that question was much discussed by palaeontologists, resulting in several conflicting theories. Some years earlier, English researcher Dr Beverly Halstead had said: 'All dinosaurs used the same basic position to mate. Mounting from the rear, he put his forelimbs on her shoulders, lifting one hind limb across her back and twisting his tail under hers.' Minnesota academic Kristi Curry Rogers was still of a similar opinion. Pointing out that a tyrannosaurus penis is estimated to have been almost four metres long, she said: 'The most likely position to have intercourse is for the male behind the female, and on top of her, and from behind. Any other position is unfathomable.'

Brian Switek, author of *My Beloved Brontosaurus*, pointed out, however, that females could not raise their tails because the bones at the top were fused. There was also the problem of lethal spikes on dinosaurs' backs which could be a fatal hazard. A computer reconstruction in Berlin led to the conclusion that a male *Kentrosaurus* mounting from behind would face castration.

Another point of view was put forward by US biologist Stuart Landry Jr in 1994. In his opinion, dinosaurs were too heavy to make love on land and would have fallen over if they tried. He suggested that they must have had sex in mud-holes or bodies of water.

Professor Switek identified one vital reason why there is such a mystery surrounding the question of dinosaur sex: 'Soft tissues are seldom preserved during fossilisation, so we have never found a fossilised phallus, but doing so would solve many mysteries.'

138. How fast did dinosaurs move?

There are three basic ways of trying to work out how fast dinosaurs moved, but none of them really works:

(i) *Morphological* This involves looking at the shape of skeletons of modern animals and the length of their limbs and any other bodily factors, such as stance and the angles at which the limbs attach to the torso, that we think may affect their speed of movement. Then we correlate these factors with the animals' known top speeds and use the results to predict the top speeds of animals the size of dinosaurs. The trouble with this method is that we have no way of knowing whether the results obtained on living animals would scale up to something the size of the large dinosaurs. We also do not know whether speed would have been as important in the evolution of dinosaurs as it is for present-day mammals.

(ii) *Biomechanical* This is pure engineering. If we knew the muscular structure of dinosaurs, we could estimate the power they could generate and a knowledge of their weight would then enable us to work out how fast they could travel. Getting a reliable estimate of the musculature of a 65-million-year-old fossil, however, is not easy.

(iii) *Footprints* By looking at the footprints left by dinosaurs and measuring how far apart they are, we can see what their stride length was, and comparing their stride length with the length of their legs would enable us to estimate the speed they were travelling at. This sounds the most reliable method of all – as long as we know that the fossil whose legs we are measuring was the same animal that left the footprints. Unfortunately, matching dinosaur footprints to dinosaur skeletons has never been possible.

The only thing we can say with a fair chance of being right is that the tyrannosaurus in the film *Jurassic Park* was running too fast.

See also BIRDS 64; NOSES 342; PANGOLINS 354; TYRANNOSAURUSES 459–61

DISEASE

139. Did seals bring tuberculosis to the Americas?

An intriguing theory was advanced in 2014 that seals had been responsible for transmitting tuberculosis (TB) to the Americas. Until then, the similarity between strains of TB from America and Europe had led to the conclusion that it had been contact with Europeans that brought it to America, but the new theory was based on palaeoanthropological detective work.

The technique involved the examination of all known strains of TB, seeing how much they differ from each other and estimating how long it would have taken for such differences to evolve. The results suggested that TB began in Africa around 70,000 years ago and that the modern

European variant is no more than 6,000 years old. Traces of TB have, however, been found in 1,000-year-old Peruvian mummies.

Putting these dates together reveals that TB reached America well before Columbus, but long after the land bridge between Asia and America had disappeared. It must therefore have arrived by sea, and according to the paper in *Nature*, it probably came from Africa to South America and the prime suspect is seals.

140. Why does Down syndrome happen?

Most people are born with forty-six chromosomes, twenty-three from the mother and twenty-three from the father. Babies with Down syndrome, however, have an extra copy of one of these chromosomes, chromosome 21. Usually this results in the baby having three copies of chromosome 21 instead of the usual two in every cell of the body, though far more rarely the extra chromosome may only be in some cells, or even be 'translocated' to a different chromosome and not appear as an extra chromosome 21 at all.

Only this last form, translocational Down syndrome, can be inherited. In all other cases, which is around 98 per cent, the extra chromosome is seen as a random event during cell division, early in the development of the foetus. We do not know what triggers such an event and we do not know what the connection is between the extra chromosome and the wide range of features, both physical and mental, that are commonly associated with Down syndrome.

141. What caused the Dancing Plague of 1518?

In July 1518 a dancing mania affected the people of Strasbourg in the Alsace. It began when a woman, Frau Troffea, began to dance fervently in the street, continuing to do so for between four and six days. Within a week thirty-four others had joined her, and within a month there were reported to be around 400 dancers, some of whom died from heart attacks, strokes or exhaustion.

Bizarrely, local physicians decided that the Dancing Plague was a 'natural disease' caused by hot blood and could be best treated by encouraging the dancers to continue dancing. Two guildhalls, a grain market and a specially constructed stage were set aside for that purpose, and musicians were paid to accompany them.

The cause of the dancing mania has never been explained.

142. What is the cause of Tourette's syndrome?

There is a group of specialized cells deep inside the brain called the basal ganglia, which are known to help regulate movement. They are also thought to play a part in decision-making and motivation, so when a person has a sudden urge to perform an action that the conscious mind neither wants nor can explain, as happens in Tourette's syndrome, the basal ganglia are thought to have something to do with it. The result is a verbal or physical tic, beyond the control of the sufferer, sometimes consisting of the repeated utterance of an irrelevant or rude word. But that's about as much as anyone knows.

The structure of the basal ganglia in Tourette sufferers has been seen to differ from normal, but whether that is the cause of Tourette's or a result of it is unknown. Studies on twins have shown that genetics may play a part, but no specific Tourette's gene has yet been identified.

143. To what extent can Alzheimer's disease be staved off?

'Three cups of coffee a day could stave off Alzheimer's disease', reported the *Daily Telegraph* in 2012.

'Meditation can help ward off Alzheimer's disease', said the *Daily Express*.

'Viagra could be used to stave off dementia', the *Daily Mail* reported.

'Nicotine patches may help fight Alzheimer's', insisted the *Daily Mirror*.

Other recent reports from sources ranging from reputable scientific journals to the popular press have put their anti-Alzheimer's money on fish and vegetables, red grapes, knowing a second language, or nuts, seeds and olive oil.

Much of the research leading to the above claims, however, has been studies on mice or fruit flies. Whether any of the above reduce a human being's chances of developing Alzheimer's disease, and if so, by how much, is a topic which – as they are so fond of saying – requires further research.

144. What is the function of prions?

We have already discussed the mystery of how prions reproduce (→ 61), but their function is also a puzzle. Prions are types of protein that have been found to be the cause of some devastating diseases in animals and humans alike. Scrapie in sheep, bovine spongiform encephalopathy (BSE, or 'mad cow disease') in cattle, and Creutzfeld–Jakob Disease (CJD) in humans have all been shown to be caused by prions. So was the disease called 'kuru', which was spread by cannibalism in New Guinea.

Prions have been found in the brains of all mammals that have been studied. Normally they present no problems, but when they go wrong, they can be highly infectious in a unique way. Like all proteins, prions are formed of strings of amino acids folded into a three-dimensional form. Rogue prions are misfolded, and despite not having the DNA or RNA usually essential for anything to reproduce, they have the capacity to hijack other proteins and cause them to misfold. The mechanics of how this happens is not understood, but it leads to fatal results when prions start attacking the neurons in their host's brain, which leads to the death of cells and the release of more prions.

The fact that all mammals have prions suggests that they must have evolved for a purpose other than to take over our brains and kill us, but what that purpose is has yet to be determined. Studies on mice have suggested that prions may have a role in helping neurons communicate. They may even have a role in delaying mental degeneration, but what that role is and how they perform it is unknown.

145. How many people are harbouring dormant CJD?

When an epidemic of BSE, or mad cow disease, hit Britain in the early 1990s and was linked to several cases of CJD in humans, research on prion diseases increased dramatically. Cattle had been fed on foodstuffs obtained by rendering sheep that had suffered from scrapie. It was known that scrapie could not be transmitted directly from sheep to humans, which led to the assumption that it could not be transmitted from sheep to humans via cows. The new version, vCJD, proved that assumption to be tragically incorrect.

Prion diseases are known to incubate in the brains of both animals and people for long periods. In 2006 a study was published based on cases in New Guinea of kuru, a prion disease thought to have been caused by the cannibalistic practice of eating human brains. That practice died out several decades ago, but cases of kuru continued to be reported. The conclusion was that its incubation period could be as long as forty years. Since incubation periods tend to be longer in diseases spread across species, it has been suggested that vCJD may lie dormant for fifty years before symptoms appear.

One report in 2006 suggested that 'millions' could be affected in the UK alone. The first case of vCJD was notified in 1996. By 2014 a total of 229 sufferers had been identified, 177 of whom were from the UK. In recent years, the number of new cases has gone down to about two a year. Whether that is a sign that few are harbouring it, or that it has a very long incubation period, only time will tell.

146. What causes schizophrenia?

Schizophrenia is a long-term mental illness that may lead to disordered thoughts and beliefs, delusions, and generally losing touch with reality, but its causes are unknown. There is strong evidence of a genetic link: while 1 per cent of people will suffer from schizophrenia in their lifetime, that figure rises to 10 per cent of people with a close relative who suffers from it. If that close relative is an identical twin, the chances of getting the illness rise to 50 per cent or more. It seems unlikely, though, that schizophrenia is caused by a single gene or a small set of genes.

Some progress has been made in identifying differences in the brains of schizophrenics, or in their brain chemicals, but if, as seems likely, schizophrenia is caused by an interaction of genes and psychosocial factors, we could still be a very long way from being able to predict whether an individual is likely to develop it or not.

147. What is the link between vitamin D and depression?

An extensive survey in 2013 revealed a strong statistical correlation between people's vitamin D levels and whether or not they suffered from depression. Low levels of the vitamin were found to be linked to depression and risk of depression. It is an open question, however, whether low levels of vitamin D cause depression, make it worse, or are a symptom of the depression itself. There is no known mechanism which can explain how vitamin D could relieve depression.

Since our bodies produce vitamin D when exposed to sunlight, an alternative explanation of the supposed link could simply be that the people who get the least sunlight are the most likely to suffer depression.

See also ANATOMY 6; AUSTEN 34; BIOLOGY 61; CANCER 84–6; EBOLA 165–7; HUMAN EVOLUTION 235; LONGEVITY 281; MUSIC 327

DOGS

148. Is it normal for dogs to chase their tails?

Until recently, tail-chasing in dogs was seen as perfectly normal and several reasons were offered for why they might do so: it could be boredom, or fleas, or a natural response to suddenly catching sight of something usually out of its line of vision. In 2012, however, researchers in Helsinki came up with another diagnosis: obsessive compulsive disorder.

Their study, conducted among 368 dog owners, showed that tail-chasing was associated with behaviours such as timidity and fear of loud noises. It was also found to be reduced by giving the dogs vitamin supplements. They concluded that tail-chasing could be a mental health issue but thought that a genetic component probably also played a part.

149. Can dogs make inferences?

The ancient Greeks argued about whether dogs were capable of reasoning. The logician Chrysippus (280–204 BC) suggested the case of a dog tracking its prey and reaching a point where the road branches into three. After sniffing two of the paths and picking up no scent, the dog takes the third path without sniffing, apparently reasoning that its prey must have gone that way because it didn't take either of the other two roads.

In 1615 King James I of England took part in a debate in Cambridge about logical ability in dogs, and the argument continues even today. In 2014 researchers in Japan published the results of a curious set of experiments with thirty-four pet dogs. Each dog was at first presented with two containers, only one of which contained food. The containers had also been sprayed to ensure they all had the same smell, so the dog could not detect which held the food. The experimenter then pointed to the container with the food. In general the dogs seemed to understand, and when left to choose, they went for the correct container. The second stage of the experiment again featured two containers, but this time the experimenter opened them to show which one had the food, closed them again and then pointed to the empty one. The final, third, stage was a repeat of the first stage.

When the responses of the dogs at the first and third stages were compared, it was found that significantly fewer dogs followed the experimenter's pointing at stage three than had done so at phase one. The researchers concluded that: 'dogs are highly skilled at understanding human pointing gestures, but also they make inferences about the reliability of a human who presents cues and consequently modify their behaviour flexibly depending on the inference.'

Or it could just be that by the time they arrived at stage three, the dogs were really confused. Further research is clearly needed.

150. Where were dogs first domesticated?

The genetic similarity between dogs and wolves confirms that they had a common ancestor, but when the species diverged, and when the first dog-wolves were domesticated, have long been contentious matters.

According to one theory, dogs and wolves first split somewhere in East Asia around 32,000 year ago, but another study concluded that dogs were only domesticated around 10,000 years ago, when the Agricultural Revolution led to scrap heaps of food waste which wolves started scavenging.

The latest study, based on analysis of mitochondrial DNA from dog and wolf fossils and comparison of that DNA with modern dogs and wolves, concluded that modern dogs are more closely related to European fossils than to those from Asia. They also concluded that most domestic dogs last shared a common ancestor 18,800 years ago, but they last shared a common ancestor with a wolf around 32,100 years ago. Domestication must have occurred sometime between those dates, but that still leaves a window of over 13,000 years for when it first happened.

The question is further complicated by a 32,000-year-old dog skull found in Goyet Cave in Belgium. It is quite unclear whether this came from an early domestication attempt and represents a species that died out, or whether it came from an unknown species of wolf.

Since most of the earliest European dogs fossils are thought to be about 15,000 years old and the oldest Asian dog fossils are no more than 13,000 years old, that still leaves many thousands of years in which we do not know what happened in canine domestication.

151. Are dogs social eavesdroppers?

People gain information about each other by watching how we behave with others. We are more likely to choose to interact with people we see being generous than with those who display signs of meanness. This is called 'social eavesdropping' and two recent studies came to different conclusions about whether dogs do the same in their dealings with people.

The first study, in 2011, involved dogs watching two researchers eating cereal from a pot that also contained sausages. A third researcher then entered the room and begged for some cereal. One of the cereal-eaters then shared his meal with the newcomer, the other shooed him away. When the dog was then let off its lead, it was found to be significantly more likely to approach the generous researcher, apparently in the hope of being given a sausage, which the researchers apparently had not been interested in eating themselves.

Curiously, however, the experiments showed that the dog was more influenced by the tone of voice of the two researchers than by the act of giving food away. The researchers concluded: 'We found that the dogs were capable of eavesdropping on human food-sharing interactions, and vocal communication was particularly important to convey the human's cooperative versus noncooperative intent.'

In 2014 a similar experiment was conducted in which the two experimenters swapped their positions, switching sides relative to the dog halfway through the experiment. The results showed that the side the person was sitting on was the critical factor affecting the dogs' choices, not the person. The conclusion was: 'The results of these experiments provide no evidence for social eavesdropping in dogs.'

152. Can dogs tell men's voices from women's?

Research has shown that dogs can distinguish between the sound of dogs barking and sounds made by other animals or other non-dog noises, but can they tell men's voices from women's? To try to answer that question, an experiment was conducted in which a man and a woman stood on either side of a speaker through which a male or female voice was played. A dog was placed facing the two people and the speaker, and the researchers observed whether the dog, on hearing the voice, inclined its head towards the man or the woman.

Some dogs' responses seemed to indicate that they could tell the sex of the voice, but others did not. As might have been expected, dogs living in households with three or more adults looked towards the 'correct' person far more frequently than dogs living with only one person. In such cases, the dogs made the right choice 80 per cent of the time. Yet for the other dogs, 71 per cent looked towards the wrong person. Perhaps dogs from single-person households are more suspicious of people and choose to look at the person they think was silent, while dogs from multi-person households choose to incline their heads towards the supposed source of the voice. Or it may not be the supposed sex of the voice they are responding to at all.

153. Do dog owners have healthier children?

Research conducted in various countries around the world has reported health benefits associated with owning a dog. The exercise involved in walking a dog, and the increased social interaction caused by dog-walking, have both been cited as benefiting health. In 2012, however, a more direct link between pet dogs and children's health was suggested by researchers in California after a study on respiratory disease in mice.

They found that mice which had been fed house dust from homes with dogs became protected from respiratory syncytial virus (RSV), a common cold strain associated with symptoms including mucus production and lung inflammation. RSV is a leading cause of bronchiolitis and can be fatal to premature or chronically ill infants.

As the researchers pointed out, mice are not the same as humans, but the result suggests that there may be a direct link between healthy children and germs associated with dogs. Previous research had suggested that children in dog-owning homes are less likely to suffer from asthma. The RSV connection may help explain why.

154. How do dogs catch frisbees?

A good deal of study has been done on how baseball players or cricketers catch balls. Essentially the task involves making a quick prediction of the speed and flight path of the ball and then selecting a route to run that will allow interception of the ball before it hits the ground. A study in 2004 suggested that dogs catch frisbees in much the same way.

The authors of the paper 'How dogs navigate to catch Frisbees', which appeared in *Psychological Science*, report that: 'Using micro-video cameras attached to the heads of 2 dogs, we examined their optical behavior while catching Frisbees. Our findings reveal that dogs use the same viewer-based navigational heuristics previously found with baseball players.' Specifically, they say that the dogs kept the target 'along a linear optical trajectory, LOT, with optical speed constancy' using 'simple control mechanisms that utilize invariant geometric properties'.

What the dog thinks it is doing is another question entirely, but cricketers and baseball players probably don't know what's going on in their heads when they catch a ball either.

See also ANIMALS 18; EBOLA 167; PSYCHOLOGY 389; SHEEP 417; WALRUSES 486

DOLPHINS

155. Why do whales and dolphins put up with remoras?

The relationship between remoras, which are also known as suckerfish, and dolphins and whales is difficult to explain. Remoras are fish which may be over seventy-five centimetres long and which are topped with long flat fins that look rather like the soles of running shoes. These form a gripping surface that enables them to attach themselves to whales or dolphins.

Very little is known of their lives before they find such a creature to stick to, but once they have done so, the benefits are clear: they suck blood from their hosts to provide food, they hitch a free ride, giving them increased opportunity for finding a mate, and their new home offers protection from sharks and other predators.

This raises the question of what's in it for the whales and dolphins. The remoras may help clean wounds, remove dead skin or clear parasites, but it is difficult to see how such benefits over a comparatively small area can be worth the irritation and drag they cause.

Remoras are far more frequently seen on young whales and dolphins than on adults, but it is unknown whether this is because remoras prefer younger hosts or because only older ones have worked out how to get rid of them.

156. Why do some dolphins use sponges?

Dolphins come in two varieties: spongers and non-spongers. This remarkable discovery was announced in 1997 when a group of bottlenose dolphins was observed off the coast of Australia carrying sponges in their mouths. Further investigations revealed that more than half the female dolphins in the area did this, and 'sponging' had first been seen in dolphins at least 160 years earlier.

One idea was that they carried the sponges in order to protect their noses from sharp rocks or stingrays or other hazards they might encounter while foraging for food, but more recently another theory has emerged: carrying the sponges may help them find food sources that non-spongers cannot reach.

Investigations of tissue samples from both spongers and non-spongers indicated that the two groups had totally different diets. It has been suggested that carrying sponges somehow helps the spongers to locate fish that live on the seafloor. Normally these are difficult for dolphins to find as their location impedes the proper functioning of the dolphin's echolocation system, but for some reason carrying sponges seems to help.

157. Why do dolphins go deaf?

A survey in 2010 reported that nearly half of all stranded dolphins turning up on beaches from Florida to the Caribbean were suffering from severe hearing loss. Whether they had been washed up on the beach suffering from exhaustion because their poor hearing had prevented them from finding food by echolocation, or whether deafness had damaged their navigational abilities, was not known.

The cause of the deafness is also not known. It could simply be age, but shipping noise and military sonar have also been suspected as possible causes.

DRACULA

158. Did Dracula ever live in Transylvania?

Bram Stoker's fictional vampire Dracula has often been associated with the historical figure of Vlad Tepes, or Vlad the Impaler, though the evidence is unconvincing that Bram even knew of the existence of Vlad, let alone based his character on him. In early versions of his manuscript, Stoker called him 'Count Wampyr' but changed it to 'Dracula' after reading that the name, in the Wallachian language, meant 'Devil'.

Whatever the reason for Stoker's choice, and whether or not he knew it, the name 'Dracula' was shared by Vlad Tepes. His father, Vlad II, ruler of Wallachia, was inducted by King Sigismund of Hungary into the knightly Order of the Dragon. That gave Vlad II a new surname, Dracul, which was the old Romanian word for 'dragon' (and later came to mean 'devil', as Stoker had read). As his son, Vlad Tepes, or Vlad III as he became, was known as 'Son of the Dragon', or 'Draculea'.

At the time of the younger Vlad's birth, thought to have been in 1431, his father definitely owned property in Sigisoara in Transylvania, where Vlad III is often said to have been born, but according to Florin Curta, a professor of medieval history and archaeology at the University of Florida, there is no real evidence that this was the case.

Vlad III also never owned any property himself in Transylvania, and Bran Castle – the modern tourist attraction in Romania also known as 'Dracula's Castle' – had no connection with him. According to Curta, Vlad III may well have been born in Targoviste, which was the royal seat of the principality of Wallachia, where Vlad II was a 'voivode', or ruler.

159. Where was Vlad Dracul buried?

One thing that is true about Vlad is that he was indeed an impaler. His favourite way of executing his enemies was by impaling them on long stakes, and the sight of 20,000 impaled corpses on the roadside was enough to persuade at least one rival leader not to confront him.

There have long been at least five versions of precisely how and where Vlad met his end, but until recently there was general agreement that he was killed in battle against the Turkish army at the end of 1476. One contemporary account reported that he was decapitated and his head sent to Constantinople.

In 2014, however, researchers from Estonia uncovered the headstone of a tomb in Naples which bore carvings of dragons and other images and symbols relating to Vlad Tepes. They point out that the graveyard of Piazza Santa Maria La Nova, where the headstone was found, is also where Vlad's son and daughter were buried. Their belief is that he was not killed by the Turks but captured and held for ransom, which was eventually paid by his daughter. They say this claim is supported by documentary evidence, and they have asked permission to investigate the grave.

DREAMS

160. What happens when we 'see' things in our dreams?

Some people say they dream in black and white while others claim to dream in colour. People who are blind often report seeing things in their dreams. But our eyes are closed when we are asleep, so what is this 'seeing' that we claim to be doing?

One factor that makes this difficult to answer is that we cannot report our dreams while we are dreaming. Our accounts of them are our conscious interpretations of the sensory stimulations and sensations generated while we were asleep. What we say we see in dreams we could not have seen at all, as our primary visual cortex was out of commission at the time. Our secondary visual cortex, however, which is where we interpret visual stimuli, is still working, trying to make sense of the images thrown up by our dreaming brains.

On the question of whether dreams are in colour or black and white, research has suggested that people's responses to that question are age-related: young people report dreaming in colour; the elderly dream in black and white. It has been suggested that this is related to the pictures on TV screens when one was growing up. Colours in dreams have also been linked to high emotions, but whether such colours were there at the time of the dream or have been painted in afterwards is not known.

161. Is dreaming a conscious state?

The trouble with consciousness was beautifully expressed by Stuart Sutherland in the *Macmillan Dictionary of Psychology* in 1989: 'Consciousness is a fascinating but elusive phenomenon: it is impossible to specify what it is, what it does, or why it has evolved. Nothing worth reading has been written on it.'

We all have a strong feeling that we know what it means, however, and it's something to do with being aware of the external world and disappears when we fall asleep. But where does that leave dreams? Our brains, during dreams, are using memories and knowledge of the world, albeit sometimes in a rather perverse way, to generate thoughts. We are not consciously aware of those thoughts at the time, but we can often reconstruct them when we regain consciousness.

And then there are questions about lucid dreaming, when we seem to be both conscious and dreaming at the same time, and hypnosis, when we react to the external world but not in a conscious way. We need to know a good deal more about the nature of consciousness itself to formulate answers to such questions as these.

See also BRAINS 79; SLEEP 423–9

EARS

162. How do our genes affect our earlobes?

Arguments about earlobe genetics are almost as old as genetics itself. In 1922 – just seventeen years after the word 'genetics' had been coined by William Bateson, in 1905 – a study was published giving a highly simplistic view of earlobes, based on a small and inadequate sample. The neat but fallacious conclusions of the study formed an earlobe myth that has persisted to the present day: that earlobes may be classified as either free (F) or attached (A), and that trait is controlled by a single gene with the two alleles F and A, of which F is dominant.

The study had indeed shown that among the families studied, all children of two A parents had attached earlobes, but there were no children in the study with two F parents, so there was insufficient evidence to say that the F allele was dominant.

An even greater problem lay in the classification of earlobes into those two categories. Any close inspection of a significant number of ears reveals a full spectrum of ear attachments, with the height of the attachment point (technically known as the 'otobasion inferius') varying from total lobe freedom given by attachment at the top right down to no freedom at all when it is attached at its lowest point (the 'subaurale').

Later studies identified many A offspring from two F parents, as well as many F offspring from two A parents. Researchers differ in the percentages quoted, but they all agree that earlobes cannot be controlled by a single gene.

Summarizing the results in 2011, the Delaware geneticist John H. McDonald wrote: 'While there is probably some genetic influence on earlobe attachment point, family studies show that it does not fit the simple one-locus, two-allele myth.' He then added the cautionary advice: 'You should not use earlobe attachment to demonstrate basic genetics.'

See also ANATOMY 4; CHINA 103

EARTH

163. Why is the Earth's magnetic field weakening?

In July 2014 data from European Space Agency satellites indicated a weakening of the Earth's magnetic field. While the field had strengthened in some areas mainly in the Indian Ocean, these were heavily outweighed by a decrease over most of North and South America and surrounding regions.

Previously it had been estimated that the Earth's magnetic field was weakening by about 5 per cent a century; the new results suggest that it could be ten times faster. The cause of this is unknown; some have suggested that a slowing-down of the liquid metal in the outer Earth's core beneath America is responsible, others that it is an indication that the Earth's magnetic poles might be about to flip, as has happened in the past. The Earth's magnetic polarity reverses every few hundred millennia, with the north and south poles swapping location, but what causes the flip or how long it takes is unknown.

164. When and where will the next super-volcano erupt?

Around 640,000 years ago, a massive volcanic eruption occurred in what is now Wyoming, ejecting more than 1,000 cubic kilometres of ash and lava into the atmosphere. It created a huge crater, called a 'caldera', in what became Yellowstone Park. For comparison, the biggest recent volcanic eruption was at Mount Pinatubo in the Philippines in 1991, which ejected only about 10 cubic kilometres of ash and lava. Pinatubo decreased the global temperature by 0.4 °C for a few months; a super-volcano eruption of the size that occurred in Wyoming is predicted to lead to a fall in temperatures of 10 °C lasting for a decade. In short, a super-volcano eruption is far worse than any natural phenomenon humans have ever experienced, but we know very little of where and when such a thing might happen.

Volcanoes are fuelled by underground chambers of molten rock called magma. When the pressure in these chambers grows too much, the rock is pushed upwards through fissures in the Earth's crust, exploding in an eruption. The magma chambers of super-volcanoes are much larger and much deeper, and their depth makes them difficult to detect and measure.

At the end of 2013 a study reported that the magma chamber beneath Yellowstone was two-and-a-half times the size previously thought. It is 55 miles long and 18 miles wide, runs at depths of between 3 and 9 miles, and is thought to contain at least as much magma as it did at the time of its last eruption. Other sites of ancient super-volcano eruptions have been identified around the world, but in most cases we do not know the size of their magma chambers or even if they still exist. We also do not know how they store such vast volumes of molten rock for so long, or what triggers an eruption.

See also ANTS 21; COSMOLOGY 120; EVOLUTION 181; GEOLOGY 212; GLOBAL WARMING 216; INTELLIGENCE 253; MARS 285–6; MERCURY 304; METEOROLOGY 308, 310; SALMON 399; SOLAR SYSTEM 443–4; WATER 488

EBOLA

165. Did Ebola pass from bats to humans, and if so, how?

Following the Ebola outbreak in West Africa in 2014, the disease became the subject of a great deal of research, but how it started is still a mystery. A year earlier, a toddler in Meliandou in Guinea died of an unknown disease. Soon after, his sister, mother and grandmother also died, and they are thought to have been the first victims of the epidemic. How the toddler caught Ebola in the first place is unknown, but bats are the prime suspect.

Several species of bat are known to survive experimental infection with the virus, and Ebola virus RNA has been found in at least three species of fruit bat. The toddler in Meliandou is known to have liked playing in a hollow tree in which bats roosted, but there is no evidence that he was bitten by a bat, and it is not known whether his family were in the habit of eating bats. Unfortunately, before researchers arrived in Meliandou, the tree burnt down, preventing any investigation of the bats beyond reports that a 'rain of bats' came from the burning tree and that they were a small smelly species with long tails.

166. How have some people managed to survive Ebola?

Ebola kills people by attacking their immune system. Not only does the virus deplete the white cells of the immune system, but it turns the immune system against itself, making it release inflammatory molecules, which cause tiny blood vessels to burst, leading in turn to a drop in blood pressure and multi-organ failure. Of all the people infected with Ebola, over half have died, but how the others survive has been a matter of urgent research.

One gene, known to be important in the functioning of the immune system, has been linked to Ebola survival, and another genetic mutation has been found to produce cells that resist Ebola infection in the laboratory. The majority of the survivors tested, however, display neither of the genes, so other as yet undiscovered factors must also be involved.

167. Why doesn't Ebola have any bad effects on pigs, bats and mice?

The Ebola virus has been detected in chimpanzees, gorillas, monkeys, antelopes, porcupines, rodents, dogs, pigs, bats and humans, but it is only fatal to primates. The other animals, bats in particular, seem to have developed an immune response to the virus which prevents it infecting host cells. What it is about their immune systems, or the nature of the Ebola virus itself, that has led to this response is not known.

EGYPT

168. When was the Great Library of Alexandria destroyed?

The Royal Library of Alexandria was founded in the third century BC by Ptolemy I Soter, a Macedonian general who was one of the successors to Alexander the Great. With a vast collection of papyrus scrolls, it was a major centre of scholarship and perhaps the largest library in the world.

The contents of the library are not known, and it is most famous today for its burning down, which resulted in the irretrievable loss of a great deal of ancient knowledge. When that destruction took place, however, has long been a matter of great speculation. Some say it burnt down as a result of Julius Caesar setting fire to his ships when he was besieged at Alexandria in 48 BC, while others say it was destroyed in AD 391 according to a decree by the Coptic pope Theophilus.

Some Arab sources, however, say the library, or at least some of it, survived until the Muslim conquest of Egypt in AD 640 or 641. For an event that has always been seen as a major intellectual tragedy, we know very little about the destruction of the Great Library at Alexandria.

See also MUMMIES 322; RELIGION 394; SEX 407; TECHNOLOGY 450

EINSTEIN

169. What happened to Einstein's illegitimate daughter?

In 1986, more than thirty years after the death of Albert Einstein, the discovery of letters between him and his first wife, Mileva Marić, revealed for the first time the existence of their daughter Lieserl, who had been born in 1902, the year before Einstein and Marić were married. Lieserl is mentioned several times in the correspondence in 1903, but then disappears and is never mentioned again.

One theory is that she was put up for adoption, another that she was brought up by a friend of her mother, but there is no clear evidence of what happened to her or whether she ever knew she was Einstein's daughter. In the book *Einstein's Daughter: The Search for Lieserl*, published in 1999, the novelist Michele Zackheim concludes that Lieserl died of scarlet fever when young, but others have suggested that she had Down syndrome or may have been blind.

170. How many illegitimate children did Einstein have anyway?

In *Einstein's Daughter: The Search for Lieserl*, Michele Zackheim suggested that Einstein suffered from syphilis and fathered an illegitimate son who lived in Prague, but another alleged love child is the subject of a different story.

In 2011 the death was announced in New York of Evelyn Einstein. Allegedly adopted as a baby by Hans Einstein, son of the great physicist, Evelyn had always maintained that she had actually been fathered by Einstein himself and was the result of his affair with a ballet dancer. She was, she said, brought up by his son to avoid any embarrassment. No DNA evidence was ever offered to support her claim.

See also COSMOLOGY 122, 126; ENERGY 172–3; MATHEMATICS 292; MILKY WAY 317; PHILOSOPHY 362–3

ELEPHANTS

171. Can elephants show insight when solving problems?

In 2006 the American Psychology Association reported a study on elephants under the heading 'Asian elephants do not show insight'. In 2011 another study appeared in the online journal *PloS ONE* with the title 'Insightful problem solving in an Asian elephant'. So do elephants show insight or not?

The earlier experiment involved training elephants to retrieve food from a bin. First the bin had no lid and the elephant was shown the food inside it, then it was trained to retrieve the food with its trunk. Then a lid was placed on the bin and the elephant was trained to throw the lid off and then retrieve the food. Finally the lid was placed on the ground a short distance from the bin. The elephant then walked over to the lid and threw it away before going to the bin and taking the food out. The conclusion was that the elephants were not learning through reasoning but were just following their training blindly and showing no insight.

The later experiment also involved elephants retrieving food, but this time with the use of tools and cubes which the elephant had to stack and climb on to accomplish the task. The animals' success in this was described as 'consistent with the definition of insightful problem solving'. Furthermore, the researchers suggested that: 'Previous failures to demonstrate this ability in elephants may have resulted not from a lack of cognitive ability but from the presentation of tasks requiring trunk-held sticks as potential tools, thereby interfering with the trunk's use as a sensory organ to locate the targeted food.'

See also AVOCADOS 37; HUMAN EVOLUTION 242; TECHNOLOGY 450; WHALES 492

ENERGY

172. What is energy?

Physicists, mathematicians and engineers have been making calculations involving energy for centuries. Stationary objects may have potential energy, which can be converted into kinetic energy. A rise in temperature increases an object's thermal energy, while the atoms in the object itself are held together by nuclear energy. We know, thanks to Einstein, that $E = mc^2$ and in general we know how to calculate the effect of turning one form of energy into another, but that does not help explain what energy itself is. Thinking of energy as a state or a condition helps get round this problem, but still leaves other questions such as...

173. How much energy does space contain?

Ever since the Big Bang the universe has been expanding. On the one hand, this expansion energy is forcing galaxies further apart; on the other hand, gravitational forces are drawing them together. In 1998 observations of distant galaxies from the Hubble Space Telescope revealed that the rate of expansion of the universe was increasing and had been doing so for about 7.5 billion years.

The only explanation was that space itself possessed a 'dark energy' that was forcing galaxies apart. However, when we try to calculate how much energy that consists of, we run into huge problems. If we calculate it according to Einstein's gravitational theory, we can work out the energy needed to account for the measured rate of expansion. Alternatively, we can use the quantum theory of matter in which the energy of space is provided by virtual particles which are constantly appearing and disappearing. The trouble is that the second of these methods gives an answer that differs by a factor of around 10^{120} from the answer given by the first method.

We shall return to this problem when we discuss the vacuum catastrophe (→ 371).

174. Does dark flow exist?

In 2008 an extensive survey of galaxy clusters reported a very surprising discovery: they were all heading in the same direction. Since shortly after the Big Bang, a flash of light known as the cosmic microwave background (CMB) has pervaded the universe. Relative to the CMB, all galaxies should, on average, show no preferred direction, but the new findings seemed to show evidence of an unexpected flow of clusters along a line joining the Solar System and a point between the constellations Centaurus and Hydra Vela.

Since the evidence for this 'dark flow' affecting the motion of galaxies was produced, several papers have appeared both challenging the original finding and confirming it. If dark flow exists, there is nothing that would explain it in terms of our current view of the universe. It has even been claimed as the first evidence of the existence of other universes, which provide the gravitational pull behind the dark flow. Like dark matter and dark energy, dark flow has left us in the dark.

ENGLISH HISTORY

175. Who were the green children of Woolpit?

Sometime in the twelfth century, two children described as brother and sister appeared in the Suffolk village of Woolpit. According to two English histories written in 1189 and 1220, they spoke in a language that could not be understood, they would only eat beans, and their skin was a greenish colour. They learnt to eat other food and lost their green colour, but the boy became ill and died. The girl grew up in the village, learnt English, and said that they had come from an underground land called St Martin's Land, where all the inhabitants were green.

The curious thing about this story is that the accounts of it date from only shortly after the events they describe. Fantasies, myths and legends usually date from 'long, long ago'. One theory giving a precise suggestion of the children's origin is that they might have been the offspring of Flemish settlers who had been killed in civil conflict, and that the 'St Martin's Land' they referred to may have been a reference to Fornham St Martin near Bury St Edmunds. If that were so, however, one would have expected someone to recognize the language they spoke.

176. What happened to the body of Alfred the Great?

On 26 October 899 Alfred the Great died. He was buried in the Old Minster in Winchester, but four years later his body was moved to the New Minster. In 1110 the monks of the New Minster were transferred to Hyde Abbey, along with Alfred's body and those of his wife and children.

The graves survived the dissolution of the abbey and demolition of the church in 1539 and were rediscovered by chance in 1788 during the construction of a prison by convicts. The coffins, however, were stripped of lead, and the bones were lost. In the mid-nineteenth century the prison was demolished and a number of bones were found which were said to be those of Alfred and were buried in an unmarked grave in a local church graveyard.

In March 2013 these bones were exhumed and were later radiocarbon-dated, but the results showed that they were from the 1300s and therefore not Alfred's. In 2014, however, a fragment of pelvis unearthed in a 1999 excavation of the Hyde Abbey site was radiocarbon-dated to the correct period. It is not known whether this was Alfred's, but in any case the location of the rest of his remains is unknown.

177. What happened to Queen Cartimandua?

All that we know about Cartimandua, queen of the Brigantes, comes from the writings of the Roman historian Tacitus. She ruled the Brigantes, who were a Celtic people of northern England, at the time of the Roman invasion and was one of the British rulers who announced loyalty to Rome.

Tacitus tells of the English chieftain Caratacus seeking sanctuary with Cartimandua after his defeat by the Romans, and Cartimandua putting him in chains and handing him over to the Romans, who rewarded her well. Despite that, Tacitus describes her behaviour as treacherous and criticizes her for leaving her husband Venutius and replacing him with his armour-bearer Vellocatus.

In AD 69 Cartimandua was overthrown by Venutius and left the area. Nothing is known of her after that date.

'It is a good morning exercise for a research scientist to discard a pet hypothesis every day before breakfast. It keeps him young.'

Konrad Lorenz

EVOLUTION

178. How did the brain evolve?

The trouble with brains is that they consist of soft tissue which does not survive fossilization. We can guess, from the size of their skulls, how big the brains of early animals were; we can also infer, from examining primitive organisms such as bacteria and sea sponges, similarities between their nervous systems and mechanisms in mammalian and human brains. Cells in bacteria communicate with each other through ion channels, which are similar to the channels through which neurons in the brain communicate. Sea sponges use chemical messengers similar to some of those in our brains to detect aspects of their environment. There is a long way to go, however, to fill in the gaps to get a picture of the entire evolution of the brain as we know it.

179. Where did angiosperms come from?

Charles Darwin once described the evolution of flowering plants as 'an abominable mystery'. At the time there seemed to be a sudden abundance of fossils of flowers in the geological record within a relatively short period of time with no evidence of where they had originated. We know a great deal more now, but there are still many questions.

Plants are divided into gymnosperms, which have no flowers or fruits and have unenclosed or 'naked' seeds on the surface of scales or leaves, and angiosperms, which produce flowers or fruit and have seeds enclosed within an ovary. Gymnosperms are unisexual and their seeds are spread by the wind; angiosperms require pollination to reproduce.

It is now known that, while angiosperms evolved significantly later than gymnosperms, they did not develop from them but evolved independently around 130 million years ago. Pollinating insects are thought to have evolved in parallel with them around the same time. While we now know that gymnosperms evolved from seed ferns during the Palaeozoic era, about 390 million years ago, there is still no agreement on what were the evolutionary predecessors of the angiosperms.

You could say that the evolution of flowering plants is still a mystery, though not quite as abominable as in Darwin's day.

180. How did wings evolve?

There is general agreement that wings must have been an example of exaptation, an adaptation of something that previously evolved for a different use. What that use was in the case of wings, however, is a matter of speculation. Suggestions include the following:

(i) Wings evolved from front limbs when quadrupeds started running on two legs, which left the front legs free to catch small prey.

(ii) Wings were an adaptation of front limbs which had been used to help animals leap into the air.

(iii) Wings evolved primarily for sexual display, with females preferring larger ones.

(iv) Wings evolved after scales had turned into feathers, which kept the animal warm, and flying evolved from gliding, which was an accidental bonus of the aerodynamic features of feathers.

181. To what extent has the evolutionary process been inevitable?

What would happen if we could rewind the universe to the moment of the Big Bang, or even the creation of planet Earth, and let it all run again? When Stephen Jay Gould raised that question in his 1989 book *Wonderful Life*, he had no doubt we would see a totally different world develop. The entire process of evolution is so dependent on random mutations and the occasional asteroid colliding accidentally with Earth, that anything could happen.

Certain features of evolution, however, appear inevitable. Life, we like to feel, was bound to happen sooner or later, and with the passage of time more and more complex organisms were likely to come into existence, culminating with the evolution of intelligent life. Believers in God and intelligent design will embrace that argument to explain how He created the world knowing that it would inevitably lead to the evolution of man in His own image.

Others, however, might ask whether mammals and man would ever have evolved and survived if an asteroid hadn't fortuitously wiped out the dinosaurs about 65 million years ago.

182. Why were sauropods so successful?

The sauropod dinosaurs of the Jurassic and Cretaceous periods were the largest terrestrial animals ever by a long way. They weighed up to 120 tons, could be over 30 metres (100 ft) long, and roamed the Earth for around 150 million years. Evolutionarily speaking, as no animal has grown to such dimensions in the 65 million years since, there must have been some environmental features in the Mesozoic era that were particularly favourable to animals of such huge dimensions, but it has proven difficult to pinpoint anything that could have been responsible. In 2011 a paper in the journal *Biology Review* suggested that the long neck, long tail and small head of the sauropods may have combined to allow more efficient food uptake than in other large herbivores. The fact that they didn't chew their food was also cited as a possible contribution to the large size of their bodies compared with their heads. Unfortunately the absence of chewing leaves a big gap in our understanding of their digestive systems, which would affect any calculations about their rate of extracting energy from food, so even this new theory brings us little closer to understanding how they got away with being so large.

183. Which came first: feathers or warm blood?

Two long-running arguments on which opinions have changed several times concern the blood temperature of dinosaurs and the question of whether they had feathers. If, as is now generally thought to have been the case, some of the smaller dinosaurs evolved into birds, they must have had feathers. That idea has been supported since 1980 by findings, particularly in China and Siberia, of feathered dinosaur fossils.

It has been argued, however, that large dinosaurs would have over-heated if they had had feathers. So large cold-blooded dinosaurs may have evolved into smaller warm-blooded, feathered dinosaurs, which became the first birds, but whether the warm blood or the feathers came first is not known.

In 2014 another theory emerged that dinosaurs may have had neither cold nor warm blood – it was somewhere in between. Where feathers fit into that theory is unclear.

184. How much interbreeding went on between ancient human species?

Recent studies of the DNA of Neanderthals suggest that at least two bouts of interbreeding went on between early *Homo sapiens* and Neanderthals. Modern Asians have more Neanderthal DNA than Europeans, which suggests that the interbreeding took place between different migrant groups at different times.

Neanderthals and *Homo sapiens*, however, were not the only species of early human. From *Australopithecus afarensis*, which lived in Africa between 3 and 4 million years ago, to the hobbit-like *Homo floresiensis*, which only died out about 17,000 years ago, fossil evidence has identified around twenty human-like species. The only one, apart from the Neanderthals, that *Homo sapiens* is known to have interbred with are the recently discovered Denisovans, of which fossils were unearthed in Siberia. Whether modern humans did, or even could, breed with other species is unknown.

See also ANATOMY 4, 6; ANIMALS 19; BEES 45; BONES 72; BRAINS 78; CHICKENS 97; DINOSAURS 136–8; FISH 190; GENETICS 210; GORILLAS 221; HUMAN EVOLUTION 234–43; HUMOUR 244; INTELLIGENCE 253; LANGUAGE 268; LEGS 271; LEOPARDS 274; MAMMALS 283; MOTHS 320; MUSIC 329; PANDAS 353; PANGOLINS 355–6; PSYCHOLOGY 386; SEX 408; SLEEP 424, 429; SNAKES 439; WHALES 492

EYES

185. How do we tell black from white?

Look up the terms 'Cornsweet illusion' and 'lateral inhibition' on the Internet and you are liable to be treated to a whole range of visual illusions in which black is made to appear as white, and vice versa. In one of the most striking examples, a portion of a checkerboard is displayed with a shadow cast diagonally across it. In the shadowed area, both the light and dark squares look darker. In fact, a light square in the shadowed area is exactly the same shade as a dark square in the unshadowed area, but our brains refuse to accept that. Even when we know what is happening, the shadowed light square looks much lighter.

This is due, in part at least, to 'lateral inhibition', which is the term given to the capacity of an excited neuron to reduce the activity of its neighbours. Put simply, black looks darker when surrounded by white. But some versions of the illusion cannot be explained by any physiological theory of perception. Telling the difference between black and white is not, as we may have thought, a simple matter of judging how much light they are reflecting.

186. Why do reindeer's eyes change colour in winter?

In 2013 a team from University College London and the University of Tromsø, Norway, announced their discovery that Arctic reindeer's eyes change colour in winter. Reindeer, like many animals, have a layer of tissue behind the retina in the eye called the tapetum lucidum, which reflects light back through it to enhance night vision. In the bright light of summer this layer is gold, but by winter it has turned blue.

The researchers can explain the advantages of this in helping the reindeer to see predators and find food in the murky winter light, but they are unsure how the colour change is accomplished. They suggest that it may be due to increased pressure caused by pupil dilation.

187. What colour were Eleanor of Aquitaine's eyes?

Eleanor of Aquitaine was one of the wealthiest and most powerful women in Europe during the twelfth century. She was wife first to Louis VII of France, then to Henry II of England, and was widely praised for her beauty. In her youth she was described as 'perpulchra' – more than beautiful; when she was thirty, the troubadour Bernard de Ventadour extolled her 'lovely eyes and noble countenance'; even in her seventies, the monk and chronicler Richard of Devizes called her 'beautiful'. Despite all this praise, however, nobody seems to have recorded the colour of her eyes or hair.

See also AUSTEN 33; CANCER 84; DEATH 133; DREAMS 160; HAIR 227; HENRY VIII 229; HUMAN EVOLUTION 239; LOBSTERS 278; SLEEP 425

FASHION

188. Who designed the tuxedo?

The suit known in the USA as a tuxedo and in the UK as a dinner jacket takes its American name from the Tuxedo Park Club, a social club for the New York gentry where the garment made its debut in 1886. One version of its origin gives the credit to Pierre Lorillard IV, a tobacco magnate and one of the developers of Tuxedo Park, who is said to have become irritated by the long tails of the frock coat that was the standard formal wear, so designed a shorter garment that did not interfere with sitting or dancing. It was not Pierre Lorillard but his son Griswold who is credited with being the first to wear it, when he shocked all at the 1886 Autumn Ball at Tuxedo Park by appearing with a group of friends dressed in the outrageous new garment.

Another version, however, gives the credit to James Brown Potter, a co-founder of the Tuxedo Club, who is said to have encountered the style in England when he was invited to Sandringham by the Prince of Wales (later King Edward VII). When he asked what he should wear, the prince sent him to the London tailors Henry Poole & Co. Unfortunately, the records of what Potter ordered have been lost, so we cannot be sure whether this was the dinner jacket which he later introduced to Tuxedo Park.

The archives of Poole & Co. do, however, show that the Prince of Wales himself ordered a 'short celestial blue evening coat' for informal dinners at Sandringham as early as 1865, and this is thought to have been the garment on which dinner jackets were based. Pierre Lorillard is also documented as a customer of Poole & Co. in the 1860s. In the absence of clear records for the designs, it is impossible to say whether the tuxedo, as introduced at Tuxedo Park, was created by Pierre Lorillard, Griswold Lorillard, James Brown Potter, the Prince of Wales or Henry Poole himself.

FISH

189. Why do goldfish like the colour blue?

In 1966 researchers trained goldfish to discriminate between blue, green and red painted panels and reported that all the discriminations were easily learnt by the fish. They also said: 'The results also suggest that the goldfish has a preference for blue.' Why this should be the case is unclear, particularly when seen in the light of later research which has shown that juvenile goldfish have great difficulty discriminating blue from both green and red.

190. Why did fish give up sex?

Recent research has shown that penetrative sex evolved much earlier than had previously been thought. Examination of fossils of a group of fish called antiarchs, which lived around 385 million years ago, has revealed them to have been the first vertebrates to evolve an organ for internal fertilization. Their front limbs are also thought to have been used to hold a mate while fertilization took place.

Antiarchs became extinct, but their descendants appear to have reverted to external fertilization, with penetrative sex evolving again a long time later. This apparently backward evolutionary step had previously been considered highly unlikely, if not impossible. The reasons fish gave up sex are still unknown.

191. Why do convict blennies take mouthfuls of their young and then spit them out?

The convict blenny is a curious eel-like fish that can grow up to sixty centimetres in length. It lives in tunnels or coastal reefs in the western Pacific and the adults seem unusually house-proud. While the young swim out of their nest during the day to feed on plankton, the adults feed in their tunnels and keep the place clean by gathering mouthfuls of debris which they then spit out of the nest.

Adults have also frequently been seen gathering up mouthfuls of their young and spitting them out again. The function of this curious behaviour is not known.

See also BRAINS 78; DOLPHINS 155; SALMON 399; SALT 400

FLORIDA

192. How did Edward Leedskalnin build his coral castle?

Edward Leedskalnin (1887–1951) was a gloriously eccentric Latvian immigrant to the United States who single-handedly built a massive monument in Florida known as the Coral Castle.

After spending six years working in various lumber camps in North America, he contracted tuberculosis and moved to Florida for his health. There, he spent the next twenty years building his Coral Castle, which he dedicated to the sixteen-year-old Latvian girl who had left him the day before their planned wedding.

The castle was made from around 1,000 kilograms of coral which Leedskalnin had quarried himself at night. His tools were basic, made from wood and parts of an old car, and when he was asked how he did it all on his own, he would reply, 'I understand the laws of weight and leverage and I know the secrets of the people who built the pyramids.'

See also DOLPHINS 157

FOOD

193. How should restaurant menus be set out?

In their splendid book *The Perfect Meal* on the science of food and dining, Charles Spence and Betina Piqueras-Fiszman devote fifteen pages to discussing the design of restaurant menus. How does the format of the menu affect diners' choices and, specifically, where should a restaurant owner place the details of an item he is particularly keen for them to order?

Much research has been conducted on how people scan menus and which areas they spend longest looking at. Apparently, the right-hand page of a menu, about a third of the way down the page, is the place that gets the most attention. Enclosing an item in a box is also known to draw people's attention to it. How this affects people's choices, however, is unclear. Spence and Piqueras-Fiszman give an example of a restaurant that applied those findings to the design of their menu, which featured two items in boxes on the supposedly most effective places on the menu. They report: 'This strategy had no effect whatsoever on the sales of the boxed items.' They go on to say: 'We guess that further research is needed here.'

194. Does food taste better when eaten with the fingers?

When I met Charles Spence, I asked him what else he didn't know about the psychology of food. Initially he seemed reluctant to disclose details of his forthcoming research, but then told me they were planning a study to discover whether food tastes better when eaten with the fingers.

Finding myself shortly after in a burger restaurant in which knives and forks were provided in a glass in the centre of each table, I asked a waitress what proportion of people chose to use them. She told me that it was about 50/50, but men are far more likely to eat with their fingers than women. Whether this is a matter of perceived taste or a question of relative size of hands and burger is, I feel sure, a question Professor Spence will address in his research.

195. Why do our taste buds dull in space?

Experience has shown that after a few days in space astronauts may start craving spicy foods much more than they did on Earth. This may partly be accounted for by evidence of a lessening of their sense of smell, which accounts for a good deal of our perception of taste. Why being in space should diminish smell or taste, however, is by no means clear.

One theory is that it may have something to do with weightlessness. In a gravity-free environment, the fluids in a person's body are no longer pulled downwards. This results in more fluids in the head, which apart from giving it a rounder appearance may result in a feeling of congestion similar to the feeling of having a cold. A sniffy inability to smell may then result.

196. Why does champagne from a magnum taste so different from champagne from a standard bottle?

There is general agreement among connoisseurs that champagne from a magnum tastes better than the same wine from a standard bottle. This is even found to be the case in blind tastings, so it cannot be due to a psychological effect of seeing the size of bottle it is poured from: the taste is definitely different and magnums generally taste better.

It must have something to do with the process of ageing in the bottle, and it has been suggested this is to do with the rate of oxidation and the relative surface area of liquid exposed to the air in the different sizes of bottle. What this effect consists of precisely, however, is not known.

197. What is the origin of the Yorkshire pudding?

The earliest recorded recipe for a Yorkshire pudding is to be found in the 1737 edition of a book entitled *The Whole Duty of a Woman*, with the author's name given only as 'A Lady'. The book calls it 'Dripping Pudding', but a very similar recipe appears under the title 'Yorkshire Pudding' in *The Art of Cookery Made Plain and Easy* by Hannah Glasse in 1747.

Cooked in the oven under a roasting joint of meat (the earlier book specifies a shoulder of lamb), this is clearly the model for today's Yorkshire pudding, but it seems to have been made all over Britain at the time and how it became associated specifically with Yorkshire is unknown.

198. Do the microbes in our foods affect the microbes in our guts?

Makers of probiotic foods have long claimed that microbes in the food we eat can have a beneficial effect on the microbes in our guts. Everyone has around 1.5 kilograms of gut bacteria, and it is known that it can affect our appetite, health and even brain function, but there is far less evidence to support the idea that microbes in our diet can affect the microbe content of our guts.

For this to happen, the live bacteria in our foods would first have to survive being eaten and passing through the stomach, which is highly acidic. They would then have to survive and breed in the gut. Ideally, they would also have to have a real effect on our health.

The most that has so far been proved is that live bacteria from probiotic products can survive their passage to the stomach, but unless one keeps taking them, they get flushed out of the system and do not establish a long-term presence. The European Food Safety Authority has therefore ruled that makers of such products may claim, in their advertising, that they can have a short-term medical effect, but any claim of long-term health benefits must await better evidence.

FOOTBALL

199. Do soccer referees have a rightward bias?

Research has shown that speakers of languages that are written from left to right tend to think of events unfolding from left to right. There is therefore a propensity to be more suspicious of events that are seen as happening from right to left. In 2010 a study was published on whether this has an effect on soccer referees when deciding whether a foul has been committed. This was based on an experiment in which referees were shown pictures from real football matches and asked to rule on whether the picture displayed a foul being committed. The referees were found to call more fouls for pictures of left-moving events than for right-moving events.

The research has, however, only been done on referees whose native language is written left to right. Whether Arabic-speaking referees have a right-to-left bias is unknown. If they are found to share the rightward bias of the referees in the study, it would suggest that, like chickens (→ 97), the rightward bias is innate rather than language-based.

200. Does sacking the manager help an unsuccessful soccer team?

Statisticians have long debated the evidence for and against sacking the manager of a poorly performing soccer team. A survey of the academic literature in 2012 reported that, of nine studies from six countries, five concluded that replacing a manager does improve a club's results, while four found that hiring a new manager did not improve team performance on average.

In 2013 the Dutch economist Dr Bas ter Weel compared the results of teams doing badly that changed their manager and teams doing badly that did not change manager. His conclusion was: 'Changing a manager during a crisis in the season does improve the results in the short term, but this is a misleading statistic because not changing the manager would have had the same result.'

In 2014, however, a ten-year study of sixty managerial changes among the thirty-six clubs in the English Premier League between 2003 and 2013 reached the opposite conclusion, at least as far as teams struggling to avoid relegation were concerned. The question of whether it is beneficial for a football team to change manager is therefore still open.

FRANCE

201. Who was the comte de Saint-Germain?

Scholar, linguist, violinist, composer, alchemist, philosopher, diplomat, dandy, braggart and probable impostor, the comte de Saint-Germain – the Count of St Germain – was one of the most extraordinary figures of eighteenth-century society, wherever he went in Europe, yet nobody knows who he was or where he came from.

He claimed to be the son of Francis II Rákóczi, the Prince of Transylvania, and was clearly well educated and rich enough always to appear well dressed and often festooned with jewels. Horace Walpole wrote in praise of his abilities in diverse fields, but also described him as a 'great Pretender'. He thought Spanish or Portuguese was his native language, though he also spoke French and Italian and understood Polish. Casanova described him as a 'learned impostor' and said: 'Notwithstanding his boastings, his bare-faced lies, and his manifold eccentricities, I cannot say I thought him offensive.'

Saint-Germain made a laboratory for Louis XV of France and travelled to Holland in 1760 to try to open negotiations between Britain and France during the Seven Years' War, though neither side had commissioned him to do so. According to different accounts, he told people he was either 300 or 500 years old and had solved the secret of eternal life. He died in 1784 and nobody has ever discovered his true identity.

202. What was the relationship between Marie Antoinette and Count Axel von Fersen?

The Swedish count Axel von Fersen (1755–1810) is celebrated for distinguishing himself on the battlefield during the American War of Independence and for his defence of the royal family during the French Revolution, but most of all, he is remembered for the mystery concerning his relationship with Marie Antoinette.

The two met at the Paris Opera in 1774, and within a few years he had become a member of her intimate circle of friends. Thanks to her influence, he became a colonel in the German infantry and later a colonel in the Royal Swedish Regiment. Their secret correspondence shows the strength of the feelings between them, and he once wrote to his sister telling her that he would never marry as 'I cannot belong to the one person whom I would truly wish to be mine'.

After the French Revolution began, he organized the flight of the royal family to Varenne in 1791, but when Marie Antoinette was guillotined in 1793, he wrote: 'I have now lost everything that I had in the world.' But how close they really were we shall probably never know.

See also DEATH 134–5; EYES 187; MURDER 323; RELIGION 394; SEX 407

FROGS

203. What killed the frogs in Windham, Connecticut, in 1754?

On a dark night in June 1754, the residents of the town of Windham, Connecticut, were woken by a hideous, shrieking roar. Some thought they were being attacked by Indians; others thought it must be Judgement Day. Many fired their muskets in the direction of the noise, but none dared venture to see what it was.

By morning the noises had died away and the source of the din gradually became clear: the shores of the mill pond and the stream leading from it were covered with the bodies of hundreds, perhaps even thousands, of dead bullfrogs. Since then, the event has been known as the Windham Frog Fight (or Windham Frog Fright) and is now commemorated by many sculptures of frogs in the town.

The cause of it all was probably a drought in the region which had left the local frog population desperate for water, but what had drawn so many of them to one small pond in Windham, and whether there was indeed a huge battle or whether they died from exhaustion and dehydration, is still rather unclear.

FUNDAMENTAL PARTICLES

204. Is the particle discovered at CERN really a Higgs boson?

In 2012 there were great celebrations at the Large Hadron Collider (LHC) at CERN in Switzerland when it was announced that they had discovered the elusive Higgs boson, the elementary particle said to account for why some particles have mass and others do not. But was it really a Higgs boson they discovered?

Shortly after the announcement of the discovery, scientists at CERN admitted that the particle they had discovered was totally in accordance with predictions about the Higgs boson, but they could not rule out the possibility that it was in fact some other particle with similar properties. The other main suspect is a particle known as the techni-higgs. A crucial difference between the Higgs and the techni-higgs is that the Higgs is an elementary particle, which means that it cannot be broken down into smaller particles; the techni-higgs, however, is made up of techni-quarks which are thought to be elementary.

Finding out whether the particle they discovered is indeed a Higgs boson is one of the tasks on the agenda for the recently upgraded LHC.

205. Do protons decay?

One of the difficulties in finding a Grand Unified Theory (GUT) that would explain all the fundamental forces known to physics is that the universe does not seem to behave quite the way it should. Any GUT would rely on a symmetry between the various fundamental particles and the various forces. We have matter and antimatter, electrons and anti-electrons, neutrinos and anti-neutrinos and anything-else-you-care-to-name matched by an anti-anything-else-you-care-to-name. In particular, the strong force ought to be equivalent to the weak force, and baryons, such as protons and neutrons, ought to be equivalent to leptons, such as electrons and neutrinos.

For the most part, such symmetry seems to exist, but the proton presents an apparent anomaly. According to most ideas of how a GUT would work, a proton should eventually decay into a positron and a pion. The trouble is that no evidence of proton decay has ever been observed. If protons do decay, however, calculations suggest that it could take a very long time: an average of around 10^{33} years in fact. Since the universe has only been in existence for just over 10^{10} years, it could simply be that there has not been enough time for more than a very few protons to decay, but the search for a decayed proton continues.

206. Is there anything smaller than quarks and gluons?

A century ago, atoms were thought to be the smallest components of matter. The very word 'atom' was borrowed from the ancient Greek philosophers who had argued that there must be a limit beyond which matter could not be divided (the word 'atom' is from the Greek meaning 'that which cannot be divided'). Then, in 1917, Ernest Rutherford built on the theoretical work of contemporaries such as J. J. Thomson and split the atom.

The world of subatomic physics began with protons, neutrons and electrons, of which atoms were thought to be composed. Then, in the 1960s, by which time the zoo of subatomic particles had a bewildering plethora of different types, Murray Gell-Mann introduced the idea of quarks, which came in six varieties and were shown to be the building blocks of other particles.

But are quarks themselves indivisible? There is no direct evidence that quarks are composite, but in 1974 the theoretical physicists Jogesh Pati and Abdus Salam conjectured the existence of a particle called the preon. Their calculations showed that several problems in particle physics could be explained if, as they suggested, quarks were themselves made of preons.

The preon has, since then, been in a position similar to that of the quark from the mid-1960s until around 1980: its existence would solve several problems, but there was no hard evidence that it existed at all. For the time being, therefore, the quark is the smallest particle. But nobody could rule out the existence of a smaller one.

207. What is the mass of a neutrino?

Neutrinos are among the most puzzling of all subatomic particles. Trillions of them pass unnoticed through our bodies every second, some dating back to the Big Bang, others more recently generated by nuclear reactions in the Sun. Neutrinos are very similar to electrons but carry no electric charge.

According to the Standard Model of elementary particles, the neutrino should have no mass, but in the 1980s it was discovered that neutrinos could oscillate, which suggested that they had mass, and in 1998 it was indeed confirmed not only that neutrinos had mass, but that the three known types of neutrino had different masses. These masses, however, are so small as to be almost undetectable and attempts to discover precisely how much a neutrino weighs have not yet produced an answer.

See also ASTRONOMY 27; BIG BANG 54–6; BLACK HOLES 71; COSMOLOGY 117, 119–22, 126; ENERGY 172, 174; GRAVITY 223; PHILOSOPHY 363; PHYSICS 372; UNIVERSE 463, 467

GAMES

208. Can video games improve intelligence?

Playing video action games has long been shown to increase people's speed of perceptual processing and reactions, but research in 2013 concluded that it may also lead to a more general improvement in cognitive function.

Subjects, who were selected specifically for their relative lack of video-gaming experience, were divided into three groups. One group played an easy version of an action game; another played a more complex version of the same game; the third group engaged in another video-game activity which placed little or no demand on memory or tactical skill.

All groups played for forty hours spread over six to eight weeks, after which they were tested on various problem-solving tasks. The results showed that the participants who had been trained on the complex action game did better than the players of the simple game, and players of the simple action game did better than those who had been engaged in the even less challenging game.

The researchers conclude that playing video action games can enhance cognitive flexibility and performance. They do, however, point out that all seventy-two participants in the experiment were female students at the University of Texas, as they could not find any male students who had the required low experience of video games. There is also the question of whether the observed improvement in performance is temporary or long-lasting.

209. Is playing good for us?

Research at Oxford in 2014 concluded that children who played video games for up to an hour a day were happier and more sociable, had fewer emotional problems, and were less hyperactive than those who didn't play at all. It has also been claimed that playing video games can reduce addictive cravings in other areas. Other research, however, has concluded that players can become obese, lazy, slovenly, unproductive, aggressive, antisocial and addicted to the games themselves.

Clearly further research is needed before we can decide whether the benefits or drawbacks are greater.

See also INTELLIGENCE 252; PSYCHOLOGY 385

GENETICS

210. Can fear be inherited?

Before the work of Darwin led to the development of the science of genetics, there was a general belief in the inheritance of acquired characteristics, or Lamarckism as it came to be known. The French naturalist Jean-Baptiste Lamarck (1744–1829) believed that evolution functioned through changes that took place during a creature's lifetime being passed on to its offspring. As the science of genetics grew, this idea was abandoned, but since the 1990s the new science of epigenetics has produced increasing evidence that – to some extent at least – Lamarck may have been correct.

A striking example was given in an experiment in 2013 in which mice were conditioned to associate a particular smell with an electric shock and therefore to show signs of fear when the smell was perceived. The conditioning was performed before the mice mated and the resulting offspring were subsequently found to be liable to exhibit signs of fear when exposed to the same smell, and so were the grandchildren of the original mice. The offspring were also found to have more receptors for the smell in their brains and therefore to be more sensitive to it.

While an acquired characteristic, such as fear of a particular smell, cannot alter the DNA of an animal, it seems that it can alter the way genes express themselves. Whether humans can acquire fears from their parents and grandparents in a similar way is unknown.

211. Is there a genetic secret to a long life?

Research has shown that living to an old age seems to run in families. Studies on twins have even reported that 40 per cent of longevity is genetic, but the quest to identify the genes responsible has not been successful.

In 2014 the genomes of seventeen supercentenarians (110 years old or more) were sequenced to explore the genetic basis for longevity. No significant evidence was found that their genes differed from those of a normal population. In common with other elusive genetic traits, it appears that longevity is not controlled by a single gene, or even a simple combination of genetic factors.

See also ASPARAGUS 26; BIOLOGY 62; CANCER 84; DISEASE 142, 146; DOGS 148, 150; EARS 162; EBOLA 166; HAIR 226; HUMAN EVOLUTION 234, 237–9; LONGEVITY 279; MEDICINE 298; MICE 313; PANGOLINS 355; PREHISTORY 383; SALAMANDERS 398; SEX 406; SMELL 435

'One of the greatest joys known to man is to take a flight into ignorance in search of knowledge.'

Robert Staughton Lynd

GEOLOGY

212. What caused the Permian mass extinction?

Around 252 million years ago, at the end of the Permian period, an estimated 93 to 97 per cent of all species became extinct. It was the most intense extinction event ever known and has been called the 'Great Dying'. Various theories have been put forward to explain this near-extinction of life on Earth, including glaciation, global warming, volcanoes, an asteroid or comet impact, catastrophic methane release from the ocean floor, or a massive drop in oxygen levels.

In other words, in terms of identifying the cause for certain, we are still at the stage of rounding up the usual suspects.

See also COSMOLOGY 125; EVOLUTION 179; RUSSIA 397; TURKEY 457

GERMANY

213. Who was Kaspar Hauser?

In May 1828 a teenage boy wearing tattered clothing was found wandering in a public square in Nuremberg, Germany. He was clutching an envelope with two letters in it but seemed unable to read or write anything other than his name, which he gave as Kaspar Hauser. The only sentence he spoke was 'I want to be a cavalryman, as my father was', and in reply to questions he would just say 'Don't know'. When offered food and drink, all he would eat was bread and water. Later he claimed to have been brought up alone in a cell and to have never seen another person until he was set free in Nuremberg. The letters were allegedly from his mother and a man who had taken care of him, but both seemed to be in the same handwriting and many thought that Kaspar Hauser had written them himself.

This mysterious boy attracted international attention and the British nobleman Lord Stanhope later gained custody of him. Stanhope paid his living expenses and made considerable efforts to find out where he had come from, but later declared it his duty 'openly to confess that I had been deceived'. In December 1833, when Hauser was about twenty-one years old, he appeared with a deep stab wound in his left breast and a story that he had been attacked by a stranger. He died of his wound shortly after.

Some theories at the time suggested that he was an heir of the grand ducal House of Baden, but recent DNA investigations have failed to confirm this (though they do not totally rule it out). Another theory is that he was a pathological liar. The truth has never been discovered.

214. What is the Salzburg Cube?

In 1885 an employee named Reidl at a foundry in Austria discovered a mysterious hunk of metal in a seam of coal estimated to be 20 million years old. Roughly cubic in shape, with rounded sides and a deep groove apparently cut into it, the Salzburg Cube, as it came to be known (it was also called the Wolfsegg Iron after the place the coal had come from), aroused great interest.

At first, it was thought to be an ancient meteorite, but later investigations showed it to have been artificially manufactured and to be made of iron. The question of how it found its way inside a 20-million-year-old coal seam produced several theories:

- It may have come from a lost human civilization.
- It may have been left by alien visitors.
- It may have fallen from an alien spacecraft.

Or it may all have been a hoax, which seems the most likely explanation. But who the hoaxers were and why they did it have never been explained.

See also BIRDS 64; NAZIS 338–40; SLOTHS 434; USA 477

GLOBAL WARMING

215. Why is atmospheric methane rising?

Most efforts to control global warming have concentrated on reducing carbon dioxide emissions, but recent years have seen a rise in levels of methane in the atmosphere, which is a considerably more potent greenhouse gas.

Several causes of methane emissions are known, but puzzlingly measurements of the changes in atmospheric methane levels do not seem to correlate with known changes in emissions. Coal production, for example, is known to produce methane emissions, yet between 2000 and 2006, when Chinese coal production was known to be increasing at 7 per cent a year, there was no change in methane levels. It could be that the increased methane from Chinese coal has been balanced by a reduction in methane emissions from wetlands, which are a major source of the gas, but there are no global figures to verify that idea.

Since 2007 atmospheric concentrations of methane have been rising quickly, but whether this is due to fossil fuel emissions, or the melting of Arctic ice leading to an increase in the area covered by wetlands, or high rainfall having the same effect in tropical regions is unknown.

216. What is the relationship between global warming and oceanic anoxic events?

The geological record shows that mass extinctions in the Earth's history have frequently coincided with oceanic anoxic events (OAEs), which occur when the oceans become depleted of oxygen. These OAEs in turn have been associated with global warming. The logic is simple: not only is oxygen less soluble in warmer water, but warming decreases the density of the surface water, leading to greater stratification and less mixing of the surface layers, which have high oxygen content, with the deeper levels where the oxygen is lower.

Research in 2014 revealed anomalies that cast doubt on this process. While the oxygen content of the oceans was found to have decreased between 1990 and 2010 when the waters were warming, it increased from 1950 to 1990, which was equally a period in which the waters were getting warmer. Measurements in the North Pacific suggested that another process was occurring which had the opposite effect from the conventional theory.

The argument was that the old theory ignored the effect of winds on the production of phytoplankton which consume the oxygen. A heavy concentration of such organisms at the surface of the water decreases the amount of oxygen underneath. Phytoplankton production is increased by strong winds because they result in the availability of more nutrients from deeper waters. This theory was supported by measurements of oceanic oxygen content, which were found to be higher during periods of high trade winds.

Although such winds have been higher since 1990, global warming is predicted to lead to weaker trade winds in the future and thus to an increase, not a decrease, in oceanic oxygen levels.

See also GEOLOGY 212; METEOROLOGY 306–7

GOLD

217. Who discovered gold in the Klondike?

On 16 August 1896 gold was discovered in the Klondike region of north-west Canada, which led to a stampede of prospectors from all over North America. The team credited with the discovery comprised George Carmack, his wife Kate Carmack, who was a member of the Tagish Native American tribe from the Yukon region, her brother Skookum Jim, and their nephew Dawson Charlie. They had been travelling south of the Klondike river on a recommendation from Robert Henderson, another prospector.

It has never been clear who was first to make the discovery. The group apparently agreed to list George Carmack as the discoverer, as it was feared that mining authorities would not approve a claim made by a Native American. Robert Henderson's basis for advising the group on where to look has also never been explained, so it is possible that he was indeed the first to discover the Klondike gold.

218. Where are the 93 tons of gold moved from Romania's National Bank to Russia in 1916?

During the First World War, when Romania was occupied by Germany, the Romanian government decided to move a collection of national treasures, including an estimated 120 tons of gold coins, ingots and objects, to Russia for safekeeping. A deal was signed that the Russians would keep the treasures safe until the end of the war.

After the Russian Revolution of 1917, however, the new Soviet government severed diplomatic relations with Romania and confiscated the treasures. Since then, successive governments of Romania have tried to recover the treasures and the gold, but with only very limited success. In 1935 and 1956 almost 40,000 artworks were returned among the treasures in seventeen railway wagons, but most of the gold was not among them. Some of the crates were also found to have been tampered with. What happened to the gold has never been discovered.

In 2012 Romania tried to raise the matter in the Council of Europe, but Russia was reported to have 'expressed regret' over Romanian attempts to raise the issue and called on Bucharest not to 'stir up the past'. The Council said that such a return could start with the return of the National Bank of Romania's gold reserves consisting of 93.4 tons of gold. Russia responded by saying that the subject of Romanian gold should be consigned to history.

219. Does Yamashita's gold exist?

Since the end of the Second World War, many treasure-hunters have travelled to the Philippines in search of the so-called Yamashita treasure, but nobody is even sure whether it has ever existed.

The story behind the alleged treasure concerns the Japanese general Tomoyuki Yamashita, who commanded Japanese forces in the Philippines from 1944. Yamashita is said to have been in charge of a massive campaign of looting which involved people ranging from the Japanese imperial family to gangs of Yakuza gangsters; valuables were looted from banks, commercial buildings, private homes and even religious institutions to finance the Japanese war effort. The loot is said to have initially been concentrated in Singapore but later moved to the Philippines, though no clear evidence of its existence was ever found.

Yamashita himself was convicted of war crimes and executed by the US Army in 1946, and others said to have been involved were killed during the war. In 1988, however, an extraordinary case was heard in a court in Hawaii brought by a Filipino treasure-hunter Rogelio Roxas against Ferdinand Marcos, former president of the Philippines, and his wife Imelda. Roxas claimed that he had discovered the Yamashita gold but had it stolen from him by Marcos.

The court found that Roxas had indeed found a treasure which had been stolen by Marcos, but ruled that they were not required to determine whether this particular treasure was the legendary Yamashita's gold. In 1992 Imelda Marcos claimed that the basis of her late husband's fortune (Ferdinand Marcos died in 1989) was indeed Japanese gold which he had found at the end of the Second World War. She was quoted as saying: 'I understand there was some Yamashita gold.' Marcos kept it secret, she said, because the amount was so large 'it would have been embarrassing'.

Many others, however, have dismissed the whole story of the Yamashita gold as a myth.

See also ALCHEMY 2; BIBLE 53; CODES 109; COSTA RICA 127; HITLER 232; TREASURE 455; USA 470

GORILLAS

220. Is there an albino gorilla Amomongo hiding in the Philippines?

The British have the Loch Ness Monster, North Americans have the Sasquatch or Big Foot, the Nepalese have the Yeti, and the Filipinos have Amomongo. Described as a man-sized ape or albino gorilla with long nails, Amomongo is said to live in caves near the foot of the Kanloan volcano.

Generally considered to be a mythical creature, Amomongo was the subject of renewed interest in 2008 following reports of at least two sightings, including one at which the creature was said to have attacked goats and chickens and eaten their entrails. There were also reports of its having attacked humans, one of whom was said to have needed treatment for scratches at various places on his body.

221. Are gorillas predominantly right-handed?

Why most human beings are right-handed has long been debated, and evidence from the teeth of Neanderthals suggests this preference dates from an early time in our evolution. To find out how early, a good deal of research has been done on handedness in apes and monkeys. Chimpanzees, gorillas and bonobos have been reported to have right-handed tendencies, while orangutans have been found to be predominantly left-handed.

Several studies have reported that gorillas are the closest to humans in this respect, with about 90 per cent of them exhibiting right-handedness, but some doubts have been raised about this claim. Most of the studies have been on captive gorillas, while observation of gorillas in the wild has generally been less convincing in demonstrating a right-hand preference. It has been suggested that the captive gorillas being studied are not showing a natural hand preference, but are simply mimicking the hand usage of the experimenters or their keepers.

We eagerly await a study conducted only on gorillas brought up by left-handed zoo-keepers to resolve this matter.

See also BRAINS 77; EBOLA 167; WALRUSES 486

GRAVITY

222. What is the strength of gravity?

More than 300 years ago, Isaac Newton discovered the law of gravity: any two objects in the universe attract each other with a force proportional to the product of their masses divided by the square of the distance between them:

$$F = Gm_1m_2/r^2.$$

All that remained was to calculate the value of G in the formula, and scientists have been arguing about it ever since. Research into the values of other scientific constants has followed a pattern of getting better and better estimates, allowing the answer to be known with ever-increasing accuracy. Different experimenters, however, have obtained, and continue to obtain, values for G that differ by more than can be explained by the limitations of their experiments. In some cases, the identical experiment performed at different times has given slightly different results.

In 2010 the International Council for Science gave a new figure for its recommended value of G, while also increasing the margin of uncertainty about the figure.

223. How can quantum theory and gravity be reconciled?

The biggest problem in physics is explaining why there seem to be different sets of rules governing the world at the scale we are used to dealing with it and the micro-world of atoms and subatomic particles. First we had Newton, explaining the macro-world with his theory of gravity; then came Einstein, who modified Newton's ideas with the theory of relativity; but soon after that quantum theory arrived to explain the micro-world in terms not of tangible objects and certainties but of waves and probabilities.

Any theory of everything, or Grand Unified Theory (GUT), will need to come up with something that reconciles the physics of Newton and Einstein with that of quantum mechanics. In particular, it needs a single theory that brings together all the fundamental forces. The trouble is that the electromagnetic, strong nuclear and weak nuclear forces are all best described by quantum mechanics, but the much weaker gravitational force is explained within the framework of classical physics.

See also ASTRONOMY 28; BLACK HOLES 71; BONES 73; COSMOLOGY 124; FOOD 195; MILKY WAY 317; PHYSICS 371; SLOTHS 431; UNIVERSE 465–7

GUILLOTINES

224. Did Dr Guillotin know about the Halifax gibbet?

In the sixteenth century the Lord of the Manor in the town of Halifax in Yorkshire had the right to sentence any criminal who had stolen more than 13½ pence worth of goods to be summarily executed by decapitation. Until the mid-seventeenth century, the sentence was carried out by means of a device consisting of an axe-head fitted to a wooden block that ran in grooves between two tall uprights. The block and axe-head were raised by means of a rope, then allowed to fall on the hapless victim's neck.

In 1791, as the French Revolution progressed, the French physician Joseph-Ignace Guillotin was a campaigner against capital punishment, but accepting that it would not be abolished, he advocated that the death penalty should be carried out as humanely as possible. The result was the device that became known as the guillotine – a nice feminization of his own name. Its similarity to the Halifax device is striking, but whether Dr Guillotin knew of the earlier device is unknown.

See also FRANCE 202

GUINEA-PIGS

225. To what extent do guinea-pigs have personalities?

Guinea-pig owners, to judge from many websites, are generally convinced that their pets have distinct personalities, but animal behaviourists are less sure. To show personality, an animal would have to exhibit forms of behaviour that distinguished it from others of its species and were also stable over time. Research in 2013 investigated the social behaviour and emotionality of adult male guinea-pigs on two occasions eight weeks apart. Comparison of their behaviour on the two occasions revealed that there was individual stability with respect to social behaviour, but none with respect to emotional behaviour.

The researchers said their results 'suggest that the concept of animal personality is applicable to domestic guinea-pigs'. Without the factor of emotionality, however, guinea-pig personality may seem limited.

HAIR

226. How do hair whorls influence handedness in humans?

In 2003 the geneticist Amar Klar published a study relating the clockwise or anti-clockwise direction of a person's hair whorl at the back of their head and whether they were left-handed or right-handed. He reported that in a normal sample of mainly right-handed people, only 8.4 per cent had anti-clockwise whorls, while in a sample of people who were left-handed or ambidextrous, 44.9 per cent had anti-clockwise whorls.

This finding led to a theory that a single gene is responsible for both the direction of hair whorl and determining whether a person is left- or right-handed. Later attempts to reproduce Klar's results, however, have met with only limited success. Of six studies performed between 2005 and 2010, only two reported a significant correlation between whorl direction and handedness. Putting all the studies together, however, does reveal a slight tendency for left-handed people to have anti-clockwise whorls.

227. Do hair whorls influence cattle development?

Research at the University of Colorado has identified several factors relating to cattle that appear to correlate with aspects of the location and direction of their hair whorls. In 1995 the researchers found that spiral hair whorl position on the forehead may be associated with a calm temperament, while whorls above a bull's eyes indicated excitability. In general, the odder and more untidy a whorl looked, the more likely the animal was to be unmanageable.

Research at the University of Limerick in Ireland in 2008 also found that horses with clockwise hair whorls were significantly more likely to move toward the right, or start trotting with their right-sided hooves.

It has been suggested that whorl development is associated with brain development in both animals and humans, but more evidence is clearly needed.

See also ANATOMY 4; CHINA 99; CRIME 129; EYES 187; NAPOLEON 337; PANGOLINS 354; SLOTHS 432; WAITRESSES 484

HENRY VIII

228. What was the illness that killed Henry VIII's elder brother Arthur?

Arthur Tudor, eldest son of Henry VII of England, was born in 1486, married in 1501 and died in 1502. A contemporary account of the illness that killed him refers to 'a malign vapour which proceeded from the air'. This may have been the mysterious 'sweating sickness' that killed thousands in the 1480s, but at the time of Arthur's death had not been heard of since 1492.

His wife Catherine had also been suffering from the illness, but she recovered and seven years later married Arthur's younger brother, who became Henry VIII. That marriage didn't work out very well for her either.

229. Did Catherine of Aragon and Prince Arthur consummate their marriage?

On Sunday 14 November 1501 the sixteen-year-old Catherine of Aragon married fifteen-year-old Prince Arthur, heir to the English throne. What happened that night, however, has been argued over for more than 500 years.

Sir Anthony Willoughby, who was a 'body servant' to the young prince, later testified: 'I made the said prince ready to bed and with others conducted him clad in his nightgown unto the princess's bedchamber often and sundry times when he entered and then continued all night.' The following morning, the prince emerged from his wife's bedchamber and said: 'Willoughby, bring me a cup of ale, for I have been this night in the midst of Spain.' Twenty-six years later, however, the question of whether the marriage had indeed been consummated became a major issue for both church and state.

Arthur had died in 1502 and Catherine had subsequently married his brother Henry. She bore him six children, all but one of which died, leaving only Mary. Henry saw an explanation for this in Leviticus 20:21, which says, 'And if a man shall take his brother's wife, it is an unclean thing: he hath uncovered his brother's nakedness; they shall be childless.' Henry sought an annulment of the marriage on the grounds that it went against biblical teaching. Catherine, however, maintained that her marriage to Arthur had never been consummated and it was therefore that marriage which was automatically dissolved, making her marriage to Henry perfectly legitimate in the eyes of both the state and the church.

Despite his strong efforts to have his marriage annulled, however, Henry VIII never stated that Catherine was not a virgin on their wedding night.

230. Was Catherine of Aragon poisoned?

When Catherine died at Kimbolton Castle in 1536, rumours were rife that she had been poisoned by friends of the king or Anne Boleyn. When her body was being prepared for burial, the chandler at Kimbolton reported that all her organs were normal except her heart, which had a large black and hideous growth.

On hearing of this, the Spanish ambassador, Eustace Chapuys, wrote to the emperor of his suspicions at no doctor or surgeon having been present at the opening of the body. Chapuys also quoted the queen's physician as saying that he was in no doubt that the queen had been poisoned, as she became ill after drinking a glass of Welsh beer.

However, the black growth on the heart could also be taken as a description of a cancerous tumour. Cancer was not recognized in those days, but making a reliable diagnosis after 500 years is not possible.

See also EYES 187; SHAKESPEARE 415; SHIPS 421

HITLER

231. How many testicles did Hitler have?

Surprisingly, the British wartime song 'Hitler has only got one ball' (sung to the tune of 'Colonel Bogey') may have had some basis in fact. Medical records confirm that during the First World War Hitler was wounded at the Battle of the Somme. A man who was a German army doctor at the time is on record as saying that he saved Hitler at the battle and saw that he had a groin injury and had lost a testicle.

In 1970 the Soviet autopsy on Hitler's body was released, revealing that 'the left testicle could not be found either in the scrotum or on the spermatic cord inside the inguinal canal, or in the small pelvis'. On the other hand, Hitler's personal physician and another doctor who had treated him while he was alive are on record as saying there was nothing wrong with his testicles.

232. What happened to Hitler's gold?

In 2013 a collection of 1,500 paintings said to be worth almost £1 billion was found in an apartment in Munich. The collection, reported to include works by Picasso, Matisse and Chagall, had been hidden by Cornelius Gurlitt, the eighty-year-old son of an art dealer trusted by the Nazis to dispose of plundered artworks.

That, however, was only a very small part of the loot plundered by the Nazis which they are thought to have hidden as defeat in the war became inevitable. Hitler is known to have had a personal diamond collection which is thought to have gone missing, together with the entire gold reserves of the Reichsbank.

233. Who was Hitler's paternal grandfather?

Adolf Hitler was the son of Alois Hitler Sr, who was born Alois Schicklgruber, but there is great doubt over who Alois Schicklgruber's biological father was. At his baptism, the space for his father's name was left blank and the priest recorded that he was illegitimate. When Alois was five, his mother married Johann Georg Hiedler. By the age of ten, however, Alois had been sent to live with his stepfather's brother, Johann Nepomuk Hiedler, but he continued to use the surname Schicklgruber. At the age of thirty-nine he applied to change his surname to that of his family, which (perhaps through a mishearing of 'Hiedler') was recorded as 'Hitler'.

Who Alois's real father was has always been a mystery. When he applied to change his name, he said that Johann Georg Hiedler was his biological father, but it has been suggested that the real father was Johann Nepomuk Hiedler, which would explain why he was sent to live with him.

Finally, another rumour centres on a story that Alois's mother, Maria Schicklgruber, became pregnant while working for a Jewish family in Graz. That account names the prime suspect as Leopold Frankenburger, the heir to the family's wealth. No evidence has ever been produced to support this story, which may have been invented solely to support a claim that Adolf Hitler was one-quarter Jewish.

See also NAZIS 338, 340

HUMAN EVOLUTION

234. Who were the Palaeo-Eskimos?

DNA evidence was found in 2014 of a previously unknown race of people which inhabited the Arctic north of America for more than 4,000 years before they died out about 700 years ago. These Palaeo-Eskimos, as they have been dubbed, were not related to the Native Americans, who were there before them, nor to the Inuit, who arrived later.

These three groups are all thought to have reached North America from Siberia across the Bering Strait, but the genetic evidence shows that the Palaeo-Eskimos lived in total isolation and did not reproduce with the other groups. Such long-lasting isolation and the apparent stability of their culture make them quite unlike any other group of humans of the past few thousand years.

Curiously, what we now know about them is similar to an ancient Inuit myth of a magical giant race called the Tunit, who are said to have lived in isolation, making no contact with others.

There is also no evidence to explain why the Palaeo-Eskimos died out.

235. What happened to the Neanderthals?

There is evidence that Neanderthals lived in Eurasia around half a million years ago. According to the latest estimates based on carbon dating, they died out about 40,000 years ago. Why they died out has long been a subject of dispute, but many theories link their extinction to the arrival of modern man in Europe between 45,000 and 43,000 years ago. Possible theories include the following:

- Violence: *Homo sapiens* and *Homo neanderthalensis* just didn't get on and the brighter *Homo sapiens* killed off their rivals.
- Disease: it was the diseases that *Homo sapiens* carried that wiped out the Neanderthals, who had little resistance to them.
- Food shortage: *Homo sapiens* had superior animal-hunting technology which resulted in their Neanderthal cousins being left with insufficient food to survive.
- Interbreeding: *Homo sapiens* and *Homo neanderthalensis* got on so well together that they interbred and the two species simply merged, with the result that the Neanderthal genes became diffused and the pure Neanderthals disappeared.

On the other hand, it could be that *Homo sapiens* had very little to do with it. There is much evidence of climate change around 40,000 years ago which resulted in severe cooling. This would have resulted in less food being available and the Neanderthals may have simply been unable to adapt their hunting methods to the demands of the new conditions.

236. Why do we have five fingers?

For the past 340 million years or so, the vast majority of land mammals have had five digits on their limbs. Before that, there is evidence of six-, seven- or eight-fingered animals, especially in the sea, but evolution seems to have settled on five as the best number. But why five? Might not four or six be preferable under certain circumstances?

The mechanics behind finger formation was discovered in 2014 and outlined in a paper with the rather forbidding title 'Digit patterning is controlled by a Bmp-Sox9-Wnt Turing network modulated by morphogen gradients'. Taking an idea originally proposed by the mathematician and code-breaker Alan Turing, the authors of the paper showed that there are three groups of molecules, called Bmp, Sox9 and Wnt, which interact with each other and turn each other on and off to control the growth of fingers in an embryonic hand. Between them, Bmp and Sox9 are responsible for the growth of fingers, but importantly, Wnt is responsible for the spaces between them, blocking Sox9 from having an effect where another finger would just get in the way.

The final number of fingers thus becomes dependent on the size of the hand. If our hands were 20 per cent larger, we would grow another finger, which is why around one in 500 people is born with an extra finger or toe. The mechanism controlling the formation and number of a creature's fingers seems firmly set to such an extent that even if a sixth finger were an advantage, its evolution might be ruled out. Pandas have shown the need for a thumb to help them grasp bamboo, but instead of evolving a sixth, opposable finger, they adapt a wrist bone into a pseudo-thumb to help them in that task.

James Sharpe, one of the authors of the paper mentioned above, described the question of why our bodies have evolved to give us hands with room for exactly five fingers as 'the ultimate meta-problem on top of everything', and he goes on: 'I often say that if we understood why five, we'd probably understand everything.'

237. When did human speech evolve?

The trouble with language is that it leaves no fossils. All evidence of the origins of language must therefore be indirect, relying on anatomy, genetics or calculations based on linguistic diversity, none of which can give a definitive answer.

The anatomical approach is based on the evolution of the vocal tract. Before this evolved, we lacked the apparatus necessary to make the sounds associated with language. Between 100,000 and 50,000 years ago changes are known to have taken place in the shape and capabilities of the human mouth, tongue, pharynx and larynx, which had profound effects on our abilities to produce a wide range of sounds, but whether our sound production could have supported a primitive language much earlier is disputed. There is even considerable uncertainty about the position of Neanderthals' larynxes, which would have strongly affected the question of whether they spoke or not.

The figure of 50,000 to 100,000 years ago for the origins of speech was recently supported by a study of the diversity of modern languages. Using a statistical technique for estimating the time-scale on which linguistic changes take place, a similar figure was reached for the appearance of the earliest proto-languages.

Different approaches, perhaps taking a more lenient view of the question of when grunting turned into talking, have come up with figures of up to 1.75 million years ago. The recent discovery of the FOX2P gene, which plays an important part in language formation, and the fact that chimpanzees possess a similar gene, have been cited as evidence that human language skills date back to soon after our divergence from chimps. Another recent study of blood flow in the brain has claimed to show that the mental processes associated with language evolved in parallel with the evolution of tool use.

So the best answer we can give to the question of when human speech evolved is somewhere between 1.75 million and 50,000 years ago, which is a very wide range indeed.

238. What sparked Upper Palaeolithic culture in human evolution?

From 40,000 to about 11,000 years ago, Upper Palaeolithic culture transformed Europe and the world. The people at the start of that period were skilled hunters, but the stone tools they used developed not only great diversity but began to show ornamentation in their designs. This was also the period of the earliest ivory carvings and rock paintings, which date back to around 35,000 years ago. At the end of the period, the era of agriculture began, in which humans began to take control of their environment.

What was responsible for these huge advances is unknown. Human brain size had not increased and no specific genetic changes have been identified that could account for it.

239. What did the Denisovans look like?

In March 2010 it was announced that a fragment of a finger-bone had been discovered in the remote Denisova Cave in the Altai Mountains in Siberia, a cave which was also known to have been inhabited by Neanderthals and modern humans. Analysis of the DNA of the bone revealed that it was genetically distinct from both those groups.

Further investigations, and the discovery of similar DNA in specimens from northern Spain, led to the conclusion that modern humans, Neanderthals and Denisovans, as this newly discovered human species was called, had shared a common ancestor around a million years ago. The Denisovans broke away from the Neanderthals about 400,000 years ago.

The coldness of the cave in which the finger-bone fragment was found was responsible for preserving the DNA, which has allowed scientists to build up a detailed picture of the evolutionary history of the Denisovans. This, however, tells us very little about their lifestyle or appearance. Indeed, with only a bit of bone to go on, together with two teeth that were discovered later, the only conclusion reached is that the female from whom the finger-bone came probably had brown eyes.

240. Who did the Denisovans mate with?

By comparing the genomes of Neanderthals, Denisovans and modern humans, much has been learnt about the inter-group mating patterns. We know that the Denisovans are more closely related to Neanderthals than to modern humans; and we know they must have made their way to South-east Asia, as their DNA shows signs of interbreeding with Melanesian and Aboriginal populations of New Guinea and Australia. But their genes also show evidence of their having bred with an even older human species than the Neanderthals.

Nobody knows who these mysterious early humans were who seemed to co-exist with Neanderthals and Denisovans. No fossils or other evidence of their existence have yet been found, other than the DNA they passed on, even to several groups of people alive today, via the Denisovans.

241. What was the most recent ancestor of both Neanderthals and modern humans?

Examination of the DNA of different species has revealed a great deal about the evolutionary path of mankind, but one question that has never been resolved is the nature of our evolutionary relationship to the Neanderthals. *Homo heidelbergensis*, *Homo erectus* and *Homo antecessor* have all been suggested as the common ancestor from which *Homo sapiens* and *Homo neanderthalensis* developed; some have even classified *Homo neanderthalensis* as a subspecies of *Homo sapiens*, but recent research has cast even greater doubt on the closeness of the relationship.

In 2013 a study was made of the shape of the teeth of various human species. In all, approximately 1,200 molars and premolars taken from thirteen hominid species were compared, and none of the three species mentioned above was found to have teeth compatible with the shape expected of an ancestor of both *Homo sapiens* and *Homo neanderthalensis*.

According to the writers, the evidence of the teeth suggests that Neanderthals diverged from modern humans as much as a million years ago, which is more than twice as long as had previously been thought. If this is right, then perhaps our search for a common ancestor has been in the wrong time period.

242. How many kinds of humans co-existed 100,000 years ago?

Homo sapiens first appeared around 200,000 years ago and by 100,000 years ago had begun to dominate other species of human. At that time, *Homo neanderthalensis* was still around and *Homo erectus* was probably not yet extinct. *Homo heidelbergensis* may also not have completely died out.

That had been the picture generally accepted for some time when remains of *Homo floresiensis* were found on the Indonesian island of Flores in 2003. Nicknamed 'Hobbit' because of its small stature, *Homo floresiensis* was found to have made stone tools, hunted dwarf elephants and large rodents, and even coped with predators such as Komodo dragons. He may also have used fire.

Some have suggested that *Homo floresiensis* may have been a dwarf species of *Homo erectus*, but the comparative recency of this discovery raises the question of whether there are other species of humans yet to be discovered which were around when *Homo sapiens* began throwing his intellectual weight around.

243. Why don't humans have tails?

Monkeys have tails; apes don't. The existence of the coccyx, or tail-bone, at the end of our spines is strong evidence that we lost our tails at some point in our evolution, but what crucial factor was responsible for the loss is a matter of speculation.

Animals with tails put them to a variety of uses: tails can swat flies, aid locomotion, act as a rudder while swimming, help preserve balance, and (if the tail is prehensile) enable its owner to swing from a branch while keeping its hands free. It has been suggested that we ceased to need a tail when we started walking on two legs instead of four, but it could equally be argued that having a tail would have been a useful aid to balance when we were becoming bipedal.

The advantages of having a tail may seem small for a modern human, but the disadvantages of having one seem to be even smaller. Why we lost it therefore seems to require some explanation.

See also ANATOMY 4, 6; ANIMALS 19; BONES 72; BRAINS 78; CHICKENS 97; EVOLUTION 181; GORILLAS 221; HUMOUR 244; INTELLIGENCE 253; LANGUAGE 268; LEGS 271; MUSIC 329; NOSES 344; PSYCHOLOGY 386; SEX 408; WORDS 498

HUMOUR

244. What are the evolutionary origins of humour?

There are three main theories that are commonly given to explain the existence of humour:

- Relief: humour is based on the alleviation of tension. A joke or humorous situation begins by setting up an unresolved conflict between two ideas; the resolution of that conflict in a non-damaging way results in relaxation.

- Superiority: humour is a way of asserting or emphasizing one's superiority over others. It thus has a social function of uniting or strengthening the bonds in a group by making others, who are the subject of the humour, look silly.
- Incongruity: an aspect present in almost all forms of humour is an unexpected outcome or a form of behaviour that goes against previous experience. The perception of incongruity may be advantageous in daily life to detect threats. It could be argued that humour helps develop that ability.

Such a categorization, however, seems more to be an attempt to analyse the content of humour than to explain its evolution. It could be argued that life is sufficiently full of stress without creating more tension and laughing at it; asserting one's own superiority could be potentially damaging as well as bond-strengthening; and laughing at incongruity could be seen as encouraging a tendency to take signs of potential threats insufficiently seriously.

In short, no convincing case has yet been made for the evolutionary benefits of humour.

245. Do animals have a sense of humour?

Much research on the topics of humour and laughter treats the two topics as two sides of the same phenomenon: humour is a cognitive reaction to a situation; laughter is our physical reaction to it, or our means of communicating that reaction. Research on humour in animals suffers from a similar confusion.

Young animals of various species have been observed having play-fights and making high-pitched laughter-like sounds as they do so. Rats have been shown to produce a giggling sound when tickled that is similar to the noise they make when they appear to be enjoying themselves. Apes have been documented apparently playing tricks on both their keepers and other apes and apparently laughing at the results.

In all such cases, however, we do not know whether there has been a cognitive humour response that led to the laughter. Indeed, we do not even know if it can be called 'laughter'. Some researchers have concluded that many animals have a sense of humour, but more cautious ones will only say that the animal's response to a situation has been a positive display indicating pleasure.

HYPNOSIS

246. Is hypnosis a distinct state of consciousness?

Consciousness and sleep are two states everyone recognizes. In addition there are trance states that may be induced by meditation, and there are drug-induced states. All of these may be detected by both behavioural and physiological signs. Whether hypnosis is a distinct state or is simply a heightened or lessened version of those already mentioned is something that even hypnotists have argued about for more than a century.

One theory is that hypnosis enables (or causes) people to divide their consciousness into two parts, one responding to the outside world, the other observing but not participating. By turning off the part that responds, the hypnotic subject may, for example, not consciously feel pain.

Another theory is that hypnosis can be explained by an individual's suggestibility. Good hypnotic subjects, this theory maintains, are simply people with high suggestibility who therefore behave as they believe they are expected to, even if that involves not feeling pain.

Supporters of the hypnotism-is-a-state hypothesis point to effects produced in subjects under hypnosis which can be neither explained nor replicated by other means. Their opponents, however, point to a lack of neurological evidence that hypnosis differs from other states. They also point to experiments that have demonstrated that when asked to simulate hypnosis, subjects can be even more consistent in producing hypnosis-like results.

This seems to be another of those questions that will not be resolved until we know much more about the functioning of the brain.

See also BRAINS 79; DREAMS 161

INCAS

247. Why did the Incas build Machu Picchu?

In the middle of the fifteenth century, the Incas built the magnificent city of Machu Picchu on a mountain ridge surrounded by a turbulent river in Peru. A century later, at the time of the Spanish conquest, it was abandoned and was not discovered again until 1911. Having no written language, the Incas left no record of their reasons for building the city or what it was used for.

One early theory was that it was a nunnery devoted to worship of the Sun. This idea now seems unlikely since investigation of remains from Machu Picchu in 2000 revealed that there had been about equal numbers of males and females.

Another theory is that it was a royal retreat, but this idea is based on a sixteenth-century Spanish document that mentions a royal estate called Picchu, but it is known that the Spanish never discovered the city.

Two more theories suggest that Machu Picchu had religious significance, either as a re-creation of a creation myth or simply as a place to honour the sacred landscape in which it was built. With around 500 buildings in a remote and generally inaccessible location, it must have had some special significance and purpose, but there is too little evidence to say what they were.

See also ANCIENT CITIES 11

INTELLIGENCE

248. What is intelligence?

We are all happy in our use of the word 'intelligent', but arriving at a definition of it is not so easy. Are problem-solving ability, learning ability, verbal fluency, spatial ability and a good memory all separate components of intelligence, or are they different ways of demonstrating some underlying trait? Early in the twentieth century, the psychologist and statistician Charles Spearman proposed the existence of a factor which he called '*g*' that lay behind any human ability. This theory led to the development of intelligence tests which were designed to measure that factor. Anyone with a high *g* score might be expected to be good at any mental task as long as he had the specialist skills appropriate to that task, while anyone with low *g* would face difficulty whatever mental task he set his mind to.

Later the psychologist Raymond B. Cattell proposed that there are two types of intelligence which he called 'fluid' and 'crystallized'. Fluid intelligence is a measure of one's capacity to think logically and analyse and solve new problems; crystallized intelligence is the ability to use acquired knowledge, skills and experience.

More recent research, based on brain scans taken during mental tasks, suggests that there may be even more types of intelligence, but whether Spearman's *g* factor underlies them all is still a matter of debate.

249. Are we getting cleverer?

In 1984 the political scientist James Flynn published his research comparing intelligence test results in a wide range of studies throughout the world. His results showed that people's average IQ scores were rising by about three points per decade in whatever country one looked at. This observation, which has become known as the Flynn effect, has been cited as evidence that human beings are getting more intelligent.

This conclusion, however, is by no means the only possible explanation. Whatever intelligence tests measure, it can hardly be denied that above all they measure the ability to do intelligence tests. As such tests have become more common, one might expect people to become more attuned to them and able to perform better at them. Before asserting, from this evidence, that people are becoming more intelligent, one would need to be able to separate pure intelligence (whatever that is) from the 'intelligence' measured by intelligence tests, and that is something we have been unable to do.

250. Can plants be intelligent?

Researchers in the field they call plant neurobiology have shown that plants can react in a manner that would be called intelligent if it was done by animals. Plants, of course, do not have brains or neurons, so the expression 'plant neurobiology' is a bit of an oxymoron, but they do gather sensory information and react to it in a logical manner.

In one recent experiment, plants were played a recording of a caterpillar chewing on leaves. The plants responded by secreting anti-caterpillar defensive chemicals. Somehow, the plants 'heard' the sounds, associated them with the caterpillar threat and took appropriate action. Another controversial experiment seems to show that mimosa plants can learn from experience.

Finding a definition of intelligence that excludes plants is not as easy as it may once have seemed.

251. Are sea lions brighter than primates?

Sea lions have been taught to perform tricks and even to recognize a sign language, but over the past twenty years experiments on sea lions in California have shown that they are capable of more unusual feats of logic. In one experiment, sea lions had to choose between two symbols, one of which was a number, the other a letter. The numbers from 0 to 9 and the letters from *a* to *j* were used, so there were ten of each. If the sea lion pressed the number with its nose, it was given a fish; if it pressed the letter, it received nothing. The sea lion soon learnt to discriminate between the winning symbols (the numbers) and the losing symbols (the letters).

When it was consistently displaying a high level of accuracy, the experimenters played a mean trick on the animal: they reversed the condition. Now it was the letters that won a fish and the numbers that received nothing. Naturally, the sea lions started making the wrong decision, but after a time they realized what had happened: everything that had previously won now lost and vice versa. They could now be shown a number and a letter that they had not seen since the rule reversal, and they would make the right decision and pick the letter. The only animals that had previously shown this ability to swap entire classes were humans and pigeons.

In another experiment, a sea lion was taught to associate a picture of a crab with a picture of a tulip and then to associate a tulip with a radio. The sea lion then showed that it associated the crab with a radio. In mathematical terms, this is the law of transitivity:

If $A = B$ and $B = C$, then $A = C$.

The sea lion is the first non-human animal to show that it understands this law. Whether other primates have the same logical skills is unknown.

252. Can human minds influence machines?

For the last thirty years the Princeton Engineering Anomalies Research Laboratory has been conducting research on whether the human mind can influence computers. In particular, experiments have been performed with random number generators (RNGs) to determine whether humans can make the numbers they generate less random than they ought to be.

The earliest results suggested that such machines produced subtly different results when attended by a human than when left alone. Further experiments suggested a small but significant difference in their output when humans were asked to concentrate and will them to produce higher numbers or lower numbers.

A scientific basis for this phenomenon, if it really exists, has been suggested in a possible interaction between the electrical fields generated by the human and the machine, but there are no suggestions of quite how that would work. The subject is particularly interesting to gamblers, as RNGs are at the heart of all computerized card games and slot machines. Research will no doubt continue into this subject.

253. If there is intelligent life elsewhere in the universe, why haven't they got in touch?

Everything we know about the evolution of intelligent life on Earth suggests that there should be intelligent life elsewhere in the universe. It may need very special conditions for life to develop, and it may take a long time for intelligence to develop, but there are billions of galaxies each containing billions of stars, many of which will have planetary systems. The Solar System itself is only about 4.6 billion years old, compared with the 13.8 billion years since the Big Bang, so even if we are only talking about life in Earth-like conditions, there is every reason to believe that intelligent life should have evolved in plenty of places.

Such an argument led the great physicist Enrico Fermi in 1950 to pose the question that subsequently became known as the Fermi paradox: 'Where is everybody?' Suggested answers include the following:

- They have been in touch with us, but we are too stupid to understand their messages.
- They know all about us but think we're insufficiently advanced to be worth contacting.
- They are higher-dimensional beings and we're too three-dimensional to notice that they are here.
- They all developed long ago and destroyed each other in intergalactic wars.
- What we think of as intelligent life is just a short phase in the development of matter and the alien life forms moved on billions of years ago.
- We've got it all wrong and we are alone in the universe after all.

254. Are bonobos cleverer than chimpanzees?

In 2011 scientists at Antwerp Zoo conducted a puzzle-solving contest between a group of chimpanzees and a group of bonobos. Each group was posed six timed tests, all involving puzzle boxes which required the use of tools to obtain the walnut rewards. The bonobos won the contest by four to two, thanks largely to the star of their team, a female named Djanoa, who is said to have concentrated on the puzzles while the chimpanzees were getting involved in fights with one another over dominance.

Chimpanzees, however, have long been known to be more aggressive than bonobos and to resolve conflicts in their male-dominated society by fighting, while the matriarchal bonobos resolve problems by having sex. The Antwerp contest therefore hardly adds to our knowledge on which species is cleverer. If Djanoa had not been particularly hungry or had not liked walnuts so much, the result could have been very different.

See also BIRDS 66; COMPUTERS 115–16; EVOLUTION 181; GAMES 208; WAITRESSES 484

INVENTIONS

255. Where were mechanical clocks invented?

From the ancient Egyptians around 1600 BC until the thirteenth century, time-keeping relied on the clepsydra, or water-clock. By allowing water to drip into a container at a constant rate, the passage of time could be measured to an accuracy up to about fifteen minutes a day, which was good enough for most purposes for almost three millennia.

The replacement of such devices by mechanical clocks was more a slow evolution than a sudden invention, which is why dates given for the invention of the first mechanical clock vary from AD 723, when the Chinese mathematician and monk I Hsing is credited, to 1344, when the Italian doctor, astronomer and clock-maker Jacopo de' Dondi (also known as Jacopo dell'Orologio) installed a clock in the tower of the Palazzo Capitaniato in Padua. The French architect Villard de Honnecourt is also sometimes mentioned as the inventor of the mechanical clock, while other sources claim that it was invented in England in 1275.

Part of the reason for the confusion lies in the development of the escapement, which is the clicking weight- or spring-driven wheel or pendulum that gradually replaced dripping water as the clock's essential time-keeper. From China in the eighth century to Europe in the thirteenth, several hybrid clocks appeared, still driven by water but using the ticking escapement for time-keeping. In Europe the first purely escapement-driven time-keeper was Villard de Honnecourt's astronomical device that tracked the Sun's motion across the sky.

For a real clock, however, we need a dial and hands as well as an escapement, and these first appeared in many places in Europe in the early fourteenth century so close to each other in time that it is impossible to say which place was first.

256. Who invented the door-knob?

On 10 December 1878 the black American inventor Osbourn Dorsey was granted US patent No. 210,762 for his 'Door-holding device'. On the basis of this, Dorsey is often credited with being the inventor of the door-knob, but around 100 door-knob patents had been issued in the forty years before Dorsey's device. Even earlier, glass door-knobs had been popular, while the French and English had used ceramic ones before cast-metal knobs and knobs made of potter's clay began to appear.

The *Oxford English Dictionary* dates the earliest recorded use of the word 'door-knob' to a US patent of 1847, but Dorsey's may indeed have been the first door-knob that had more than a decorative use and could actually be turned to close and open a door.

See also CHEWING GUM 96; SEX 407

IOWA

257. What was the Van Meter Visitor?

For several days in 1903, the town of Van Meter, Iowa, was terrified by nightly visits from a creature described as half-man, half-animal with enormous bat wings. It was first spotted flying over the roofs of buildings, and the sightings were by respected and reliable people, including a doctor and bank cashier. The creature was reported to have let off a powerful stench and shot a blinding light from its horned head.

On the third night, the townsfolk armed themselves and followed it to an abandoned coal mine, where it let out a noise 'as though Satan and a regiment of imps were coming forth for battle'. They chased it down the mine and it was never seen again.

The story has no doubt been embellished over the years, but it seems certain that something was seen in Van Meter over those days. More than a century later, however, there is still no idea of what it might have been.

ITALY

258. How and why were the tunnels at Baiae built?

In the early 1960s the British amateur archaeologist Robert Paget started to investigate a mysterious doorway in the rocks at the old Roman resort of Baiae on the Bay of Naples. It had been discovered about a decade earlier after having been left undisturbed and hidden for around 2,000 years. The doorway was narrow and led to a pitch-black, fume-filled passageway which had deterred anyone from venturing inside. Paget and an American colleague Keith Jones, however, started investigating the passageway, which turned out to reveal an astonishingly complex system of tunnels.

The initial passageway ran exactly east–west, which suggested a ritual purpose probably connected with the equinox. For its first 400 metres it had a slow incline downwards, with niches every metre or so, probably for oil lamps. There followed a much steeper passageway downwards, leading to an S-bend which revealed an underground stream filled with hot, sulphurous water. An ascending passage on the other side of the stream led to an ante-chamber from which hidden staircases led to the surface.

How the ancient Romans could possibly have built an underground complex on such a scale is one mystery, but even greater is the question of how they could possibly have known of the existence of the underground stream which seems to have been the justification for the work. One suggestion is that whoever built it may have modelled its construction on myths of Hell, with the underground stream representing the River Styx, which was the boundary of the underworld, or the River Phlegethon in Hell itself. Or perhaps they even believed that they had discovered a real entrance to Hades. It was not until the 1970s that it was finally discovered that the stream led not to Hell but out into the Gulf of Naples miles away at Cape Miseno.

See also ATILLA 31

'Beware of false knowledge: it is more dangerous than ignorance.'

G. B. Shaw

JESUS CHRIST

259. How did Joseph and Mary, the parents of Jesus Christ, die?

The New Testament is very sparing in the details it gives about the lives of Joseph and Mary. The last we hear of Joseph is when Jesus was twelve years old and went missing on a trip to Jerusalem and was found by Joseph and Mary in the temple. According to the 'Story of Joseph the Carpenter' in the Coptic Apocrypha, Joseph died at the age of 111, on 20 July AD 18 or 19. St Epiphanius gave his age as ninety when he died and the Venerable Bede wrote that he was buried in the Valley of Josaphat. Their sources for these claims are unknown. It seems reasonable, however, to assume that Joseph had died before the Crucifixion, or Jesus would not have entrusted his mother to John's care.

Mary's death is also not recorded in the scriptures, but both the Catholic and Orthodox churches say that she was taken bodily into heaven and did not die at all. According to the seventh- or eighth-century writer Hippolytus of Thebes, she lived for eleven years after the Crucifixion and died in AD 41.

260. Did the manuscript of Jesus' sayings known as Q ever exist?

The Gospels of Matthew and Luke have much in common. Their writers are thought to have both used Mark's Gospel as a source, but they also share a good deal that is not in Mark. Much of this consists of the sayings of Jesus which, it has been conjectured, they obtained from a hypothetical document known as Q (from *Quelle*, German for 'source').

Whether Q was an actual document or just represented the oral tradition of the early Christian church has been argued since about 1900. Opponents of the theorized existence of Q say that no direct evidence of such a document has ever been found and such an important piece of writing would never have been allowed to disappear. Supporters of the Q theory, however, point to the close similarity of a large number of references in Matthew and Luke, which would have been very unlikely to occur if they were relying on spoken and remembered accounts.

261. How many brothers and sisters did Jesus have?

Both Matthew and Mark tell us that Jesus had four brothers – James, Joseph, Simon and Judas – and they also mention that he had sisters, but neither names them nor tells us how many. When Matthew (13:56) reports Jesus' followers asking in the synagogue, 'His sisters, are they not all with us?', the use of the word 'all' would seem to imply that he had at least three.

Some have argued, however, that the words 'brothers' and 'sisters' may refer to the children of Joseph by a previous marriage, or the cousins of Jesus rather than later children of Joseph and Mary.

262. Did Jesus ever work as a carpenter?

There is an eighteen-year gap in the Gospels in their account of Jesus' life between the ages of twelve and about thirty. All we are told of that period is that he 'advanced in wisdom and stature, and in favour with God and men' (Luke 2:52). One suggestion is that he entered the family business and learnt the skills of a carpenter from Joseph.

In Mark 6:3 the question is asked, 'Is not this the carpenter, the son of Mary', which suggests that Jesus was recognized as a carpenter, while Matthew 13:55 poses the same question as: 'Is not this the carpenter's son?' This suggests that Jesus was recognized at best as an apprentice to his father, or even as 'the kid we used to see playing at the carpenter's place'.

There is also a problem about the word 'carpenter', which is a translation of a Greek work signifying a more general type of handyman than we now associate with the word 'carpenter'.

263. How many contemporaries of Jesus were direct descendants of King David?

Both Matthew and Luke make a point of establishing that Jesus was a direct descendant of King David whose own genealogy is traced back to Adam. Both give very similar lists from Adam to David, but they diverge considerably in the way they trace the family tree from David to Jesus. Matthew's list gives twenty-seven generations from one to the other, Luke gives forty-two generations. When you do the maths, however, this ought not to be surprising, for there would probably have been many ways to trace back Jesus' ancestry to David.

Tracing anyone's ancestors will reveal two parents, four grandparents and, in most cases, eight great-grandparents. The number of great-grandparents may be lower if inbreeding took place. As we go further and further back, the numbers of direct ancestors will continue growing until we reach a stage when almost everybody is an ancestor. The only exceptions will be those in closed communities who never married outside, and those who never had children or whose lines of descendants died out.

The population of the Holy Land at the time of Jesus was about a million, and calculations based on a plausible mathematical model of reproduction show that King David would have been a common ancestor of the entire population of the Holy Land somewhere between twenty and thirty-five generations after his own. So almost everyone alive in the Holy Land at the time of Jesus would have been able to claim David as an ancestor.

See also ANATOMY 7; ASTRONOMY 30; BIBLE 52–3

> 'Research is what I'm doing when
> I don't know what I am doing.'
>
> Werner von Braun

JUPITER

264. Why are Jupiter's clouds so colourful?

From an artistic point of view, Jupiter is beautiful. From the Great Red Spot in its atmosphere to the wide range of colours in its clouds, from white to yellows and ruddy browns, and even occasional hints of green and blue, it presents an ever-changing technicolour rainbow. From a scientific point of view, however, it is a mystery, because we do not know about the chemistry that is producing these colours.

Jupiter's atmosphere is known to be mostly frozen ammonia, but ammonia ice is white and cannot account for the colours. There are plenty of chemicals which might, but theories about how the colours are produced do not match the data obtained from either the Infrared Space Observatory in the 1990s or the Cassini fly-by of Jupiter in 2000/1.

Even the Great Red Spot is unexplained, as this indicates the presence of something absorbing blue light and we do not know what it is.

See also ASTRONOMY 30; SOLAR SYSTEM 441

KANGAROOS

265. Were giant kangaroos too big to hop?

Until about 30,000 years ago, a species of giant kangaroo called sthenurines roamed Australia, but how exactly they did the roaming is a matter of some dispute. Research on modern kangaroos has shown that hopping is for them the most energy-efficient means of locomotion at speeds of more than 29 km/h. Giant kangaroos, however, were three times the weight of even the largest species of kangaroo today, and a recent study of the bones of both modern and extinct species has suggested that the giant kangaroo might have swaggered rather than hopped.

The authors of the study suggested that the muscles used to flex the spine in giant kangaroos were too small to allow efficient hopping. Their conclusion was that as kangaroos grew larger, they started to walk on two legs rather than bending down to bounce. If that is all true, however, it raises the question of how the kangaroos managed in the first place to evolve to a size that interfered with their primary means of locomotion.

See also MAMMALS 283

KISSES

266. Who was the first to use X as a symbol for a kiss?

According to the *Oxford English Dictionary*, the earliest recorded use of an X to signify a kiss was in 1763, when the naturalist and cleric Gilbert White ended a letter: 'I am with many a xxxxxxx and many a Pater noster and Ave Maria, Gil White.'

It is not clear, however, whether Gilbert White's Xs signified a string of kisses or Christian blessings. An X had long symbolized the Crucifixion as well as being the first letter of 'Christ' in Greek, so when a cleric strung several together in conjunction with a Pater noster and an Ave Maria, it could be that he wasn't thinking of kisses at all.

In any case, some have derived the use of X to symbolize a kiss back to a much older practice of illiterates signing documents with an X and then kissing the X to show sincerity. Some say that an X is simply designed to suggest the coming together of two puckered-up lips, while perhaps the most romantic idea of all is that a letter-writer might place a kiss at the end of the script, then add an X over the kiss to let the recipient know where it was so they could place it to the lips and receive the kiss. But when the practice began seems not to be known.

LANGUAGE

267. Is language ability hard-wired into our brains?

In the 1960s the US philosopher/linguist Noam Chomsky popularized the idea that language is hard-wired into the human brain. His idea was not that we are pre-programmed to understand and speak a particular language but that we are all equipped with what he called a 'universal grammar', which is the underlying structure behind all languages.

The idea that language ability is innate has been argued for half a century, and papers continue to appear both for and against Chomsky's view. Supporters of the innateness theory cite evidence of the way children learn languages, apparently picking up and generalizing rules without needing to be taught them. Opponents, however, have questioned the existence of a universal grammar, and, after comparing the structure of different languages, have concluded that there is nothing they all have in common. They also claim that the so-called innate linguistic abilities of children are not language-specific at all, but are simply examples of our general innate skills of concept formation and pattern recognition.

268. Did every language evolve from a single primitive mother tongue?

Similarities between different languages have led to the conclusion that some must have had a common origin. We know that many English words had their roots in Latin and Greek, while others were borrowed from French or Germanic languages. Pursuing the trail further back has led to the belief that all those languages, together with Hindi, Gaelic, Russian and a host of other tongues, had a common ancestor in an unknown ancient language known as Proto-Indo-European.

Similar comparisons between language groups have led to notional languages from which all others, including those that have now died out, evolved. Knowledge of human evolution suggests that the physical ability to utter sounds dates back to the earliest days of *Homo sapiens*. Even Neanderthals had the basic anatomy needed for speech, so it seems likely that some sort of language may have existed before the earliest modern humans emerged from Africa. Tracing the fifty or so proto-languages back to a single common ancestor, however, has so far been no more than pure guesswork.

See also ATILLA 32; AZTECS 38; COMPUTERS 114; ENGLISH HISTORY 175; HUMAN EVOLUTION 237; MARRIAGE 284; MEERKATS 302; PREHISTORY 383; WORDS 498

LEGS

269. Why do centipedes have so many legs?

Centipedes may have more than 300 legs or fewer than twenty, but the evolutionary advantages of having so many is unclear. A large number of legs is no doubt helpful in letting them move quickly, or in using some legs to hold captured prey while using others to grab more, but numerous legs are also liable to get in each other's way and at the best of times their co-ordination will take up considerable mental resources.

Interestingly, millipedes, which have more legs, move more slowly than centipedes, so the question of why they have so many is even more difficult to answer.

270. Why do centipedes never have a hundred legs?

A centipede's body is divided into segments and each segment has two legs. The number of legs is therefore always even, but the number of segments is always odd, so the number of pairs of legs is odd. This may be explained by the way the centipede's body grows. It does this by adding segments, and each time it adds a segment, that segment divides into two. This leaves an even number of pairs of legs on the added segments, which becomes an odd number when we include a pair of legs on the head segment which are used as pincher-legs.

Whether the pincher-legs are formed on a segment that divides, however, is not known. If that is the case, another reason would need to be found why the number of pairs of legs is odd and why a centipede with exactly 100 legs (i.e. fifty pairs) is impossible.

271. Why did apes start walking on two legs instead of four?

Writing about the evolution of bipedalism in 1871, Charles Darwin said that the early hominids walked on two legs in order to leave their hands free. He said that 'the hands and arms could hardly have become perfect enough to have manufactured weapons, or to have hurled stones and spears with a true aim, as long as they were habitually used for locomotion'.

This sounds plausible enough, but later evidence showed that apes started walking on their hind legs about 7 million years ago, which was about 4.5 million years before the earliest stone tools came into use.

Another theory has linked bipedalism with environmental changes leading to deforestation, when walking on two legs across open country could have been more energy-efficient. It has also been suggested that bipedalism evolved alongside monogamy, enabling males to carry food back to females who were looking after the young.

Until further evidence is found of early hominids and the environments they lived in, the origins of their bipedalism will remain a mystery.

See also DINOSAURS 138; MEDICINE 300; SLOTHS 431

LEMURS

272. Why do fat-tailed dwarf lemurs hibernate?

The fat-tailed dwarf lemur of Madagascar is the only primate known to hibernate. According to research published in 2013, it is also the only animal known to fall fully asleep while hibernating and was the first tropical mammal known to hibernate. Other animals when hibernating enter a state of torpor when metabolism almost stops. Lemurs fall properly asleep and metabolism continues. Unlike other animals that hibernate because of the cold, the behaviour in lemurs seems to be an adaptation to drought, when food and water are scarce. During their six- or seven-month hibernation period, they live off the fat stored in their tails. Even more unusually, their body temperature does not stay low during the hibernation period, but fluctuates quite dramatically.

Other lemurs have recently been found to hibernate, but their hibernation is more like that of other mammals. How the fat-tailed dwarf lemurs of Madagascar evolved this unique behaviour and what triggers it when they decide to curl up in a tree trunk and fall asleep for half the year are not yet known.

LEONARDO

273. Were Leonardo da Vinci's catapults ever used in battle?

In the 1480s Leonardo da Vinci made at least two detailed sketches of designs for catapults. Although gunpowder had already been introduced to Europe, da Vinci is known to have been concerned about its safety and general unreliability and believed that there was still a need in military battles for more traditional weapons such as catapults.

One of his designs features a single-arm catapult using a ratchet system to move the swing arm into a position from which it could unleash a projectile with great power. The other design was for a double-arm catapult which used gears to allow the throwing arm to be drawn back. Both designs featured improvements on anything that had been seen previously.

Da Vinci is known to have touted his ideas to kings and noblemen, who we may assume would have been very interested in any device that might have enhanced their prospects on the battlefield or the defence of their castles. There is no evidence, however, whether or not da Vinci's catapults were ever even made during his lifetime, let alone used in battle.

Later reconstructions have confirmed that they may have been difficult and expensive to construct at the time, but would almost certainly have been effective if someone had taken the trouble to do so.

See also ART 25

LEOPARDS

274. Why do leopards kill their young?

A recent survey covering a thirteen-year period in South Africa's Kruger National Park revealed that of 280 dead leopard cubs recorded by the researchers, forty-five had been killed by male leopards which then ate them. There have also been accounts of female leopards eating their own babies, but that is much rarer. So what is the evolutionary advantage of such behaviour? There are several theories:

(i) They may be driven to it by a food shortage.

(ii) They may do it to keep the family to a manageable size.

(iii) They may be driven to it by stress, possibly caused by human behaviour.

(iv) They may just be aggressive animals, with the cubs just collateral damage from fights between adults.

(v) Males may be killing off babies of a potential mate to give their own future offspring a better chance.

In view of the fact that most such killings are done by males, the most likely of these is the last, with the eating of the babies just a nutritional, opportunistic by-product of the killing, but the other explanations seem equally possible if females are simply less inclined towards infanticide.

LITERATURE

275. Was Wordsworth's Lucy a real person?

Between 1798 and 1801, when William Wordsworth was living in Germany, he wrote a series of five poems expressing his love for 'Lucy', an English girl who 'dwelt among th' untrodden ways beside the Springs of Dove' and who died young. The passionate melancholy in these verses about the 'maid whom there were none to praise, And very few to love' is very striking, but the question of whether Lucy was a real person or an idealized figment of Wordsworth's imagination has never been resolved.

The poet himself never revealed any details about Lucy, leaving others to speculate on her possible identity. It has been suggested that Lucy represented his childhood sweetheart Peggy Hutchinson, who died young in 1796. Wordsworth later married Peggy's sister Mary, but it has also been suggested that Lucy in fact was based on his own sister Dorothy, who went on to live to the age of eighty-three.

276. Did the Book of the Wars of the Lord ever exist?

The King James Bible, in Numbers 21:14, refers to the 'Book of the Wars of the Lord' and goes on to quote lines from a song and sayings of poets, without making it clear whether these quotations are taken from the same Book of the Wars of the Lord.

It has been conjectured that the book referred to may have been a collection of victory songs or poems, or it may have been a military history. It has also been suggested that the phrase 'Book of the Wars' was not the title but only a quotation from the book, but since no trace of the book has ever been found, it may not have existed at all.

277. What does the first word of *Beowulf* mean?

The opening words of the epic poem *Beowulf*, which begins 'Hwæt! We Gar-Dena in gear-dagum...', are usually translated 'Listen! We have heard of the might of the kings...', but there has long been dispute over the meaning and significance of the opening word.

In 1837 Jakob Grimm (one of the brothers Grimm, who collected fairy tales when not pursuing their linguistic researches) wrote that 'Hwæt' was purely an interjection. For many it was seen simply as a way of telling the reader or listener to take notice, which later writers translated as 'Listen!' or 'Attend!' or even 'So!' (which was the choice of Seamus Heaney in his acclaimed 2000 translation).

In 2013, however, Dr George Walkden of Cambridge University gave a very different view based on an analysis of 141 other clauses using the word 'Hwæt', combined with general evidence of the Anglo-Saxon use of exclamation marks. His conclusion was that 'Old English *hwæt* (as well as its Old Saxon cognate) was not an interjection but an underspecified wh-pronoun introducing an exclamative clause'. In other words, 'hwaet' is not an exclamation on its own, but only becomes one when taken in conjunction with the words that follow. The translation he suggests for the opening line was: 'How we have heard of the might of the kings.'

Some 1,200 or 1,300 years after *Beowulf* was written, we are still arguing about what its first word means.

See also TROY 456

LOBSTERS

278. How long can a lobster live?

Lobsters have very long lives. For a long time, some people even believed they were immortal. They do not even seem to age, and lose neither strength nor reproductive abilities as they grow older. The reason for this seems to lie in the lobster's habit of discarding its shell quite frequently and growing a new one, which enables it to grow while renewing the parts of itself that might be considered susceptible to ageing.

The same process, however, makes it very difficult to assess the age of a lobster. Unlike both trees and other animals, it does not have obvious growth rings, such as have been found in dinosaur bones and fish scales, marking the years of its development. The best way to judge a lobster's age until recently was from its size: multiply its weight in pounds by four, add three and you have an approximation of its age in years.

In 2012, however, a more scientific way of estimating a lobster's age began to be developed. Although moulting destroyed the exoskeleton and all the hard parts of a lobster which would normally be relied upon to bear the marks of ageing, growth rings were found in their eye-stalks and the gastric mills in their stomachs which are used to grind up food. The build-up of neurolipofuscin in their brains was also found to give an indication of age. The reliability of such measures continues to be investigated in order to establish whether the metabolic age, as measured by such ring-counting, correlates with chronological age.

Since shedding their shells demands increasingly large amounts of energy as lobsters get bigger, eventually they stop shedding and die, so they are definitely not immortal, but how long they can live is still not known. In 1977 a lobster weighing over 20 kilograms was caught in Nova Scotia, which, by the old formula, would have made it at least 179 years old. But nobody counted the rings on its eye-stalks at the time.

'Is an intelligent human being likely to be much more than a large-scale manufacturer of misunderstanding?'

Philip Roth

LONGEVITY

279. How long can humans live?

In 2004 BBC News reported a story under the headline: 'We will be able to live to 1,000.' The story centred on the SENS (Strategies for Engineered Negligible Senescence) project which consisted of 'a very detailed plan to repair all the types of molecular and cellular damage that happen to us over time'. The Cambridge geneticist Aubrey de Grey was quoted as saying: 'I think the first person to live to 1,000 might be 60 already.'

Some other scientists dismissed such claims as more fantasy than science, but in 2013 the *Daily Mail* published a report of research in California under the heading: 'Could humans live to 500 years old? Scientists believe genetic tweaks could significantly extend our lifespan.' The research, however, was on worms, not humans. By modifying the genes of *Caenorhabditis elegans* lab worms, the researchers had been able to increase their lifespans by a factor of five. If a similar technique could be applied to long-lived humans, the newspaper report said, we could live to the age of 400 or 500. 'The next step is to investigate if the effects occur in mice,' it said.

Today worms, tomorrow mice, maybe one day humans, but in the meantime our worldwide life expectancy is still 68.5 years for males and 73.5 years for females.

280. Is human immortality out of the question?

Is death an inevitable part of life? Ever since alchemists started looking for an elixir of immortality, that question has been asked and the comparatively recent discovery of telomeres is the nearest we have yet come to an answer. Telomeres are chains at the ends of our DNA molecules which become shorter every time the cell replicates. When the telomere becomes too short, the cell loses its vital DNA code, its ability to replicate is damaged, and the process of dying begins.

The number of times a cell can divide without damage is called the Hayflick limit, after US anatomist Leonard Hayflick, whose study of cell reproduction in 1961 put an end to the belief that human cells were in principle immortal. Later it was found that the Hayflick limit correlated with telomere length, and the quest for immortality began to concentrate on looking for ways to prevent the shortening of telomeres with each cell division.

The good news in that regard is an enzyme called telomerase which can turn telomere production on and off. You might say that telomerase is potentially the elixir of immortality for our cells. The bad news, however, is that telomerase is precisely what makes cancer cells keep reproducing. Thanks to telomerase, cancer cells are, in fact, the nearest thing we have to immortality. Anything that increases our production of telomerase, boosting our telomeres and maintaining the reproduction of our cells, will also lead to an increase in cancers.

Immortality by this route would therefore seem to need something that blocks the action of telomerase on cancerous cells while not interfering with its action on normal cells.

281. Are short telomeres a sign of ageing or a cause of ageing?

In 2002 a study at the University of Utah confirmed that shorter telomeres in humans are associated with shorter lives. People with shorter telomeres were three times more likely to die within the next year from heart disease and eight times more likely to die from infectious disease. In healthy people, however, it has been shown that telomeres do not shrink significantly until old age thanks to the production of telomerase. The net shortening of telomere length seems to be caused by a combination of cell division and lessening telomerase production.

The 2002 study showed that only 37 per cent of the variation in the risk of dying among the over-sixties was accounted for by a combination of age, gender and telomere length. The other 63 per cent was attributed to other causes such as oxidative stress and glycation, caused by our intake of oxidants and glucose, which can damage DNA, proteins and fats.

Ageing and shortened telomeres undoubtedly go together, but which is the cause and which is the effect remains unproven. Mice, after all, have much longer telomeres than humans, but live much shorter lives.

282. How long do fangtooths live?

Members of the ugly fang-toothed Anoplogastridae family – commonly known, appropriately enough, as 'fangtooths' – are among the least-known fish in the oceans. There are two species, the common fangtooth and the short-horn fangtooth; they live at depths of up to 5,000 metres (but more often at 500–2,000 metres), growing to just over eighteen centimetres in length, and have no known close relatives.

Fangtooths have very poor sight and seem to locate prey through their chemical receptors, latching on to it with their huge teeth when they bump into it. The upper parts of their mouths have holes in them through which their lower fangs slot to enable them to close their mouths.

The depths at which they live have hampered attempts to find out more about them. All that is known about their mating behaviour is that females seem to deposit eggs in the water at the same time as males deposit sperm. And nobody seems to have any idea how long they live.

See also GENETICS 211; SHARKS 416

'Science... is made up of mistakes, but they are mistakes which it is useful to make because they lead little by little to the truth.'

Jules Verne

MAMMALS

283. Why do only placental mammals have a corpus callosum?

Mammals come in three varieties: monotremes, such as the platypus and echidna, which lay eggs; marsupials, such as the kangaroo and koala, which have pouches; and placental mammals, such as humans and rats, in which the mother nourishes the foetus within a placenta until it is fully developed. As mentioned earlier (→ 5), all the placental mammals, and only the placental mammals, have brains divided into two halves joined by a thick bundle of neural fibres called the corpus callosum.

The evolutionary split of mammals into these three classes is thought to have occurred between 65 and 100 million years ago, which is roughly when the corpus callosum is thought to have evolved. So was the evolution of the placenta in some way connected to the evolution of the corpus callosum?

Nobody has yet suggested a way the two might be connected, but the fact that all mammals have either both or neither seems to demand an explanation.

See also ANATOMY 5; BONES 72; BRAINS 78; DINOSAURS 138; DISEASE 144; EVOLUTION 178, 181; HUMAN EVOLUTION 236; LEMURS 272; PANDAS 353; PANGOLINS 354; PLATYPUSES 375; RATS 393; SALAMANDERS 398; SLEEP 423–4; WALRUSES 486

MARRIAGE

284. When and where did the first marriage ceremony take place?

The earliest recorded formal marriage ceremonies between a man and a woman took place in Mesopotamia about 2350 BC. In the language of the Sumerians of southern Mesopotamia, the word for 'to love' was even a compound verb connected with the marking-off of land, suggesting that the concept of love and marriage had a primarily legal aspect. Indeed, in the Code of Hammurabi, which around 1750 BC laid down 283 laws and punishments for breaking them, more than fifty were concerned with the legal rights and wrongs of marriage, polygamy, dowries and adultery.

With such long and detailed regulations surrounding the concept of marriage, it seems reasonable to suppose that the idea of it had already been around a long time before the Mesopotamians formalized it so precisely. Very early human societies are thought to have consisted of communal groups in which women and responsibility for children were shared, so they would have had little use for marriage. How these societies developed from promiscuity to pair-bonding is not known, but it must have happened long before the Mesopotamians had advanced enough to draw up copious laws and procedures related to it.

See also ATILLA 31; HENRY VIII 229; SHAKESPEARE 414

MARS

285. What turned Mars into a dry planet?

Evidence from space research has revealed water vapour in Mars's atmosphere as well as a vast amount of ice and even a freshwater lake on the planet's surface. The planet is now predominantly desiccated, but around 4 billion years ago, when the Solar System was in its infancy, Mars is thought to have been kept warm by a thick atmosphere and to have had rivers flowing into lakes and seas. NASA's Mars Atmosphere and Volatile Evolution (MAVEN) orbiter is currently trying to get to the bottom of the question of what dried Mars out when it seemed to be firmly on the path to producing life in a way similar to what happened on Earth.

One idea is that the Martian atmosphere may, over billions of years, have been blown away by the solar wind. The reason this has not happened on Earth is that we have a global magnetic field to protect us. Mars has just a few areas similarly protected by its own magnetic properties.

Another suggestion is that the greenhouse gas carbon dioxide (CO_2) may have been absorbed by the planet's surface with a resulting cooling effect. It is hoped that MAVEN will be able to measure the rate of escape of CO_2 and other gases and extrapolate the figure backwards to get an idea of what has been going on for the past 4 billion years.

286. What is the source of the methane on Mars?

Ever since 1909 we have known there is a small amount of methane in Mars's atmosphere. This cannot be the remains of ancient methane because methane molecules last only 300 or 400 years in Martian air before they are broken down by sunlight. So the planet must still be releasing methane. In December 2014 the Martian methane question became still more intriguing when NASA's *Curiosity* rover reported the discovery that Mars was periodically belching out clouds of methane from its surface.

On Earth most methane is produced as a waste gas from the consumption of food by living organisms, so the Martian methane was seen as a possible hint of life on the planet. It could also be produced by the remains of long-extinct organisms being heated in the Martian interior and vaporized.

There are plenty of ways, however, that methane could be produced that do not involve life of any form, and the gas on its own will never be enough to prove that there is or is not life on Mars. Nevertheless, investigation of the rocks on Mars and the gases in its atmosphere may suggest or rule out other possible causes for the methane.

See also MERCURY 304

MATHEMATICS

287. Does a perfect cuboid exist?

Given any three positive integers, we can imagine a cuboid (that's a rectangular box) whose length, breadth and height are given by those integers. Pythagoras' theorem lets us work out the lengths of the diagonals on the faces of the box, and if the lengths of all three such diagonals are also integers, the cuboid is known as an 'Euler brick' after the great eighteenth-century Swiss mathematician Leonard Euler.

The first such Euler brick was discovered in 1719, with sides of lengths 44, 117 and 240 (where the diagonals work out at 125, 244 and 267 exactly). But what about the internal diagonal, from the bottom, front, left corner to the top, back, right? Can that have an integer length too?

What we're looking for is three integers, a, b and c (the side lengths), for which not only are $a^2 + b^2$ and $b^2 + c^2$ and $c^2 + a^2$ (the squares of the diagonals) perfect squares, but $a^2 + b^2 + c^2$ (the square of the internal diagonal) is also a perfect square. If such numbers can be found, then the result is called a 'perfect cuboid', but so far nobody has either discovered one or proved that none can exist.

288. Can every sufficiently large number be expressed as the sum of six cubes?

One cubed = 1 x 1 x 1, which is 1, two cubed is 2 x 2 x 2, which is 8, and we can go on with the sequence of cubes: 27, 64, 125, 216, 343, 512, 729...

What happens, though, if we try to express any number as the sum of positive cubes? It was proved about a century ago that every number can be expressed as the sum of at most nine cubes, and the only numbers that required nine were 23 (= 8 + 8 + 1 + 1 + 1 + 1 + 1 + 1 + 1) and 239 (= 125 + 27 + 27 + 27 + 8 + 8 + 8 + 8 + 1). Later it was proved that, apart from these, the only numbers needing at least eight cubes were 15, 22, 50, 114, 167, 175, 186, 212, 231, 238, 303, 364, 420, 428 and 454, so it follows that any number greater than 454 can be expressed as the sum of at most seven cubes.

But can we make a similar statement about six cubes? Is there a number beyond which we can say that any larger number is the sum of at most six positive cubes?

289. Are there infinitely many Fermat primes?

The great French mathematician Pierre Fermat, who died in 1665, spent much effort looking for a formula that would generate prime numbers. The nearest he got was the so-called Fermat primes, which are numbers of the form $2^{(2^n)} + 1$.

Fermat conjectured that all such numbers were prime, and for the first few values of n, he was right. The first five values given by the formula are 3, 5, 17, 257 and 65537, and these are indeed prime numbers. Unfortunately, as Euler discovered in 1732, the next number in the series, 4294967297, is equal to 641 x 6700417.

Since that time, no Fermat prime apart from the first five has ever been discovered, yet whether there are any more, or even possibly an infinite number of them, is still unknown.

290. Does the number 10 have any friends?

Think of a number; find all the numbers (including itself) that divide into it exactly; add them all together and divide by the number you first thought of. Now try to find another number that gives you the same answer if you do the same thing. If you find one, then the two numbers you started with are called 'friendly'. For example, 30 and 140 are friendly:

The sum of the divisors of 30 is

$1 + 2 + 3 + 5 + 6 + 10 + 15 + 30 = 72.$

Dividing that by 30 gives 72/30, which equals 12/5.

The sum of the divisors of 140 is

$1 + 2 + 4 + 5 + 7 + 10 + 14 + 20 + 28 + 35 + 70 + 140 = 336.$

Divide that by 140 and we get 336/140, which (dividing top and bottom by 28) equals 12/5.

If we start with the number 10, we get $(1 + 2 + 5 + 10)/10 = 9/5$, and nobody has ever found another number that gives the same result. Nobody has ever proved that no such number exists, however, so we do not know whether 10 has any friends or not.

291. Is there a 3 x 3 magic square all of whose entries are distinct perfect squares?

A magic square is a square array of numbers, all of whose rows, columns and diagonals add up to the same number. Here's an example in which they all add up to 15:

4	9	2
3	5	7
8	1	6

Here's another more complicated example devised by Euler in 1770:

4624	841	1681	1369
289	961	6241	1024
3481	783	529	3721
121	5929	64	2401

But Euler was not just fooling around with large numbers, for his square has a really magical property: not only do all lines add up to 8515, but all sixteen numbers in it are themselves squares.

The question is, can the same trick be done with a 3 x 3 square? Does a magic square of that size exist that is made up of nine different square numbers? Nobody has ever found one or proved that no such square exists.

292. Why is mathematics so effective at explaining the world?

Why do two bodies, according to Newton's law of gravity, attract each other with a force proportional to the product of the masses of the bodies and inversely proportional to the square of the distance between them?

Why do Maxwell's equations tell us all we need to know about electricity and magnetism?

Why does $E = mc^2$?

In short, as Einstein put it: 'How is it possible that mathematics, a product of human thought that is independent of experience, fits so excellently the objects of physical reality?'

According to mathematical Platonists, maths is a pure and idealized language that is in effect the mother tongue of the real world and everything must yield to its power or make no sense. According to non-Platonists, maths is, as Einstein said, a product of the human mind, a mental construct that can at best give a rigid approximation to what is really happening.

Mathematics, even the non-Platonists must agree, has made a pretty good job of explaining the world, but many of the unanswered questions in this book could be cited as evidence that its explanations are never complete.

See also BIG BANG 55; COSMOLOGY 123, 126; JESUS CHRIST 263; NUMBERS 346; SOLAR SYSTEM 444; UNIVERSE 464

MAYANS

293. What caused the collapse of the Mayan civilization?

In the ninth century the Mayan empire stretched right across Central America. Their cities had large populations and were ruled by a strong and dominant elite. Its temples and stone carvings were evidence of a thriving culture. Even long-distance trade was flourishing. Yet within about 150 years, everything fell apart, leaving the cities in ruins and abandoned. So what happened?

One theory suggests a natural disaster, an earthquake or volcano, or terrible disease perhaps, but while the collapse was fast, it was too slow to suggest a dinosaur-like sudden extinction. Another idea is warfare: perhaps the various Mayan city-states went to war and wiped each other out. But that hardly explains what happened to the victors in such wars.

It could have been famine; it could have been environmental change; it could have been floods; it could have been drought; but there is little evidence of any of these.

It may have been a combination of any or all of the above that destroyed the Mayans, but the lack of evidence suggests that there is something we have not yet discovered.

See also CHOCOLATE 105

MEDICINE

294. Does acupuncture work?

Supporters of acupuncture cite studies in which subjects suffering from pain or depression or other conditions are treated with acupuncture and report a significant level of improvement. Opponents of acupuncture insist that the results in such studies are no better than those achieved with placebos.

In 2009 and again in 2012, analyses were published assessing the results of numerous studies in different countries in which the effects of no acupuncture, acupuncture and sham acupuncture were compared. In the last of these, the patient is 'treated' by having needles inserted into him acupuncture-style, but the places they are inserted are randomly chosen rather than being placed at the so-called 'meridian points' advised in traditional acupuncture. The results showed a very small difference between acupuncture and sham acupuncture, and a rather larger difference between no acupuncture and acupuncture (real or sham).

Supporters of acupuncture say it proves what they've been saying all along, as acupuncture proved itself significantly better than no acupuncture. Opponents point out that the differences between the trials involving acupuncture and no acupuncture are exactly what one would expect from what we know about placebos, and while the differences between real and sham acupuncture may be *statistically* significant, that is mainly because the sample sizes, when the various studies are all taken together, are so large that a tiny difference may account for it. For a treatment to be worth employing, it needs to be *clinically* significant, which is a different matter entirely. In any case, the effect of the person conducting the trials, who would normally be a trained acupuncturist, can influence the results.

So on the question of whether acupuncture works, we would have to say that the jury is still out.

295. Are bacteria good for us?

We have already touched on this subject when discussing probiotic foods (→ 198), but there is far more to it. We like to think of our bodies as nice all-human entities, but our non-human cells outnumber our human cells by about ten to one (though admittedly the non-human ones are much smaller). The question is whether this co-habitation agreement is to our benefit.

Our non-human microbiota, which are mostly bacteria, have an important part to play in the regulation of our health, but not all of this is good. To take one example, there is a bacterium called *Heliobacter pylori* which is known to cause ulcers and has also been implicated in the development of stomach cancer. Zapping it with antibiotics was a standard treatment until a study in 2011 showed that it may also have a role in warding off asthma.

Such findings, suggesting that even the 'bad' bacteria may be good for us, make it difficult to form a definitive view on whether our bacteria are good for us.

296. How do antidepressants decrease pain?

Antidepressants, as the name suggests, were created in order to treat depression. In cases of depression caused by chronic pain, however, a surprising benefit – that the drugs appeared to reduce the pain as well – was discovered. So antidepressants started to be prescribed for the treatment of pain when normal analgesics were having insufficient effect.

Since then, a vast number of papers have appeared in the medical literature on the question of whether antidepressants are effective in treating pain. Even those who are convinced of the efficacy of antidepressants in this respect, however, are liable to disagree on the details of which particular antidepressants are effective against which types of pain.

One of the underlying problems is that we do not know how antidepressants perform their function as analgesics. Those most generally used are serotonin uptake inhibitors (SUIs), which lead to increased concentrations of the neurotransmitter serotonin. Since serotonin is associated with feelings of well-being and happiness, it is easy to see how it could treat depression, but reasons for SUIs to be effective in treating pain are more elusive.

In a 2008 report, Sansone and Sansone say 'multiple mechanisms are likely to be involved' and go on to mention 'adjunctive thera-peutic influences through histamine receptors', 'modulation of sodium channels' and mechanisms exerting their effects on the neurotransmit-ters serotonin and norepinephrine, 'particularly along the descending spinal pain pathways'.

Or, to put it more simply, we don't know.

297. How do placebos work?

For hundreds of years both medical practitioners and quack doctors have known that if patients think their condition is going to improve, then it is liable to do so. For this reason, whenever a new drug or other treatment is introduced, its effect on one group of subjects is compared with the results on another group given a harmless placebo. Neither the subjects nor the doctors administering the treatments know who is getting which. On average, about 30 per cent of the subjects receiving the placebo treatment will report an improvement in their condition, so for a new treatment to be considered effective, it has to outperform that figure.

But why are those 30 per cent getting better? For a long time it was thought that the improvement was only in the mind. People were being treated; they expected to get better; so they reported improvements. Later studies, however, showed that in many cases they really were getting better. Patients with stomach ulcers who were given placebos were found to recover more quickly than those who received no treatment. Patients given a placebo which they were told would raise their heart rate and blood pressure were found to have higher heart rates and blood pressure, and the reverse effect was found in patients who were told the same placebo would lower their blood pressure and heart rate.

Clearly our bodies' defence mechanisms can be stimulated into performing more effectively by our believing that they will do so. Most curiously, one study has even reported a placebo effect in patients who were told they were being given a placebo, but perhaps they did not believe what the experimenters had told them.

If placebo treatments can lead to real improvements in health, as seems to be the case, potentially it would be very beneficial to know how they work, but we really have no idea.

298. Why are autism rates rising?

In the 1970s and 1980s, around one in 2,000 children in the USA was diagnosed with autism. Now the figure is about one in 150. This raises two important questions:

Is autism really rising, or do the statistics merely reflect a growing awareness of the condition and a recent tendency to refer to an 'autistic spectrum' ranging from mild Asperger's syndrome to severe autism?

If autism is rising, as seems to be the case, what is causing the increase? Is it diet, genetics, environmental changes, or some unsuspected medical treatment, all of which have come under suspicion?

299. Does marijuana reduce pain?

In the USA, under the Controlled Substances Act, marijuana (cannabis) is a Schedule I drug, the strictest classification, yet several states have legalized the medical use of marijuana for pain relief, and more are likely to follow. The Food and Drug Administration (FDA) classification is based on the drug's high potential to lead to abuse, addiction or other harm, but are they right in saying that it has 'no currently accepted medical use'?

Supporters of legalized marijuana point to the pain reliever Sativex, which is based on a natural extract of marijuana, or the drug Marinol, which is used to treat nausea in cancer patients and contains a synthetic form of a cannabinoid known as THC, which is found in marijuana. Both of these have been approved by the FDA, so how can there be doubts about marijuana's effectiveness?

The doubters, however, were supported by a study in Oxford in 2013 based on brain-imaging scans to see exactly what effect cannabis had. The results showed that the drug did not affect the areas of the brain that interpret pain to any significant degree, as conventional pain medicines do. The areas cannabis affected were those that are responsible for the emotional reaction to pain. In other words, cannabis does not reduce pain, it just makes it more bearable.

300. What is the cause of muscle cramps?

Muscle cramps, which tend to occur at night and wake us up in sharp pain, are sudden spasms or tightening, usually in the calf muscles of the leg, which may last anything from a few seconds to several minutes. They tend to occur just as you are falling asleep or waking up; they are sometimes associated with recent exercise, or dehydration, or pregnancy, or blood-flow problems, or mineral deficiency, or simply sleeping in an awkward position.

But sometimes they just happen, and we really do not know what causes them.

See also CHEMICALS 95; NAPOLEON 337; PANGOLINS 356; SOCRATES 440

'The doorstep to the temple of wisdom
is a knowledge of our own ignorance.'

Benjamin Franklin

MEERKATS

301. Why do meerkats stop begging?

Young meerkat pups make begging calls to which adults respond by bringing them food. Eventually, the young meerkats stop begging, the adults stop bringing them food, and the young go and find their own. Three reasons have been suggested for the young stopping their begging:

(i) The adults think it's time for the young to become self-sufficient, so stop responding to the calls.

(ii) The young decide they'd prefer the wider choice they might get if they took charge of the foraging.

(iii) The young simply lose the ability to make the begging calls.

A study in 2008 showed that adults who had ceased their food delivery service could be induced back into it by being played a recording of pups begging. This suggested that the initiation of the pups' foraging was not forced on them by the adults. The experimenters also found acoustical differences in pups' begging sounds as they grew older and showed that adults responded better to sounds made by younger pups. They concluded: 'We suggest that older pups are unable to produce stimulating begging calls.'

302. What do meerkats talk about?

Meerkats have a variety of about thirty sounds with which they communicate with each other. They chatter, they squeak, they growl and they purr. They seem to purr when content, growl when looking for food, chatter when anxious, and squeal when danger threatens. They have also shown signs of being able to recognize each other's voices.

They also communicate by scent and posture, but with at least thirty words in their language, and recorded utterances apparently having between one and four syllables, they must have the capacity to convey reasonably detailed information. We just haven't learnt their language yet.

MERCURY

303. What caused the Pantheon Fossae in the Caloris Basin on Mercury?

When the Messenger spacecraft went into orbit around Mercury, the pictures it sent back revealed a huge set of grooved valleys radiating outwards from a central crater. It was first informally dubbed 'The Spider', but the International Astronomical Union later officially named it 'Pantheon Fossae', as the pattern of its grooves or ditches (*fossae* is Latin for 'ditches') resembled the dome of the Pantheon in Rome. They also named the central crater 'Apollodorus', after the architect of the Pantheon.

What caused the grooved pattern is still a matter of debate, as is the question of whether its formation is connected with the Apollodorus crater at all. With the crater not at the exact centre of the radial grooves and some evidence that the crater was formed later than the grooves, it may be just a coincidence that they are in the same place.

304. Why is the planet Mercury so dense?

We know the size of Mercury and we know, from calculation of its gravitational pull, what its mass is. These figures allow its density to be calculated and the result is much higher than that of Venus, Earth and

Mars. The conclusion is that the planet's metal-rich core must account for about 60 per cent of its mass, which is twice as much as the other three planets.

For this to have occurred, Mercury must have lost some of the lighter elements early in its formation. It could be that solar nebular gas dragged off the lighter silicates before Mercury was formed, leaving mainly the heavier metallic elements. It could be that when Mercury was in its early stages of formation, the heat from the Sun vaporized part of its outer layers. It could be that Mercury was once similar to the other planets, but was the victim of a giant impact that stripped off its crust.

Each of these theories would predict a different composition of the rocks on Mercury's surface, and it is hoped that information from the Messenger orbiter will be enough to identify which of them is most likely to have occurred.

MESOPOTAMIA

305. What was the purpose of the Baghdad batteries?

In 1938 the German archaeologist Wilhelm König made an intriguing discovery when working just outside Baghdad. The object he dug up consisted of a thirteen-centimetre-high clay jar containing a copper cylinder with an iron rod inside it. Tests indicated that an acidic liquid such as lemon juice or wine had been inside the cylinder.

König decided this must have been a voltaic cell, leading to the suggestion that the ancient Mesopotamians had invented the battery almost 2,000 years earlier than the Europeans. It is not clear how many of these 'Baghdad batteries' were unearthed, but some estimates put the number at around twelve.

Replicas of these objects that have been made in recent years show that they could, with lemon or grape juice in the jar, have generated a current of between 0.5 and 2 volts. They could, König suggested, have been used for electro-plating, though later it was found that the objects he thought might have been treated in such a manner were in fact fire-gilded with mercury.

Hardly anyone believes the ancient battery theory now, but the only other suggestion relies on their similarity to storage vessels found at a nearby location. Those vessels, however, lack the outside clay jar.

See also MARRIAGE 284; PREHISTORY 382

METEOROLOGY

306. Why are US tornadoes occurring on fewer days than they used to?

In 2014 the National Oceanographic and Atmospheric Administration in the USA published a survey of weather data stretching back over fifty years. Their analysis revealed that the number of tornadoes hitting the US each year had not changed much over that period: it was always about 1,200. But, mysteriously, the number of days on which tornadoes struck had decreased. In fact, the figures showed that during the 1970s the number of days on which thirty or more tornadoes were recorded had been around six a year, but in the past twenty years it was only about three. In other words, there have been about the same number of tornadoes, but they tend to occur more closely together in time.

It has been vaguely suggested that this may have something to do with global warming or atmospheric changes due to pollution, but the mechanism causing the change is unknown.

307. What is the effect of polar warming on mid-latitude regions?

In 2012 research was published suggesting that the melting of the Arctic ice-cap could lead to very cold winters in mid-latitude regions in the northern hemisphere. The argument was that rapid melting of the sea ice could bring about changes in the flow of the jet stream, driving it further south and bringing colder temperatures and longer-lasting winters to more southern regions.

The argument was supported by some data on Arctic ice cover and changing paths of the jet stream, but the authors agreed that further details were needed and it was still only a hypothesis.

The research was immediately leapt on by representatives of both sides of the global warming debate. Sceptics said it was just more evidence that the global warming doom-mongers could twist anything to support their theory: whether it gets colder or hotter, they can say it's due to global warming. Adherents of the global warming hypothesis, however, criticized the research as unconvincing, saying that far more evidence was needed before we could justify any conclusions about the effect of polar ice melting on the motion of the jet stream.

So whether the melting of polar ice brings hot or cold weather to mid-latitude areas is still an open question.

308. Is there a connection between space weather and Earth weather?

The region of space surrounding the Earth is constantly being bombarded by a flow of electrons and protons from the Sun known as the solar wind. The Earth's magnetic field protects us from most potentially harmful effects by deflecting the solar wind, but changes in the Sun's activity have been linked to effects measured on Earth. Geomagnetic storms can disrupt technological systems and solar flares can disrupt long-range radio communications. The effect of such space weather on terrestrial weather, however, is less clear.

From about 1645 to 1715 observations of the Sun indicated a significant decrease in the number of sunspots (patches of relative coolness on the Sun's surface). This period is now known as the

Maunder minimum and coincided with a period known as the Little Ice Age, which was characterized by a cooling of the Earth's climate. The Sun is now known to have a magnetic cycle of around twenty-two years which is responsible for an eleven-year sunspot cycle. For more than a century it has been conjectured that sunspot activity affects the Earth's weather, but this has never been convincingly demonstrated.

Changes in the Sun's magnetic field seem to affect sunspot activity and will presumably also affect the solar wind. One suggestion is that changes in cosmic ray flux caused by the solar wind may cause changes in the amount of cloud formation, which would have a direct effect on the weather. But convincing evidence for this has not yet been demonstrated.

309. How do climate change and land vegetation affect each other?

The relationship between climate change and land vegetation is a complex one. On the one hand, plants absorb carbon dioxide (CO_2) from the atmosphere, which has a cooling effect; on the other hand, they convert the CO_2 into food, releasing energy and water into the atmosphere by transpiration, which has a warming effect. This warming effect is short-term, but the cooling effect is long-term.

Recent research suggested that the amount of water lost through transpiration by plants decreases as CO_2 rises, which would mean that the warming effect was not as large as it might be. However, this issue is again complicated by the fact that different types of plant respond differently to rising CO_2 levels.

Then there is the question of plants growing in regions where snow and ice have melted. That will make the surface less reflective and absorb more heat, which will have a warming effect. And then there is the question of the effect of greenhouse gases on the soil, which will also affect plant growth.

How the various warming and cooling effects balance out and which one comes out on top is the subject of continuing debate.

310. **How does lightning happen?**

Any elementary science book will explain the cause of lightning. An electrical charge builds up in clouds with the positive charge at the top and the negative charge at the bottom: this is called ionization. The negative charge then attracts positively charged particles on Earth, and the force between them eventually becomes so big that it overcomes the insulating properties of the air between them. Result: a flash of lightning as the positively charged particles from the ground rush up, at the speed of light, to meet the negatively charged lower side of the cloud.

It's when you start reading the small print that you realize it's not that simple. First, there is no real explanation of how the clouds become ionized other than a rather vague suggestion that water and ice droplets bump into each other and dislodge electrons that fall to the bottom of the cloud. Secondly, measurements of electrical charge within clouds often yield anomalous results that do not support the simple picture given above. And thirdly, large thunderstorms, when viewed from above, have been seen to emit other electrical phenomena called transient luminous events (TLEs), which have been given suitably exotic names such as 'red sprites' (large but weak red flashes), 'blue jets' (sudden cones of blue light) and 'elves' (large expanding glowing discs of light lasting only a thousandth of a second). None of these have been explained at all.

311. **What causes bends in the jet streams?**

The jet streams are fast-moving narrow currents of air flowing west to east high in the atmosphere which are known to have a huge influence on the motion of weather systems. They follow meandering paths known as Rossby waves, which sometimes flatten out and sometimes become more intense. When these waves are flatter, it leads to high pressure and more settled weather.

To add to these meandering waves, the jet streams themselves seem to move north or south in an unpredictable manner. In recent years, the motion of the northern polar jet stream has been closely mapped and shown to correlate with extreme weather patterns. In particular, floods in Britain in 2007 were attributed to an unusually southerly jet stream bringing depressions across the country. In the same period, however, the same jet stream was shown to exhibit a slow annual drift northwards, which suggested that the weather in Britain was caused by an unusually big bend in the stream's meandering path.

A connection has long been suspected between climate change and changes in the paths of jet streams, particularly that of the northern jet stream, but whether jet streams are causing climate change or climate change is changing the jet streams' paths is unknown. In either case, the possible role of human activity in the changes is also a matter of speculation.

See also GLOBAL WARMING 215–16

MEXICO

312. How did Gil Pérez get to Mexico City?

On 24 October 1593 Gil Pérez was on duty as a guard at the governor's palace in the Philippine capital Manila. The governor, Gómez Pérez Dasmariñas, had been killed by Chinese pirates the previous night and the guards were awaiting the appointment of his successor. Pérez is said to have leaned against a wall to rest. When he opened his eyes, however, he was in an unfamiliar place which turned out to be Mexico City's Plaza Mayor.

Pérez was reported to be still wearing the uniform of the palace guards in Manila and he told the Mexicans about the assassination of the governor. Thinking him to be a madman, a deserter or a servant of the devil, the Mexicans put him in jail. Two months later, they freed him when a ship arrived from the Philippines with news of the governor's death. Pérez was taken back home on the ship and is not known to have instantly teleported again.

This story is presumably all an urban myth, but it has been around since the seventeenth century and is allegedly backed by accounts in both Mexico and the Philippines.

See also ANCIENT CITIES 8; AVOCADOS 37; AZTECS 38; CHEWING GUM 96; VOLCANOES 482–3

MICE

313. Did the house mouse reach Australia on convict ships?

James Cook claimed Australia as part of the British empire in 1770 and British convict ships started arriving at Botany Bay in 1788. Dutch explorers, however, had discovered 'New Holland' long before in 1606, so was it the British or the Dutch who brought house mice with them? Or did the mice arrive from Asia before the Europeans came?

In 2011 a study was made of the mitochondrial DNA of mice in Australia, Britain and the Netherlands, and the results were compared with each other and with Japanese mice. Australian mice were found to have far greater similarities with European mice than with Asian mice, and there were strong indications that they came from British strains rather than Dutch ones.

The analysis, the researchers said, 'does not fully exclude the Netherlands as a possible source area for the Australian house mouse', but 'pending larger sample sizes and more detailed genetic data, a British Isles origin of Australian mice is the most reasonable interpretation of our results'.

It must also be possible, I suppose, that British mice found their way onto Dutch ships and travelled to Australia on them before the British fleet arrived.

314. Do mice like excrement?

Or, to put it less crudely, do wild mice have the luxury of avoiding faeces? That was the question posed by a research paper in 2013 which examined whether wild mice took steps to avoid the potential health risks of proximity with the faeces of others of their own species. Laboratory animals have been observed to stay away from such faecal droppings, but there has been little research of the same phenomenon in the wild.

Contact with faeces can spread parasites and lead to infection. However, the presence of faeces may also be a guide to successful foraging or finding a safe nesting place as it indicates that other members of the same species have already visited the area.

The results of the research suggested that in contrast to their laboratory cousins, wild mice do not demonstrate faecal avoidance. In fact, they preferred being near faeces and did not even distinguish between parasite-ridden and uninfected samples.

Staying healthy is clearly a good behavioural strategy, but finding a good place to eat or nest seems to count for more as far as faeces avoidance is concerned.

See also BIOLOGY 59; DISEASE 143–4; DOGS 153; EBOLA 167; GENETICS 210; LONGEVITY 279, 281; PSYCHOLOGY 389; WALRUSES 486

'The difference between stupidity and genius is that genius has its limits.'

Albert Einstein

MILKY WAY

315. When will the Milky Way collide with Andromeda?

Until recently, astronomers were unsure about a predicted collision between the Milky Way and the Andromeda Galaxy. Some said it would happen in 2 billion years; others said that it might not happen at all. The two galaxies were definitely moving closer together, but Andromeda also had a transverse component to its velocity that could make it pass by the Milky Way without a collision. Assessing this transverse component accurately was difficult until 2012, when pictures from the Hubble telescope measured it and allowed a computer simulation to be made of the galaxies' future progress. The new prediction was that the Milky Way and Andromeda would definitely collide in about 4 billion years' time.

Some reports, possibly feeling that the figure of 4 billion sounded a bit vague, said it would happen in 3.75 billion years. Others pointed out that the two galaxies would only make contact in 4 billion years and would take another 2 billion to merge completely.

Since then, however, the universe has been found to be expanding faster than had been thought, and mysterious discoveries such as the so-called Great Attractor and the Sharpley Supercluster have been found to be attracting all galaxies in our Local Group. Also, in 2015, a massive hydrogen cloud was found to be heading this way which could collide with our galaxy in about 30 million years, adding extragalactic material to the Milky Way.

Observations may still be in alignment with the predictions based on the 2012 prediction based on Hubble, but a good deal could happen in the next 4 billion years to change our minds about its conclusion.

316. What will happen when Andromeda and the Milky Way collide?

The computer simulation by NASA based on observations by the Hubble telescope shows the two galaxies passing through each other and slowing down during the collision, then being drawn back towards each other by their mutual gravitational pull. This oscillation will continue until they have merged. The stars, they say, will be thrown into different orbits around the new galactic centre. To reassure us, NASA say that 'our solar system will probably be tossed much farther from the galactic core than it is today'. They also say that 'although the galaxies will plough into each other, stars inside each galaxy are so far apart that they will not collide with other stars during the encounter'.

While it may be true that any individual star has a very small chance of hitting another, there are around about a trillion stars in Andromeda and 300 billion in the Milky Way. A rough calculation indicates that the distance between stars is similar to ping-pong balls 3 kilometres apart. The chance of two specified ping-pong balls hitting each other is therefore very slim, but with a trillion going in one direction and 300 billion in the other, the chance of a stellar collision somewhere must surely be high.

317. Did the Milky Way collide with Andromeda 10 billion years ago?

In 1981 the Israeli physicist Mordecai Milgrom suggested that some of the major problems in cosmology could be solved by making a small adjustment to Newton's second law of motion. Milgrom's Modified Newtonian Dynamics (MOND) theory suggests that gravity behaves differently on a very large scale, and if we apply his theory, it becomes unnecessary to hypothesize the existence of dark matter, which has still not been confirmed, to explain anomalies such as the rotational speed of galaxies.

In 2013 a group of European astronomers applied the MOND theory to calculate the motion of galaxies in the Local Group to which the Milky Way and Andromeda belong. Their calculations suggest that 10 billion years ago these two galaxies had a close encounter. According to the conventional Newton–Einstein theory together with the dark matter hypothesis, they would have merged, but Milgrom's methods suggest they would have passed through each other harmlessly. They could now be on the way back, heading for another collision, but the results of it could be very different from those predicted by Newton–Einstein.

See also ASTRONOMY 27; COSMOLOGY 118; QUASARS 390

MONKEYS

318. Do capuchin monkeys pay for sex?

In a classic experiment at Yale in 2005, capuchin monkeys were taught to exchange tokens for food in order to see if they could grasp the concept of money. Not only could they grasp the concept, but they were shown to take economic decisions as sensibly as humans.

One of the researchers, however, reports seeing a monkey exchanging a money token for sex. As further evidence that the monkeys knew what they were doing, the female who accepted the money then traded it in for a grape.

Sadly, this line of research was not pursued as the researchers felt that turning the monkey laboratory into a brothel might not reflect well on their research ethics. This remains the only known instance of monkeys paying for sex.

319. Why do capuchin monkeys tell lies?

In 2009 an experiment was conducted to see if capuchin monkeys will lie to other monkeys in order to get more food. Specifically, the researchers wanted to see if the monkeys would make deceptive alarm calls in order to lure more dominant monkeys away from the dinner table so that they could then grab more of the food.

Giving the monkeys access to plates of banana pieces, then counting their alarm calls, the experimenters predicted:

(i) there would be more deceptive alarm calls by subordinates than by dominants;

(ii) alarm calls would be more frequent when the food was placed in a smaller number of locations (making it more liable to be contested);

(iii) calls would be more frequent when less food was available;

(iv) calls would be made when the caller was in a good position to grab the food.

All the predictions were supported except (iii), for which the results were not statistically significant.

The researchers conclude: 'These results generally support the hypothesis that alarm calls are used by capuchins to reduce the effects of feeding competition. Whether this is intentional on the part of the caller requires further investigation.' In other words, we don't really know if they are lying deliberately or not. Whether capuchins would lie about paying for sex (→ 318) is a complex question that only future research can resolve.

See also ANIMALS 18; BONES 72; BRAINS 81; EBOLA 167; GORILLAS 221; HUMAN EVOLUTION 243

MOTHS

320. Why do moths fly towards a light?

Most attempts to explain this suggest that it is something to do with navigation by the stars or Moon. Several insects are known to navigate by a process called transverse orientation by which they keep a constant angle to a distant light source. When the light source is close, however, it is said to throw them completely off course. If you try to keep the angle constant between yourself and the Moon or stars, you'll more or less go in a straight line, but if you do the same with a light-bulb, you'll go round in circles.

This explanation, however, runs into trouble when we consider the evolutionary implications. Light-bulbs may be a relatively modern invention that moths haven't had time to adapt to, but people have been lighting camp-fires for 100,000 years or so. Flying towards a fire is a sure path to extinction, one would have thought.

Another rather bizarre theory was suggested when it was discovered that female moths' pheromones are slightly luminescent. Could it be that male moths are attracted to light because it reminds them of female moths' sex hormones? Are moths trying to mate with our candles and light-bulbs? Perhaps if the pheromones glowed at the same frequency as such artificial light sources, it might suggest that something of the sort was going on, but the frequencies are totally different, so it seems very unlikely.

See also SLOTHS 433

MOUNTAINEERING

321. Where is the body of Andrew Irvine and what can his camera tell us?

In 1924 Andrew Irvine and George Mallory died while attempting to be the first people to climb Mount Everest. They were last sighted only a few hundred metres from the summit, and it has never been clear whether they conquered the mountain and died on their way down or whether they never got to the top. Mallory's body was found in 1999; Irvine's has never been discovered.

The pair are known to have been carrying two VPK (Vest Pocket Kodak) cameras, which suggests that Irvine would probably have had charge of one of them. Photographic experts have said that if the camera is ever found, there is a good chance that printable images could be obtained from its film, as it has been frozen all the time it has been missing. The camera might not tell us how they died, but it would at least offer the prospect at last of finding out whether they reached the top.

MUMMIES

322. How did Egyptian mummies get traces of tobacco and cocaine in them?

In 1992 analysis of samples taken from Egyptian mummies revealed traces of cocaine, hashish and nicotine. Two of these substances are derived only from American plants, so how did they get to Egypt so long before Columbus? Various theories were proposed by critics of the research findings:

(i)   There was no evidence that the drugs were in the mummies before their death.

(ii) The drugs may have been absorbed into the mummy tissue from visitors to the museums where they were housed.

(iii) The mummies may have been recent fakes.

(iv) Chemical effects may have taken place in the mummies to produce substances similar to the drugs mentioned.

(v)   The drugs may have been introduced by people who had handled the mummies.

On closer examination, however, none of these suggestions seemed likely, which leaves only two possibilities:

(vi) The ancient Egyptians conducted trade with the pre-Columbian Americans.

(vii) Nicotine and cocaine existed in ancient Egypt but became extinct.

Neither of those seems very likely either.

See also CHINA 99; DISEASE 139

MURDER

323. Who killed Arthur I, Duke of Brittany?

Arthur of Brittany had a short but eventful life. Born in 1187, he was the son of Geoffrey Plantagenet, the fourth son of Henry II of England. Arthur was born after Geoffrey had died, and when he was two years old, Richard I became king of England. When Arthur was three, in 1190, Richard named him his successor before setting off on a crusade. In 1199, however, Richard changed his mind on his deathbed and named his own brother John his successor instead. This led to some friction between Arthur and his uncle John, but a great deal more between the French barons, who supported Arthur, and the English, who accepted John.

In 1202, at a battle north of Poitiers between the forces of King John of England and Philip II of France, Arthur was captured and imprisoned at Falaise. What happened then is unclear. According to one story, which Shakespeare seized on for his play *King John*, the English king ordered Hubert de Burgh, who was in charge at Falaise, to have Arthur blinded and castrated to remove him as a rival, but de Burgh refused.

Arthur was then moved to Rouen under the charge of William de Braose, who was the man who had captured him and delivered him to John in the first place. Arthur disappeared at the end of March 1203. Some say he was killed by de Braose; some say he was killed by John himself in a drunken rage. In Shakespeare's version, however, Arthur is killed when leaping from the castle battlements while trying to flee from his wicked uncle.

324. Who was the 'boy in the box' murdered in Philadelphia in 1957?

In February 1957, in the Fox Chase neighbourhood of Philadelphia, the body of a boy aged between four and six was found in a cardboard box, naked and battered. The body was wrapped in a plaid blanket and the box was from the JCPenney department store chain and had once contained a baby's cradle.

The police took the boy's fingerprints and were hopeful that his identity could quickly be established. Even when pictures of the boy were sent to every home in Philadelphia, however, no information was ever received. The case is still open.

325. Who killed the Black Dahlia?

In January 1947 the investigation of one of the most gruesome murders in American history began when the body of Elizabeth Short was found in a Los Angeles parking lot. It had been sliced in half at the waist, drained of blood and washed; her face had been slashed from the corners of her mouth to her ears; and the two halves of the body were placed about a foot apart with her intestines neatly tucked beneath her buttocks. There were multiple cuts on other parts of her body and ligature marks on her neck, wrists and ankles. The case, not unnaturally, attracted a great deal of interest in the press, which began referring to the victim as the 'Black Dahlia' after the 1946 film noir *The Blue Dahlia*.

The notoriety of the case led to at least fifty people confessing to the murder, but none was considered plausible. In 2014 a retired police detective named Steve Hodel was reported to have found evidence that his father, George Hodel, who had died in 1991, was a serial killer whose victims may have included Elizabeth Short. Apparently, however, he is not the only person to have suggested a relative as the murderer.

The case is still unsolved and no charges have ever been filed.

326. How does gun availability affect firearm homicide rates?

The number of homicides worldwide is estimated to be around half a million a year and 42 per cent of them are committed with a firearm. The US gun lobby say that the right to bear arms acts as a deterrent to potential killers; their opponents say that the more people have guns, the more are going to be shot. So who is right?

In 2011 the *American Journal of Criminal Justice* published a reassessment of the relationship between gun availability and homicide which showed that the situation is highly complex and in particular 'the relationship between gun availability, gun homicide and homicide is not stable across nations'. Gun availability, they found, made gun homicide more likely in Western developed nations and Latin American nations, but exhibited a small negative effect in Eastern European countries. 'Perhaps Western citizens view guns as a defence mechanism against the aggression of others,' they suggest, 'rather than a tool to be used with the intent of causing great bodily harm or death.' In Latin America, however, the figures suggested that the opposite was the case.

Socio-historic and cultural factors, economic inequality, and urbanization were all found to have effects on firearm homicide rates, but those effects could be very different in different countries. The authors conclude that the relationship between gun availability and gun homicide does not operate uniformly across nations.

An earlier study in the US reported that murders were more numerous in areas with more firearms, but whether it was the rise in gun ownership that led to the murders or the high murder rate that drove up gun ownership by people feeling a need to defend themselves was not answered.

See also DEATH 131, 134; NAPOLEON 337; SHIPS 420

MUSIC

327. Do vuvuzelas spread disease?

The plastic horns known as vuvuzelas achieved worldwide renown during the 2010 World Cup soccer tournament in South Africa. While most people either rejoiced in or protested at their loud honking noise, one group of researchers from London became worried by their possible propensity to spread disease by expelling aerosol particles at great intensity.

They accordingly asked eight healthy volunteers to blow vuvuzelas and to shout. In both cases, their expelled air was measured by a particle counter, and the velocity of the air and the duration of vuvuzela-playing were also measured. The results showed that vuvuzelas emit 178 times as many particles as shouting. The writers say that further research is needed 'to assess the potential of the vuvuzela to contribute to the transmission of aerosol-borne diseases' but recommend, as a precautionary measure, that 'people with respiratory infections should be advised not to blow their vuvuzela in enclosed spaces'.

328. Does the human brain have a pitch centre?

Much research has been done in recent years on how our brains perceive sound in general and music in particular. Sound is, after all, only vibrations in the air. These are picked up by our tympanic membrane (eardrum), amplified by the three small bones in our inner ear, and changed by the cochlea into neurological signals. Then it is up to the brain to react to the various structural elements of the sound, which include pitch, timbre, amplitude, duration and location, and of all these, pitch seems the most complex.

At its most basic, pitch is what enables us to tell whether one note is higher or lower than another. It is how we recognize a tune. A small percentage of people have perfect pitch (also known as absolute pitch), which enables them to recognize and remember any note without the benefit of another note to compare it with. An equally small percentage are totally tone-deaf and cannot recognize tunes at all or even say whether one note is higher or lower than another.

All sorts of brain scans, from PET (Positron Emission Tomography) to fMRI (functional Magnetic Resonance Imaging) to TMS (Transcranial Magnetic Stimulation), have been employed to try to see what's going on in our brains when we analyse pitch, but it seems that the more we look, the more complex it becomes.

Until a few years ago, a part of the auditory cortex called the lateral Heschl's gyrus was thought to be the general pitch centre. Then it was found that several other parts of the brain were, under different conditions of timbre and tonality, involved in the assessment of pitch. It has also been found that left-handers have a better short-term memory for pitch than right-handers, and ambidextrous people are best of all. Studies on absolute pitch have also failed to locate a brain region that may be responsible. Some even suggest that absolute pitch results from the suppression of activity in certain areas of the brain rather than the activation of others.

Music may be one of the most complex functions the brain performs.

329. Did human music evolve as a courtship display?

In his book *The Descent of Man*, published in 1871, Charles Darwin wrote:

> it appears probable that the progenitors of man, either the males or females or both sexes, before acquiring the power of expressing their mutual love in articulate language, endeavoured to charm each other with musical notes and rhythm.

The argument is simple: human evolution, like that of other animals, has been driven either by natural selection (which is survival of the fittest) or sexual selection (aids to reproduction). Since art in general and music in particular have no discernible survival value, their role, like birdsong or the croaking of frogs in the mating season, must have been to help attract a suitable mate.

In 2000 the evolutionary psychologist Geoffrey Miller wrote in support of Darwin's theory:

> *Consider Jimi Hendrix, for example. This rock guitarist*
> *extraordinaire died at the age of 27 in 1970, overdosing on the drugs*
> *he used to fire his musical imagination. His music output, three*
> *studio albums and hundreds of live concerts, did him no survival*
> *favours. But he did have sexual liaisons with hundreds of groupies,*
> *maintained parallel long-term relationships with at least two*
> *women, and fathered at least three children in the U.S., Germany,*
> *and Sweden.*

One Jimi Hendrix, of course, does not make a scientific theory, but Darwin's idea is probably the only one we have for the origin of human music-making.

330. What happened to Jacques Duphly and his harpsichord?

Jacques Duphly (1715–89) was a French composer and harpsichordist greatly esteemed as a performer and teacher. He published four volumes of harpsichord pieces, but shortly after the last of these, which appeared in 1768, he mysteriously disappeared from public life.

He died the day after the storming of the Bastille, on 15 July 1789, in a small apartment at the Hôtel de Juigné on the Quai Malaquais in Paris, having apparently not been heard of for twenty years. He was surrounded by his books, but there was no harpsichord in his apartment.

To add to the mystery, another man, who also lived at the same address, left Paris on the day Duphly died. This was Antoine de Sartine, ex-chief of police, ex-minister of the navy and patron of the arts, after whom Duphly had named one of his earlier harpsichord pieces.

331. Was Wagner a cross-dresser?

There are several stories about the life of Richard Wagner that suggest a strong interest in women's clothing. He is known to have ordered pink silk underwear and to have enjoyed wearing silk next to his skin, if only because he suffered from erysipelas, a condition that could lead to painful skin rashes. Yet the stories suggest that his affection for women's clothing may have been more than for medical reasons.

In 1864 it was said that Wagner escaped from creditors in Vienna dressed in women's clothes. In 1869 he placed an order with a dressmaker for a black satin costume that could be worn outside or indoors as a negligée. In 1874 he sent an order to Milan for a bodice with 'a high collar, with a lace jabot and ribbons; close-fitting sleeves; the dress trimmed with puffed flounces – of the same satin material ...' His description continues with more and more precise instructions.

Of course, he could have been ordering all these things for his wife Cosima, but she was a prolific diarist and never recorded having received any of them.

See also DISEASE 141; SUICIDE 449

MYANMAR

332. Are there any British Spitfires buried in Burma?

Since the end of the Second World War, a rumour has circulated that the British had buried between twenty and sixty unassembled Spitfires in the Burmese (now Myanmar) jungle as the war was reaching its end. In 2012 a project was initiated to try to find and recover these planes and permission was obtained to dig for them. With security concerns and bad weather hampering the excavations, however, and the two-year exploration contract running out, the search was abandoned in 2014.

No hard evidence has ever been found for the planes, but there have been accounts by British, American and Burmese eyewitnesses who say they saw them being buried. Documents detailing deliveries of aircraft parts to the RAF in Burma during the war, however, appear not to mention any Spitfires.

MYTHOLOGY

333. Where did Geoffrey of Monmouth get his stories of King Arthur from?

King Arthur, according to legend, was a British leader who fought against the invading Anglo-Saxons in the late fifth or early sixth century. The earliest known mention of him may have been in the ninth-century Latin historical compilation called *Historia Brittonum*, but the bulk of the Arthurian legend as we know it comes from Geoffrey of Monmouth's *Historia Regum Britanniae* ('History of the Kings of Britain'), written in 1135.

Geoffrey of Monmouth's work was later embellished by Chrétien de Troyes and Thomas Malory, but where Geoffrey got his story from in the first place is unclear. He claimed that he was merely copying a 'very ancient book written in the British language' he had in his possession, but he may have invented most of it, though its roots perhaps lay in Celtic myth. The ancient book referred to by Geoffrey of Monmouth has never been identified.

See also AZTECS 38; ENGLISH HISTORY 175; GORILLAS 220; HUMAN EVOLUTION 234; INCAS 247; ITALY 258; PREHISTORY 382; TROY 456

NAMES

334. What does 'Britain' mean?

Pliny and other ancient Roman writers referred to the island as 'Britannia' and the British Isles as 'insulae Britannicae', and the modern name of Britain probably stems from these, but the earlier history of the name is obscure.

One theory is that it derives from the Old Welsh 'Priten', which was the name the British called themselves. This in turn may derive from an old Celtic word 'pryd' meaning 'countenance', 'image' or 'beauty', though it has also been suggested that 'Priten' or 'Priton' may have some connection with the practice of tattooing or body art. Explanations for how the initial P changed into a B are rather vague, however, ranging from complex discussions of phonological shifts in Celtic to a possible mishearing by the Romans.

Another suggestion is that the name of Britain has nothing at all to do with Welsh, Celtic, beauty or tattooing, but derives from a word for 'tin' in a Middle Eastern language, perhaps used by Phoenician traders to describe Britain, as tin was the most important commodity brought from Britain.

335. How did Mongolia get its name?

Mongolia seems to have taken its name from the word the inhabitants used for themselves – Mongol – but where that word came from is highly uncertain. Suggestions include the following:
- It was the name of a mountain.
- It was the name of a river.
- It was an abbreviation of a phrase *Mongkhe-tengri-gal*, meaning

244

'Eternal Sky Fire'.
- It comes from a word *mong*, meaning 'brave'.
- It derives from the name *Mugulu*, a fourth-century tribal leader.

The *Oxford English Dictionary* just says 'of uncertain origin', which sounds a pretty good summary.

336. How did Edmond Halley pronounce his surname?

Hailey, Hawley or Halley (to rhyme with 'valley')? The argument about how to pronounce the name of the discoverer of Halley's Comet seems to have gone on since his own time. He lived from 1656 to 1742, and contemporary accounts are recorded referring to him as Hailey, Hayley, Haley, Haly, Halley, Hawley and Hawly.

Modern historians tend to favour the 'Hawley' pronunciation (to rhyme with 'poorly'); others, perhaps influenced by the rock singer Bill Haley and his backing group 'The Comets', rhyme it with 'daily'; while the Royal Astronomical Society in 1910 came down firmly in favour of the third possibility in a drinking song:

> *Of all the comets in the sky,*
> *There's none like Comet Halley.*
> *We see it with the naked eye*
> *And periodically.*
> *The first to see it was not he,*
> *But still we call it Halley.*
> *The notion that it would return*
> *Was his originally.*

'Real knowledge is to know the extent of one's ignorance.'

Confucius

NAPOLEON

337. How did Napoleon get arsenic in his hair?

In his will, written three weeks before he died aged fifty-one, Napoleon Bonaparte wrote: 'I die before my time, murdered by the English oligarchy and its assassin.' This accusation, coupled with the later finding of traces of arsenic in Napoleon's hair, fuelled the suspicion that the French emperor had been deliberately poisoned by his captors on St Helena. When his body was exhumed in 1840 for reburial in Paris, its remarkable state of preservation supported the theory of arsenic poisoning: arsenic is known to be toxic to the micro-organisms that cause decomposition. In Napoleon's time, however, deliberate poisoning was far from the only way to get arsenic into someone's system:

- An arsenic-laced paste was commonly used to hang wallpaper, and a sample of the wallpaper at Napoleon's prison home of Frogmore was found in 1980 to contain arsenic.
- Arsenic was also an ingredient commonly used in weed-killers, fly-paper and rat poison.
- Arsenic was commonly used to treat a number of ailments including syphilis, from which Napoleon was known to suffer.
- Even as late as the 1950s, arsenic was a common ingredient of various medicines and skin creams.

In 2008 a team of scientists in Italy compared hairs taken from Napoleon's head at various times in his life and found that the arsenic level barely changed between his boyhood in Corsica and his death on St Helena. Similarly high levels were found in the hairs of his son Napoleon II and his wife Josephine. They concluded that the results 'undoubtedly reveal a chronic exposure that we believe can be simply attributed to environmental factors, unfortunately no longer easily identifiable, or habits involving food and therapeutics'.

See also OPERA 348

NAZIS

338. Who planted Germany's swastika forests?

In 1992 a cluster of larch trees in the shape of a swastika was observed from the air growing in a forest in the German state of Brandenburg. For most of the year the larches blended in with the pine forest, but for a few weeks in spring and autumn their leaves turned bright yellow and their swastika formation stood out. Invisible from the ground and in an area only occasionally flown over by private planes, it went unnoticed for over fifty years. Then various stories emerged about its possible origins.

A local farmer said that he had been paid a small amount by a forester for planting the larch seedlings as a child. Another tale told of a member of the Hitler Youth planting the larches, possibly in tribute to Hitler on the Führer's birthday in the late 1930s. More mundanely, a Berlin newspaper reported that the trees were planted in gratitude to the Reich Labour Service for building a street in Zernikow.

Other swastika forests were later found in the German towns of Jesberg, Wiesbaden and Neukirchen, and one was even discovered near the edge of the Himalayas in Tash-Bashat, Kyrgyzstan. One theory of the swastika grown on Soviet territory was that it was planted as an act of secret defiance by German prisoners of war.

Between 1995 and 2000 the trees forming the swastika in Brandenburg were uprooted. Whether more such formations remain to be discovered, and whether they were originally planted as local tributes to Nazism or under orders from the party or the German government, are questions that have yet to be answered.

339. Who betrayed Anne Frank to the Nazis?

On the morning of 4 August 1944 a car carrying an Austrian officer and members of the Dutch Nazi Party arrived outside the warehouse and office at 263 Prinsengracht in Amsterdam. The occupants of the car went into the building brandishing a gun and demanded to know where the Jews were hiding. As a result, eight arrests were made including that of Anne Frank. They were all sent to Auschwitz and the only one to survive the war was Anne's father Otto Frank, who subsequently published Anne's meticulously kept diaries.

An investigation in 1948 into who betrayed them reached no conclusion. Anne, in her diaries, reports their wariness about the new warehouse manager Willem van Maaren, who had been very curious about the rooms at the back of the warehouse where they had been hiding throughout the war.

A cleaner at the warehouse, Lena van Bladeren-Hartog, was also suspected, having allegedly been heard gossiping with another woman about Jews hiding in the building. There was also a rumour that the call to the Gestapo betraying the Franks had been made by a woman.

Then there was Tonny Ahlers, a vicious anti-Semite known to have betrayed several Jews during the Occupation and to have been arrested for other crimes. In 2002 Ahlers' son Anton said that he believed his father, who died in 2000, had been guilty of the betrayal.

As a result, the case of who betrayed Anne Frank to the Nazis was reopened in 2003, but the investigation concluded that, while the case against Ahlers was strong, all evidence was circumstantial and, along with the other suspects named above, his name was cleared.

340. Was Fritz Todt's death an accident?

In the early years of the Second World War, Fritz Todt was one of Hitler's leading strategists. An Oberführer in the Nazi Party, he founded the Organisation Todt, which supervised the building of the West Wall, later known as the Siegfried Line, a 630-kilometre line of bunkers, tank traps and tunnels built to defend Germany from assault from the west.

While remaining close to Hitler, whom he warned against letting his army get bogged down in the Russian winter, Todt found himself increasingly in disagreement with army commanders, particularly Hermann Göring, and party chief Martin Bormann.

In 1942, shortly after taking off from an airfield on the Eastern Front, a plane carrying Todt exploded in mid-air and all on board were killed. He was buried in Berlin and decorated with the Deutscher Orden, the first person to receive this award for 'duties of the highest order to the state and party', but the circumstances of the crash that killed him have always raised speculation of an assassination plot. Albert Speer, who succeeded him as Minister of Munitions, had cancelled plans to travel on the same flight shortly before it took off.

The official Germany Air Ministry inquiry into the plane accident ended abruptly with the words: 'The possibility of sabotage is ruled out. Further measures are therefore neither requisite nor intended.'

See also DEATH 135; HITLER 231–3

NORTH DAKOTA

341. Why does the Great Seal of the state of North Dakota look the way it does?

Since the inauguration of the US state of North Dakota in 1889, its constitution has contained the same description of its Great Seal:

A tree in the open field, the trunk of which is surrounded by three bundles of wheat; on the right a plow, anvil and sledge; on the left, a bow crossed with three arrows, and an Indian on horseback pursuing a buffalo toward the setting sun; the foliage of the tree arched by a half circle of forty-two stars, surrounded by the motto 'Liberty and Union Now and Forever, One and Inseparable'; the words 'Great Seal' at the top; the words 'State of North Dakota' at the bottom; 'October 1st' on the left and '1889' on the right.

The date was when the voters approved the state's constitution, but research has failed to reveal the reasons behind the choice of the symbols.

The tree could be an elm, but the elm did not become the state tree until 1947. It has been conjectured that the three bundles of wheat may represent the three branches of government: executive, legislative and judicial. The plough, anvil and sledge may make reference to the agricultural background of the state and its work ethic, while the bow and arrows, buffalo, the Indian on horseback, and the setting sun could be reminders of its history, but, without any official explanation, all of this is speculative.

To add to the mystery, the seal is adorned with forty-two stars, which is curious as North Dakota was only the thirty-ninth state of the Union. Either they miscounted, or they were making a guess at how many other states would have joined by the time the seal was produced.

NOSES

342. Why did the hadrosaur have a big nose?

In 2014 a new species of hadrosaur (or duck-billed dinosaur) was discovered which was promptly names *Rhinorex*, meaning 'King Nose', because of its truly enormous nose. One report even referred to it as the 'Jimmy Durante of dinosaurs'. Most hadrosaurs have a bony crest extending from the skull, but not *Rhinorex*. This one has a huge nose instead, but what it did with that nose is completely unknown.

Terry Gates, a palaeontologist from North Carolina State University who was one of the team that discovered it, said:

> *The purpose of such a big nose is still a mystery. If this dinosaur is anything like its relatives then it likely did not have a super sense of smell; but maybe the nose was used as a means of attracting mates, recognizing members of its species, or even as a large attachment for a plant-smashing beak.*

They are still trying to sniff out the answers.

343. Why do we pick our noses?

According to a study published in the *Journal of Clinical Psychiatry* in 2001, only 4 per cent of students in Wisconsin never pick their noses. Half of them pick their noses four or more times a day and about 7 per cent say they do it twenty or more times a day. Of the nose-pickers, 80 per cent use their fingers, while the rest are divided equally in their use of tweezers and pencils.

Excessive nose-picking, or rhinotillexomania as it is technically known, is generally viewed as an example of obsessive-compulsive disorder, but if 96 per cent of us do it, does that mean we are almost all mildly obsessive-compulsive?

Because almost all cultures consider nose-picking impolite, or at least something that should only be done in private, most nose-pickers feel a sense of shame in doing it, yet we go on picking, even if we only do so when alone. The simplest explanation is that unblocking our nasal passages opens our airwaves and helps breathing. We do not always have a handkerchief to hand, so we pick our noses. According to the research mentioned above, only 50 per cent of students said they picked their noses to unclog nasal passages or to relieve discomfort or to relieve itching, while 11 per cent did it for 'cosmetic reasons' and another 11 per cent picked their noses for pleasure. Curiously, in view of the social stigma of nose-picking, practices were found to be the same across all social classes.

There is, however, one other aspect of nose-picking that could contribute towards an answer to this question...

344. Is it healthy or unhealthy to eat our nose-pickings?

In 2004 a report appeared on the Ananova news wires quoting an Austrian doctor saying that eating nose-pickings was good for us and recommending that society should change its attitude and encourage children to take up the practice. Eating nose-pickings, the report claimed, boosts our immune system by transferring bacteria which our nose traps into our stomach, where they can perform a useful function.

This report was widely quoted as a piece of bizarre news, and some even suspected it of being an April Fools' joke. There was no evidence cited in support of the argument other than an unsupported claim that 'people who pick their noses with their fingers were healthy, happier and probably better in tune with their bodies'. In 2013, however, Scott Napper, a biochemistry professor at the University of Saskatchewan, Canada, was reported to be investigating the 'health benefits of boogers'. His argument, however, was not that eating nose-pickings transferred useful bacteria to our stomachs but that it was a way of training our immune system by exposing it to germs. His theory follows others that have suggested that improved hygiene may have led to an increase in allergies and auto-immune disorders.

Professor Napper has even suggested a way to test his idea: put some sort of molecule in the noses of a group of volunteers, half of whom pick their noses and eat it, while the other half don't. Then look for immune responses to the molecule and see if they're higher in the booger-eaters. Perhaps, if the experiment is ever conducted, the researchers could consider getting subjects to eat each other's nose-pickings as well, to see if that is equally, or perhaps even more, effective.

If eating nose-pickings is indeed beneficial for us, however, it reflects badly on the evolution of our cultural taboos which, according to the study mentioned in the previous item ($\rightarrow$ 343), have led to only 4.5 per cent of nose-pickers eating their pickings.

345. What is the purpose of the 'nose' of the Pinocchio frog?

In 2010 a new species of tree frog was found in Papua. It has not yet been given a scientific name as its genus has not been confirmed, but it has informally been dubbed the 'Pinocchio frog' because of a strange protuberance on the end of its nose. When making energetic calls, the male frog has the ability to inflate the nose and point it upwards, while deflation takes place and the nose points downwards when the males are less excited.

Whether the nasal shape and gymnastics have any effect on its sense of smell or ability to attract a mate, or whether they have some other function, has yet to be determined.

See also ATILLA 31; AUSTEN 34; DOLPHINS 156; INTELLIGENCE 251

π=3.1415
92653589793
238462643383
279502884197169

NUMBERS

346. Is pi (π) normal?

The idea of normal numbers is one of the most infuriating in mathematics: we know that almost all numbers are normal, but we hardly know any that definitely are. The formal definition of a normal number is a little off-putting but the idea is quite simple.

Let's start by taking any number expressed as an infinite decimal expansion. One seventh, for example, is 0.142857142857142857...

The only digits this contains are 1, 2, 4, 5, 7 and 8, each of which, as we go on counting further into the expansion, approaches a total of one sixth of the digits counted. For a number to be normal, its digit count must be the same for all possible digits. In the case above, it's the same for 1, 2, 4, 5, 7 and 8, but 0, 3, 6 and 9 don't appear at all, so the number is not normal.

We can do better with 0.012345678901234567890123456789... where all the digits from 0 to 9 appear equally often, but even that won't fulfil the stern demands of normality, because in its full definition it demands not just an equal number of each of the single-digits but an equal number of all the double-digit and triple-digit numbers too. The number above clearly fails that test as every 1 is followed by a 2, so the numbers 11, 13, 14, 15 and so on are never seen.

So how about .012345678910111213141516 .... and so on, just going through the positive integers in increasing order? Now we're nearly there, for it has been proved that the above number does what is asked for. As we continue further and further down the decimal expansion, not only do all the single-digits approach the limit of one-tenth of all the digits counted, but any double-digit number approaches one-hundredth of all double-digit numbers counted, all triple-digit numbers approach one-thousandth of their type, and so on.

But we're not quite there yet. The trouble with the above is that everything we've discussed so far is expressing numbers to base 10. The last number we mentioned is called 'normal to base 10', but what if we had worked out the same number to base 2, as a string of 1s and 0s? Would there be an equal number of them? Or to base 3, or 5, or 47?

For a number to be considered normal, it must be normal to any base one chooses. It is known that if it were possible to pick a number at random, it would almost certainly be normal, but no test is known by which we could discover whether any particular number is normal or not. Indeed, only very few normal numbers have been discovered and they are all numbers that have been created by exotic and laborious procedures.

An examination of the first 6 billion digits of pi makes it highly credible that it is normal to base 10, though even that has not yet been proved. To prove that it is normal to every base is beyond all known mathematical techniques.

See also BEES 43; BIBLE 53; CHICKENS 97; HUMAN EVOLUTION 236; INTELLIGENCE 251–2; MATHEMATICS 288–91; PHYSICS 370–1

OCTOPUSES

347. How do octopuses recognize each other?

When two octopuses meet for the first time, they touch each other with the suction caps on their arms. If the same two octopuses meet again shortly after, they stay away from each other. In 2011 a study was published using this behaviour to see if octopuses recognized each other.

The first stage of the experiment was to keep octopuses in pairs in tanks. They would approach each other as expected, feel each other with their arms, then move apart. The next day, the octopuses were again placed in pairs, but some were with the same octopus as they had met the day before while others were with a different octopus. Those placed with a new tank-mate were found to be much more likely to approach it and feel it than those that were with the same octopus as on the previous day. Those with a new companion were also found to be more likely to squirt ink, which is a sign of feeling threatened.

The conclusion was that octopuses can indeed recognize other octopuses whom they have previously met, but how they do so is not known. Interestingly, the sense of touch appears to play a strong part in getting acquainted, but no part in the recognition. The researchers suggest that touch, sight and smell may all have a role to play.

OPERA

348. What happened to Baron Sciarpa, on whom Puccini's Scarpia in his opera *Tosca* was based?

The most villainous of all operatic villains is surely Baron Scarpia, the police chief who lusts after the opera singer Tosca, whose lover Cavaradossi, a painter, he arrests and tortures so that he can have his evil way with her. For all his melodramatic villainy, however, Scarpia appears to have been modelled on a real person.

In 1798, when Napoleon was marching against the various pre-unification Italian states, King Ferdinand IV of Naples had been deposed and was fighting to regain his throne against the Republicans. One of his strongest supporters was Cardinal Ruffo, who brought together various outlaw bands to fight for the king. The most powerful of these outlaws was a mercenary soldier Gherardo Curci, who was known as Sciarpa and had been the chief of the palace guard. When he was dismissed from that post, he raised his own army and offered their services to the French. When they turned him down, he adopted a career of pillaging, but was then brought back on the king's side by Ruffo.

When Ferdinand was restored to the throne, he not only granted a pardon to Sciarpa but rewarded him with estates, a valuable annuity and the title of baron. Sciarpa then oversaw a campaign of revenge against former Republicans, who would have included artists and politicians such as Cavaradossi and Angelotti, whom the painter is trying to help in the opera.

What happened to Sciarpa after that is unknown, but he is unlikely to have been stabbed to death in his own study by an opera singer. The opera, incidentally, was based on the play *La Tosca* by Victorien Sardou, which was written as a star vehicle for Sarah Bernhardt.

See also FRANCE 202

OTTERS

349. What do otters talk about?

An acoustical analysis of the vocalizations of giant otters in 2014 reported 'a sophisticated vocal repertoire' consisting of twenty-two different sounds made by adult otters and eleven by newborn otters. They bark, howl, whistle, growl or hum and make sounds identifiable as begging, or mating calls, or isolation calls (when separated from the group). The sounds made by newborn otters were seen as 'precursors of the adult repertoire' or 'babbling bouts'.

Comparing the vocalizations of otters with those of other sea or river creatures, the researchers concluded that 'the giant otters' social complexity seems to be reflected in their vocal complexity'. Their analysis of the different sounds seemed mainly to provide a general association of types of sound with types of social behaviour, rather than offering more precise insights into the nature of otter vocal communications.

With twenty-two sounds, they might be expected to be able to communicate a good deal to each other, but we still don't really know what they talk about.

OUTER SPACE

350. Why is outer space roaring at us?

In 2009 NASA scientists discovered a radio signal from outer space that was six times louder than it should have been. At the time, they were trying to explore the oldest parts of the universe by monitoring emissions from the furthest galaxies. The further away in the universe you look, the further back in time you see, owing to the time light takes to travel. Owing to the continuous expansion of the universe, however, the wavelengths of light from the most distant parts are stretched by the time they reach us and are detected not as light but as radio waves. They can therefore be heard, rather than seen, by radio telescopes.

What was actually heard when they trained their telescopes at the furthest stars, however, was a strong hiss six times louder than expected. After eliminating equipment error as the cause of the surprising power of the hiss, the scientists have been at a loss to explain why it is happening. Nothing in the known universe has the potential to generate a radio signal of such power. The space roar, as it has been called, is one of the great unsolved mysteries of cosmology.

See also COSMOLOGY 117–26

PALAO

351. When and why were the great stone faces in Palao carved?

The island group of Palao in the western Pacific is home to thirty-seven massive carved ancient monoliths, many of which have carved faces. Who built them and what they were built for is completely unknown. To add to the mystery, the stone they are made from does not appear to be from Palao, so it must have been imported over a large distance from somewhere else, but how it was brought to Palao is unknown.

The sculptures are thought to date from around AD 100. One theory is that they were part of a large construction being built for the gods or demigods which was never completed. Another legend is that they were part of a construction built by the gods themselves.

PANDAS

352. Did the giant panda in Edinburgh Zoo have a miscarriage in 2014?

On 13 April 2014 Tian Tian, the giant panda in Edinburgh Zoo, was artificially inseminated. In August it was announced that a scan had confirmed that she was pregnant and a cub was expected at the beginning of September. On 1 September, however, it was announced that she did not seem to be pregnant at all and must have suffered a miscarriage.

On 22 September the announcement came that all hope of her giving birth had gone and there was now no evidence of her ever having been pregnant in the first place. Panda specialists said they had been misled by the data on which they had relied. There was even a suggestion that Tian Tian had faked her hormonal level in order to obtain more comfortable living conditions.

So what was going on? The previous year, a similar thing had happened after a supposedly successful mating had taken place. Tian Tian was declared pregnant; then, just as the cub was due, her hormone levels had gone back to normal and she was declared to have suffered a miscarriage. Later she was said not to have had a miscarriage but to have 'reabsorbed the foetus', which is apparently something pandas sometimes do.

If the data can mislead, right up to the time the baby is due, about whether she is pregnant or not, how can it be relied upon to tell whether she has miscarried, reabsorbed a foetus, or was never pregnant in the first place?

353. How long is a giant panda's gestation period?

Another strange thing about panda pregnancy is 'delayed implantation'. Unlike the pregnancy of almost every other mammal, a fertilized egg of a giant panda does not immediately implant in the mother's uterine wall but may stay in her reproductive tract without developing for two months or more. Because of this, we cannot say that we know precisely the length of the giant panda's actual gestation period. All we can say, from observations of successful panda births, is that the time from mating to birth ranges from 95 to 160 days.

See also HUMAN EVOLUTION 236

PANGOLINS

354. What was the evolutionary origin of a pangolin's scales?

Birds have feathers, reptiles have scales, mammals have hair or fur. So where does that leave the pangolin? Apart from being one of the cutest and most endangered animals in the world, the pangolin is also one of the most mysterious, for it is the only mammal whose body is covered with scales. The scales come in very handy as a defence mechanism, for they enable the pangolin to curl up into a ball when threatened, leaving its body totally covered by an impenetrable shell of sharp, overlapping scales. The name 'pangolin' actually comes from the Malay word *pengguling*, which means 'something that rolls up'. Where its scales came from in evolutionary terms, however, continues to be a matter of speculation.

Feathers, scales and hair are all composed mainly of types of keratin. So are nails, claws and beaks. Birds' feathers are thought to have developed from the scales of dinosaurs, and it has been suggested that pangolin scales were the result of a reverse form of that evolution. Since pangolins are neither birds nor reptiles, however, the idea of them developing scales, then turning into mammals, or turning into mammals while keeping their scales, which no other mammals did, seems to require some sort of explanation.

Examination of the types of keratin in the scales of pangolins has led to the alternative suggestion that they came not from compressed feathers but from nails or claws, but again this raises the question of why the pangolin was the only mammal that performed this trick.

355. Is the pangolin descended from the stegosaurus?

The American geneticist Eugene M. McCarthy offers a radically different theory of the pangolin's scales on his macroevolution. net website. He starts by challenging the common view of what a stegosaurus looked like. 'The familiar image of *Stegosaurus*', he says, 'shows a creature with spikes tipping its tail and upright angular plates sheltering its spine', but he goes on to point out that such an image is a reconstruction based on scattered remains and guesswork. 'Suppose... the plates actually did lie flat on the skin in an overlapping fashion', he says, pointing out that such a formation would offer better defence against predators. Suppose too that the 'tail' spikes were not on the tail, but instead were huge claws on the feet. 'How would such an animal look?' he asks, and then gives us the answer: 'Clearly, it would closely resemble extant pangolins.'

The stegosaurus had very small teeth and the pangolin has no teeth at all, and both of them digest food by grinding it up in their stomachs. He lists other similarities too, but the nicest point of all is that the smallest stegosaurus ever found was only slightly bigger than the largest pangolin fossil. Perhaps the stegosaurus did not become extinct at all: it just became smaller, surviving as a dwarf species which became the animal we now call the pangolin.

356. Do pythons often eat pangolins?

Quite apart from such evolutionary questions, there are many other things we do not know about pangolins:
- How many still survive in the wild?
- What is the normal male–female ratio?
- What is their gestation period?
- How do the answers to all these questions vary among the eight known species of pangolin?
- And which came first anyway, the Asian pangolins or the African?

In 2007, at the National University of Singapore, a start was made at finding out more about this elusive creature. For his Master of Science degree, Norman T-Lon Lim captured twenty-one Malayan pangolins (also known as the Javan or Sunda pangolin), fitted them with radio transmitters, and put them back in the wild. Unfortunately, seventeen of the transmitters fell off or were otherwise got rid of by the pangolins, leaving only a sample of four that were tracked throughout the project.

One of the seventeen discarded transmitters was later tracked to the stomach of a reticulated python. The presence of pangolin scales in the same stomach indicated that the snake had eaten the poor thing. Lim writes: 'it is unclear whether pythons are able to coil around and constrict a curled-up pangolin.' Citing an earlier piece of research based on an examination of the stomach contents of 1,070 reticulated pythons in Sumatra, he says that 229 contained identifiable remains, of which only six were remains of pangolins, compared with 148 field rats, thirty-one long-tailed giant rats, eleven silvered leaf monkeys and eight domestic chickens. Conclusion: 'It is unclear whether python predation on pangolin is a common event in the wild.'

In fact, the most common predators by far – which has resulted in all eight species of pangolin being listed as endangered – are human beings, illegally trapping pangolins to sell to Vietnam, where their meat is prized as a delicacy, or to sell their scales to the Chinese for use in their medicines.

PARAPSYCHOLOGY

357. Is beginner's luck real?

When performing an activity for the first time, whether it is gambling at a roulette table, or cooking a soufflé, or playing on a putting green, or anything else where luck may play a part, people are often struck by the fact that their later attempts never seem to match the promise of the first. The good start is put down to 'beginner's luck' and no more is said about it.

One of the most consistent results in parapsychology experiments, however, seems to suggest that beginner's luck may be real. Reports of experiments on telepathy or psychokinesis or demonstrations of other supposedly psychic abilities have frequently reported subjects performing significantly above chance at the start of the experiments, but falling back as the session continues.

Those who believe in such things say that extrasensory abilities work best when the normal senses are suppressed. The early trials were therefore more successful because the subject had low expectations and wasn't really trying. Once effort came to be put in, the extrasensory abilities were overruled and ceased to function.

Or it may be that the experimenters are just more likely to remember the cases in which beginner's luck seemed to be operating.

See also SCIENCE 405

PENGUINS

358. Why do crested penguins kick their first egg out of the nest?

Crested penguins lay two eggs of which the second-laid egg is usually the larger. If they are both allowed to hatch, the second typically hatches first or at the same time as the other and produces a bigger chick. More often than not, however, the first-laid egg is kicked out of the nest by the adults before hatching time.

In the case of the erect-crested penguin, the second egg is on average 81 per cent larger than the first egg, and nearly all pairs get rid of the smaller first egg around the time the second egg is laid. What the point of the first egg is and what evolutionary quirk resulted in this phenomenon are not known. Perhaps, at some stage, the penguins' eggs were vulnerable to predators and laying a spare egg was a good survival strategy, but we have no evidence that this was ever the case.

PHILOSOPHY

359. What can a body do?

In his philosophical masterpiece *Ethics*, published in the year of his death, the Dutch philosopher Baruch Spinoza (1632–77) wrote: 'no one has hitherto laid down the limits to the powers of the body, that is, no one has as yet been taught by experience what the body can accomplish solely by the laws of nature.'

The French philosopher Gilles Deleuze (1925–95) posed that statement more succinctly as a question: 'What can the body do?' As usual with twentieth-century postmodern French philosophers, Deleuze's discussion is metaphysical and unintelligible, so let us continue with Spinoza's account:

> *No one hitherto has gained such an accurate knowledge of the*
> *bodily mechanism, that he can explain all its functions; nor need*
> *I call attention to the fact that many actions are observed in the*
> *lower animals, which far transcend human sagacity, and that*
> *somnambulists do many things in their sleep, which they would not*
> *venture to do when awake: these instances are enough to show, that*
> *the body can by the sole laws of its nature do many things which the*
> *mind wonders at.*

> *Again, no one knows how or by what means the mind moves the*
> *body, nor how many various degrees of motion it can impart to the*
> *body, nor how quickly it can move it.*

We know much more now about how muscles control the body and how our minds control the muscles by sending nerve impulses, but Spinoza's basic statement remains true: we still do not know how our minds limit the potential of what our bodies could achieve.

360. How can we know that other people have minds?

The history of robots in the movies exemplifies the philosophical idea behind this question. At the start, robots such as Robby in *Forbidden Planet* or C-3PO in *Star Wars* looked like robots and everyone knew they were robots. Then came Ash in *Alien* and Arnold Schwarzenegger in the first three *Terminator* films when robots (or cyborgs, as they were often called) looked and, when they wanted to, behaved so like humans that they could fool people. Finally, there were robots, such as David in *AI* and Marcus Wright (played by Sam Worthington) in *Terminator*

Salvation, who not only fooled everyone but actually believed they were human.

It all comes down to the question of 'philosophical zombies': how can we tell whether a human-like creature we meet has consciousness and sentience? Is it possible in theory to program a robot to behave in a manner totally indistinguishable from that of a human being?

Metaphysical solipsists will argue that we can only ever know about our own minds. The knowledge that one has a mind is a personal conscious experience, so trying to prove that someone else has a mind is futile. Physicalists, however, may say that the brain is a physical object and the mind is a product of the workings of the brain, so the mind and consciousness will one day be detectable as physical processes. Then we'll be able to tell whether the person we're talking to has a mind or not.

361. Can we experience anything objectively?

Everything we know, everything we believe, everything we think comes to us through our senses and is followed by a supposedly logical analysis of that sensory input. The analysis may be objective, but the data it is applied to must be subjective.

Plato, in his theory of forms, argued that the highest and most fundamental reality is the non-material abstract, not the material world of change we perceive through our senses. Platonic idealism involves a belief in a world of ideas that is objective, unchanging and absolute. We experience the world subjectively and abstract the objective reality from our experiences.

The opposite point of view is expressed in the Buddhist concept of 'emptiness', which, according to the Dalai Lama, is 'the true nature of things and events'. Nothing exists in the way we think it does. He also warns us 'to avoid the misapprehension that emptiness is an absolute reality or an independent truth'. In other words, we can't even experience emptiness objectively.

362. Is time an illusion?

According to Einstein, 'the dividing line between past, present, and future is an illusion'. In other words, there is no objective reality to the concept of 'now'. One of the fundamental ideas behind his theory of general relativity is that one observer may see various things happening at the same time while another sees the same things happening one after the other. My 'now' may be your past, present or future.

Until Einstein came along, we were all happy with the idea that we lived in a three-dimensional space with time ticking along happily at the same rate for all of us. Einstein showed that the passage of time may be different for all of us, though that difference may only be noticeable when we are moving at speeds close to that of light.

To resolve this apparent anomaly, Einstein changed our view of the world. It was no longer a three-dimensional entity moving through time, but a four-dimensional space–time continuum. There is no difference between what we see as a fixed past, a real present and an open future; they are all the same. We humans, however, are doomed to travel through the world along a one-dimensional, no-going-back timeline, which gives us the very reasonable illusion that time is real. It may be real to us, but time may appear to have a different reality for someone else.

Whether the flexible, personal nature of time makes the whole concept of time an illusion is a much deeper philosophical question.

363. Is reality an illusion?

As if it were not bad enough Einstein telling us that time was an illusion, the pioneers of quantum mechanics then suggested that reality itself might be an illusion. First, we were treated to particles that could be in two places at the same time. Then we realized that they might not be particles at all but sometimes were better seen as waves. Then we learnt that they might not be anywhere at all until we observed them. And now the string theorists tell us that what we think of as solid matter may actually consist of vibrating ten-dimensional wiggly things.

Once life evolved, our senses developed in a way that best enabled us to cope with the world. It looks increasingly as though the world that we perceive is just a construction – a hologram, if you like – created in our brains. It's not quite as bad as the plight of Neo in the *Matrix*, but quantum mechanics has forced all of us to take at least a small dose of the red pill that shows us what reality is really like.

364. Did David Hume believe in God?

In his book *Dialogues Concerning Natural Religion*, the Scottish philosopher David Hume (1711–76) employed a highly readable way of discussing the question of whether God exists. The form of the book is a series of discussions about the existence and nature of God among three characters named Demea, Philo and Cleanthes.

Demea argues that God exists but is incomprehensible; Philo agrees that God is incomprehensible but says that if you look at the evidence, you'd have to agree that He may be morally corrupt; while Cleanthes says that the evidence of nature confirms God's existence. For each of these characters, Hume argues their position so well that it is impossible to deduce what his own views were.

Hume's enemies often charged him with atheism, saying that his refusal to admit it was simply through a fear of the problems such an admission could cause for his career. On the other hand, throughout his life Hume argued against allowing human reasoning to overreach itself, so he may well have felt equally hostile to those who maintained that God definitely did not exist and those who were sure He did.

Perhaps the strongest conclusion we can reach is that Hume was opposed to traditional theistic views, but did not rule out the existence of a god absolutely.

365. Are free will and determinism incompatible?

Philosophers have been arguing this question for over 2,000 years and they are still no nearer to agreeing on an answer. Part of the problem lies in defining precisely what is meant by the terms 'determinism' and 'free will', but however one defines them, there seems to be an argument over whether they are compatible.

The incompatibilist line is simple: determinism means that everything in the universe is predetermined, either because God already knows what is going to happen and there's nothing we can do to change it, or because the laws of physics, including those we haven't discovered yet, determine everything in the world, including the actions of the particles in our brains that we use to make decisions. So you can't have both free will and determinism.

Compatibilists, however, will denounce the religious argument on the grounds that God, if He exists, knows everything, including what we're going to decide with our free wills. As for the laws of physics, the ancient compatibilists see no problem: the decisions we make with our free will are bound to be influenced by our upbringing, what we had for breakfast, our state of mind and all sorts of other things in the past. If I'd had three rashers of bacon instead of two with my fried egg, I might well have made a different decision later in the day. I call that free will, you call it the laws of physics. Modern compatibilists have it even easier: quantum theory, after all, is non-deterministic and has a good deal of inherent randomness.

We haven't the faintest idea, however, how quantum randomness could affect the operation of free will.

See also ANIMALS 17; BRAINS 80; COSMOLOGY 123; FRANCE 201; FUNDAMENTAL PARTICLES 206; LANGUAGE 267

PHYSICS

366. Do tetraneutrons exist?

In 2002 researchers at the Large Heavy Ion National Accelerator in Caen, France, fired beryllium-14 nuclei at a small carbon target. This was not just for fun, but to see whether they could create a tetraneutron. The beryllium-14 ion has a halo of four neutrons which were expected to break away when it smashed into the carbon.

Theory predicts that when that happens, it should produce a beryllium-10 nucleus and four separate neutrons. Instead of the four neutrons, however, only one signal was detected, suggesting that the four neutrons had bound together into a single tetraneutron.

The trouble is that according to current models of nuclear forces, a tetraneutron ought to be impossible. Attempts to replicate the Caen findings have not so far been successful and some doubts have been raised over its detection methods. There are, however, another four or five reports of tetraneutrons being produced in other experiments, so the jury is still out on whether they are possible or not.

367. Why don't moving bicycles fall over?

In a celebrated scene from the 1949 French film *Jour de Fête*, the blunder-prone postman François, played by Jacques Tati, is seen chasing his runaway bicycle as it winds its way riderless down a country road. Twisting right and left, the bicycle rolls a surprising distance without falling over. It looks like an excellent piece of trick photography, but that is what bikes do: when they start to veer off in one direction, their front wheels auto-correct and send them back the other way.

Since the film came out, various suggestions have been proposed to explain what causes this effect. Some said it was the gyroscopic effect of the rotation of the wheels that was keeping the bike upright; others said it was like the castors on a shopping trolley automatically turning the right way when the trolley was steered. The same explanations had also been advanced to account for the remarkable stability of moving bikes with riders on them.

In 2011, however, a team at Cornell University designed an experimental bicycle that had all its gyroscopic effects cancelled out by a system of counter-rotating wheels. It still stayed upright when rolling along on its own. The researchers admitted that this does not solve the problem of why bikes don't fall over, but it does rule out some possible answers.

368. Can magnetic monopoles exist?

Any magnet has a north pole at one end and a south pole at the other. Cut it in half and you get two magnets, each with a north pole and a south pole. And you can go on cutting it in half, eventually arriving at an atom with a north pole at one end and a south pole at the other. You just cannot get down to a single monopole.

Maxwell's equations for electromagnetism were even thought to show that monopoles were impossible, but in 1896 Pierre Curie pointed out that they may be possible. In 1931 the great physicist Paul Dirac proved that monopoles could only exist if electric charge was quantized (i.e. electric charge came in discrete chunks), so when that was later found to be true, interest in monopoles was renewed.

Recently, the existence of magnetic monopoles has been predicted by string theory and the search for them has intensified. In January 2014 it was widely reported that magnetic monopoles had been created in a lab in the US, but the reports proved to be exaggerated. What had been created was not an actual monopole but a physical system exhibiting the magnetic field that a monopole would produce. So we still do not know if they exist, but it is looking more likely than it did a few years ago.

369. Is there a general theory to describe the dynamics of turbulent flow?

The Nobel Prize-winning physicist Richard Feynman described turbulence as the most important unsolved problem of classical physics. Feynman died in 1988 and we are still a long way from solving it. Turbulence affects the flow of gases or liquids, turning a smooth flow into something choppy and unpredictable. It spills our tea, it makes our washing-up bowls splash all over our clothes, it terrifies plane passengers, and it even has to be taken into account in the design of artificial heart valves.

Whether we are talking about the water flowing out of a tap or a plane moving through air, everything may start smooth, then – as velocity or resistance increases – suddenly become disordered and turbulent. And once turbulence starts, it can take some time to die down, even after whatever caused it in the first place is reduced.

Despite a great deal of research and volumes of intensely complicated mathematics, we are still unable to make reliable predictions of when turbulence will occur.

370. What is responsible for the value of the fine-structure constant?

Another of Richard Feynman's 'greatest damn mysteries of physics' is the value of the fine-structure constant known as α (alpha). It's one of the fundamental constants of physics that make the universe what it is and governs the strength of the force between electrically charged particles and the energy levels of atoms.

To calculate α, you take the square of an electron's charge, divide it by the speed of light and Planck's constant, then multiply by 2π (pi), and the answer is 0.007297, or about 1/137. The extraordinary thing, though, is that if it differed from that figure by as little as 4 per cent, either higher or lower, then the nuclear reactions in stars that lead to the production of oxygen and carbon would not take place and we carbon-based life forms would not exist. Why α has this particular life-supporting value is a complete mystery.

As Feynman said: 'All good theoretical physicists put this number up on their wall and worry about it.'

371. How is the vacuum catastrophe explained?

Think of a number. Add 107 zeros onto the end of it. The difference between the number you started with and the one you now have is a measure of the so-called 'vacuum catastrophe'.

It's all to do with the energy of empty space, which is a problem we raised earlier (→ 173). According to quantum field theory, the energy of space is not zero and the theory enables us to calculate what it should be. However, when the Voyager spacecraft came to calculate its real value by measuring the gravitational pull of empty space, it came up with a much lower number. Very much lower: in fact, a number differing from the theoretical value by as much as the same number with 107 zeros on the end of it.

This has been described as the worst theoretical prediction of all time. If we were to estimate that the entire universe consisted of one atom, it would be closer than this prediction. Something is going very badly wrong here, either with quantum field theory or with our understanding of gravity, and we do not know what it is.

372. Can negative mass and negative energy exist?

In the seventeenth century, alchemists were puzzled by the fact that some things gained weight when they were burnt. We now know, of course, that burning often involves combining with oxygen, which accounts for the weight gain. Not knowing about oxygen, the alchemists came up with the 'phlogiston' theory. When something is burnt, it loses phlogiston, and phlogiston has negative mass.

After oxygen was discovered in the 1770s, the idea of negative mass disappeared for around two centuries, but it has returned recently through the work of theoretical physicists exploring the more exotic implications of physical laws. If we allow negative mass and negative energy, it could, some say, explain why we have not yet discovered gravitational waves (which could be absorbed by a combination of positive and negative mass), and it could provide an explanation of how wormholes might exist.

For many years, there was a bit of a problem that negative mass was thought to break one of the fundamental assumptions of Einstein's general relativity. In 2014, however, physicists at Montreal University found a solution to Einstein's equations that allowed mass to take a negative value.

So in theory, negative mass might exist after all, though we have no evidence for it, nor any clear idea of how it might have been produced in the first place.

See also BIG BANG 54–6; BLACK HOLES 70–1; COSMOLOGY 123, 126; ENERGY 172–4; FUNDAMENTAL PARTICLES 204–7; GRAVITY 223; PHILOSOPHY 365; UNIVERSE 463–7

PLANTS

373. How long can seeds live?

Gardeners know that if seeds are kept cold and dry, they can last for years, but in 2005 scientists in Israel announced that they had grown a date palm from a seed which carbon dating had revealed to be 2,000 years old. Around ten years earlier, a Chinese lotus plant was reported to have been grown from a seed dated to be 1,288 years old.

The date-palm seed had been dug up during excavations, so it had been kept cold and away from the sun and air, while the lotus seed had been preserved in peat. The lotus germinated easily but its seedlings grew up deformed, probably because of damage caused by radioactivity in the soil.

Examples such as these show that seeds can indeed live a long time, but exactly how long remains completely unknown.

See also AVOCADOS 37; EVOLUTION 179; INTELLIGENCE 250; METEOROLOGY 309; NAZIS 338

PLATYPUSES

374. Why are Tasmanian platypuses much bigger than North Australian platypuses?

Tasmanian platypuses are significantly larger than platypuses in mainland Australia, but in general platypuses in the north of mainland

Australia are smaller than those in the south. Why this should be so is important for a large range of animals, not just platypuses.

In 1847 the German biologist Carl Bergmann proposed that as a general rule for any species, members of that species coming from colder climates are smaller than those from warm climates. This would seem to explain the difference between mainland platypuses and Tasmanian platypuses, but the difference in size of animals in different regions of the mainland seems to go in the wrong direction. In 1986 the Ukrainian-born US environmentalist Valerius Geist suggested that Bergmann's rule was spurious. It wasn't temperature that mattered but food availability during the growing season.

In 2012, however, a study comparing platypus size in different locations came to the conclusion that the main factor affecting it was rainfall, with larger-sized individuals typically found in lower-rainfall environments. Evidently the effect of environment on platypus body size is more complex than had been thought.

375. Why do ostriches sleep like platypuses?

When most mammals or birds sleep, they exhibit two different states: slow-wave sleep (SWS) and rapid eye movement (REM) sleep. SWS is characterized by slow, high-amplitude brain waves; REM sleep has fast, low-amplitude waves accompanied by rapid eye movements. However, the egg-laying mammals, platypuses and echidnas, have only a single sleep state that combines elements of both SWS and REM sleep.

In 2011 ostriches were found to have a sleep pattern all of their own. Episodes of REM sleep were accompanied by the usual rapid eye movements, similar to those observed in other birds and mammals, but at the same time their forebrain activity would flip between the high-amplitude waves of REM sleep and SWS-like slow waves, much like the platypus.

How two animals as different as the ostrich and the platypus came to be the only ones with such brain activity while asleep is a mystery.

POKER

376. Do poker faces help poker players?

Wearing an emotionless expression has long been considered a key to success at poker, but some research in 2010 cast doubt on the value of a 'poker face'.

Subjects played a simplified version of Texas Hold 'Em poker against an opponent whose face they could see on-screen. The faces were taken from a database and each was modified by computer into three versions designed to be seen as trustworthy (smiling and optimistic), neutral (poker face), or untrustworthy (scowling). In each hand the opponent bet first and the subject had to decide whether to fold or match the bet. The decisions were correlated against the type of face depicted on the screen to see which was most effective.

'According to these results,' the experimenters concluded, 'the best "poker face" for bluffing may not be a neutral face, but rather a face that contains emotional correlates of trustworthiness.' Whether this finding will influence the facial expressions of poker players, however, is doubtful.

POLAR BEARS

377. Do male polar bears find mates by following females' smelly feet?

Polar bears are solitary animals and how they find each other for the purposes of mating has long been a matter of speculation. Males have been known to follow a female's trail for 160 kilometres or more during the mating season, and it has been presumed that scent plays a part in their ability to do so. A study published in 2015 revealed that smelly feet may be very important in this process.

Swabs were taken from the feet of polar bears and presented to a number of polar bears in zoos. Female bears in particular were found likely to approach the scent of smelly feet during the spring. Males were found to differentiate scent donor by sex and reproductive condition.

Whether smelly feet are the main guide males use to pick mates, however, is an open question.

378. Are polar bears' penises weakened by pollutants?

In 2015 a paper on the possible effect of pollutants on the density of the bone in polar bears' penises set off a wave of headlines in the popular press. 'Is pollution destroying polar bears' penises?' they asked. 'Chemical pollution is causing polar bear penises to break' or 'Polar bear penises are wilting', they stated. But is it true?

What the research behind the paper had identified was a negative correlation between the density of the bacula (penis bones) of polar bears and levels of organic chemicals known as PCBs in the bears' fat. No mechanism was suggested to explain how the chemicals might affect bone density, nor was there any evidence to suggest that bones of lower density were more likely to break. No examples of broken penis bones were found in the investigations.

See also BEARS 42

'What is research but a blind date
with knowledge.'

Will Harvey

PORPOISES

379. Do porpoises choose their friends?

Porpoises are not known to be particularly social animals, and a report in 1999 suggested that mother–calf pairs were probably the only stable social unit. That finding, however, had been based on observations of porpoises on the surface of the water, and it was challenged in 2011 by some research that monitored their underwater behaviour.

The diving behaviour of six finless porpoises was recorded to see whether they exhibited any patterns indicating preferences in which of the group they dived with. Two pairs in particular were found to dive together more frequently than other possible pairings, and later dives by such pairs were found to last longer. One of these pairs was an immature female and an adult male, the other was a young male and an adult male.

The researchers concluded that 'certain individuals form associations even if they are not a mother and calf pair'. With only six porpoises involved in the research, however, more work is clearly needed before we conclude that porpoises choose their friends.

PREHISTORY

380. What were the Carnac stones for?

Around the village of Carnac in Brittany, a collection of over 3,000 huge standing stones were erected, cut from local rock during the Neolithic period between 4500 and 3000 BC. Although many of the stones have been moved or destroyed, it is clear that they were arranged in patterns generally consisting of straight lines, with the stones increasing in height as one moves down the line.

Artefacts including axes and arrow-heads have been found in the region of the stones, as well as pearls and other gems and probable human graves and tombs. It has been speculated that the stones were arranged in some astronomical alignment to serve as a primitive observatory, but despite the large number of stones, nothing has been confirmed about the reasons for this massive construction.

381. Did something crash into the Baltic Sea 140,000 years ago?

In 2011, while looking for a shipwreck in the Baltic Sea between Sweden and Finland, a Swedish team discovered a strange formation on the sea bed. Described as looking like 'rough granite', it was round, about 60 metres in diameter, and stood on a 9-metre-tall pillar at a depth of 85 to 90 metres. A staircase and a round black hole going directly into the structure were reported on a later investigation. Also a long rough path, reminiscent of a skid mark, was seen leading up to the object.

Samples of either the object itself or rocks that had formed around it were brought to the surface and subsequently found to be around 14,000 years old (or possibly 140,000 years ago, depending which account you read). A host of theories have emerged to explain it:

- It may be a natural rock formation, though its shape looks man-made.
- It may be something that formed around a sunken German Second World War U-boat.
- It may be a meteorite.
- It may be an alien spaceship (its shape is a bit like that of the Millennium Falcon in *Star Wars*) which crashed into the Baltic during the last ice age.

382. Who or what were the lizard men of al-'Ubaid?

In 1919 the Egyptologist Harry Reginald Hall began excavations at a site called Tell al-'Ubaid in the region of ancient Mesopotamia. Among the artefacts that were dug up were a number of figurines with human-like bodies and lizard heads. Each of the figures has its own individual pose, with the strangest of them showing a naked female suckling a baby which also has a lizard head.

The figurines have been dated to around 7,000 years ago, which was when the Sumerian culture was reaching its peak in Mesopotamia. They were found predominantly at grave sites, so they are thought to have had some ritual significance. While snakes are known to have had mystic significance for the Sumerians, lizards are not thought to have featured highly, if at all, in their mythology.

Perhaps they were placed in graves to ensure safe passage to the underworld, but with no known links to what we know of Sumerian culture, any such suggestions are pure guesswork.

383. What is the origin of the Basque people?

There are two main ways of trying to find out where the Basque people of southern Europe originated: from the Basque language, which is unlike anything else spoken in Europe, or from an analysis of their DNA. Neither method has so far yielded more than tantalizing theories.

While the Basque language includes some borrowed words from Latin-based languages, it is mostly so different from other languages that it is thought to have developed from a proto-Basque that was spoken before Indo-European languages even arrived in the region. One theory is that Basque is the only survivor of a number of similar languages that were spoken in the Palaeolithic era around 16,000 BC. This is generally linked to a theory that the Basque people spread to Europe from Africa after the European climate warmed at the end of the last ice age.

DNA studies have revealed a number of markers the Basques share with other European peoples, but they seem to point in several different directions. Studies concentrating on the Y chromosome have related the Basques to the Celtic, Welsh and Irish; one study of mitochondrial DNA suggested that they have shared some features with the rest of Europe since prehistoric times; studies in Spain in 2007 and 2010 concluded that the Basques have a DNA profile indistinguishable from the rest of the Iberian peninsula; while another general DNA study in

2012 said that they have unique features in their genetic profile that do distinguish them from other groups.

See also ANCIENT CITIES 8–11; ANCIENT HISTORY 12–13; BIRDS 64; DINOSAURS 136–8; TYRANNOSAURUSES 459–61

PSYCHOLOGY

384. What is the explanation of foreign accent syndrome?

On 2 October 2014 the UK newspaper the *Daily Mirror* ran a story under the headline: 'Woman is diagnosed with Foreign Accent Syndrome after "waking up speaking Italian".' Well, perhaps 'waking up speaking Italian' was a little sensationalist, as anyone reading further would have discovered that her speech was only distorted in a manner that made some people think she was talking with an Italian accent, while others described it as French, Japanese, Polish or Lithuanian. But foreign accent syndrome (FAS), though rare, is a well-documented condition.

First described in 1907, there have been fewer than seventy cases of FAS reported in more than a century since then. They usually follow a stroke, head injury or migraine attacks and are presumed to result from damage to parts of the brain involved in speech production, or possibly to the tongue or jaw or the muscles that control them.

Despite various types of brain scan being performed on people suffering from FAS, however, no specific area of the brain has been found to be associated with the syndrome.

385. Do we make better decisions when we're hungry?

Many studies have shown that predators take greater risks when hunting for food if they are hungry. That makes sense, but the question of whether hunger generally increases risk-taking, particularly in humans, has produced contradictory results.

In 2010 a study at University College London was conducted on two groups, one of which had eaten shortly before the experiment, while the other had fasted. Subjects in both groups were asked to select lottery tickets marked with potential prizes of various sizes and the odds against winning them. The higher prizes offered lower chances of winning. The experimenters reported that the subjects who had fasted were more likely to go for the high-prize, low-chance lotteries. In other words, hunger increases risky behaviour.

In 2014, however, a study in the Netherlands reached almost the opposite conclusion. Their experiment compared the behaviour of well-fed and hungry groups at a gambling game and reported that 'hungry participants performed better in this complex task with uncertain outcomes'.

Whether one should eat before taking decisions still seems to be an open question.

386. How much of our behaviour reflects our evolutionary past?

This question underlies the recently developed subject of evolutionary psychology. An ordinary (non-evolutionary) psychologist will take the line that as conscious, thinking beings, we learn from experience. We may be born with certain skills and elementary patterns of behaviour, but as we grow, we learn about the world and other people, and our interactions with them result in our forming likes and dislikes and patterns of behaviour that make us what we are as individuals.

Evolutionary psychologists take a rather different view. Our brains and minds, they say, have evolved in a similar way to our bodies. For 99 per cent of the history of *Homo sapiens*, we were hunter-gatherers living in small groups in Africa. Many of our behavioural traits, in their view, stem from behaviour that evolved during that long period. People are afraid of snakes because that was a key to survival for our distant ancestors. Our social skills have developed from life in those hunter-gatherer groups.

Some evolutionary psychologists will even say that most of the problems of modern mankind stem from conflicts between the modern world and our evolutionary heritage. All our social skills, sexual impulses and aggression may be the result of our long evolution. On the other hand, they may be the result of our conscious, thinking ability to adapt and solve problems in real time rather than waiting for evolution to do the job for us. The question is: how much of our behaviour do we owe to evolution and how much to the man-made social structures of the world we live in?

387. At what stage does free will enter our decision-making process?

A study in 2008 raised perplexing questions about the nature of free will. Subjects were placed in front of a button and asked simply to decide whether to press it with their left hand or right hand. Before they pressed the button, they were also asked to watch a screen on which an ever-changing stream of letters was displayed and to remember which letter was shown at the moment they took the decision which hand to use for the button-pressing. While this was going on, the subjects were attached to brain-scanning equipment.

The remarkable finding was that the brain scans not only revealed which hand the subject chose, but by monitoring the scans, the researchers could predict which hand they would choose up to ten seconds before the subjects thought they had made the decision.

We like to think that we take decisions consciously after thinking about the alternatives. This simple experiment, however, seems to show that we may first make a decision subconsciously, then our subconscious tells our conscious mind about it. Where that leaves free will is very puzzling.

388. What causes déjà vu?

The only thing all scientists seem to agree about déjà vu is that it is very difficult to study in the laboratory. The feeling, when seeing something for the first time, that you have encountered it before is not only fleeting, but difficult to reproduce to order. Several theories have been advanced, but there is very little evidence to support any of them:

(i) It is caused by the split-second delay in transferring information from one side of the brain to the other: both sides may see something, then one side tells the other about it, with the result that one side gets the information twice and thinks it has seen it before.

(ii) Just as our muscles may twitch unexpectedly, so do the neurons in our brain; déjà vu is nothing more than a brain twitch.

(iii) Any face has much in common with any other face; any room is, to some extent, like any other room; déjà vu results from our brains detecting such similarities before they start concentrating on the differences.

(iv) Sigmund Freud said it was a result of paramnesia – a confusion between fact and fantasy caused by repressed memories.

In fact, around forty different explanations have been offered to explain déjà vu. I shall spare you the other thirty-six. We just don't know.

389. What is the connection between depression and serotonin?

We have already touched on this subject a couple of times when talking about depressed dogs (→ 18) and antidepressants (→ 296), but the real nature of the connection is highly elusive. One of the problems is that we can accurately measure serotonin levels in the blood, but there is no simple way of assessing serotonin levels in the brain and we do not know whether levels in the bloodstream reflect the levels in the brain. Many studies have shown a correlation between low blood serotonin levels and depression, but whether low serotonin causes depression or depression causes serotonin depletion is not known.

In 2014 research on mice threw another spanner into the workings of serotonin. To discover more about the serotonin–depression link, the researchers developed a strain of mice that lacked the ability to produce serotonin in their brains. Behavioural tests showed the mice to be compulsive and extremely aggressive, but they showed no signs of depression. Even when put under stress, the mice behaved the same as normal mice. The researchers concluded that serotonin may not play a major role in depression at all – in mice anyway.

See also BRAINS 75, 77; DREAMS 161; ELEPHANTS 171; FOOD 193–4, 196; INTELLIGENCE 248; MUSIC 329; SEX 410; SEX DIFFERENCES 412

QUASARS

390. What powers quasars?

Quasars, which is short for 'quasi-stellar radio sources', were first detected in the 1950s as sources of radio waves, but were soon shown to be immensely bright and compact regions at the centre of massive distant galaxies. In fact, barring such explosive events as supernovas, quasars are the brightest objects in the universe, emitting more energy than seems possible. The energy output of one quasar may be many times that of the entire Milky Way galaxy.

The most plausible current theory is that every quasar is powered by the existence of a supermassive black hole at its centre. The black hole is surrounded by a large, rotating cloud of gas which is hugely heated as it falls into the black hole. The gas emits thermal radiation, which may be the source of the quasar's energy.

Whether all quasars have black holes at their centre, however, is unknown, as is the way such supermassive black holes would have come about. The reason they are hypothesized as the power source of quasars is more by default than through evidence: nobody has come up with any other suggestion of a sufficiently powerful power source to do the job.

391. Where have all the quasars gone?

As far as we know, every quasar is very distant from us. More than 200,000 quasars have been detected, but the closest is about 600 million light years away. This suggests either that quasars stopped being formed about 600 million years ago, or that they ran out of fuel at that time as their black holes sucked up all the gas that was providing their power source. There could, in fact, be no quasars in the universe today, and what we detect of them is just a trace of the ancient universe that has taken more than half a billion years to reach us.

RATS

392. Does tickling a rat make it optimistic?

The science of rat-tickling began in the 1990s when research in Massachusetts revealed that rats emit an ultrasonic vocalization akin to human laughter when they seem to be enjoying themselves. This naturally led to the question of whether rats laughed when tickled and whether this was the same laughter as when they were having fun. Experiments seemed to show that they did and it was.

The next stage was to see if the positive emotions associated with laughter affect rats in the same way as people. In particular, does laughter make rats more optimistic? In 2012 an ingenious experiment was set up to explore this question.

First, the rats were trained to distinguish between two sounds. In either case, after hearing the sound, the rat was presented with a lever to press. For one sound, pressing the lever earned them a reward of food; for the other sound, they received a painful electric shock if they pressed the lever. Then the rats were divided into two groups: those in one group were tickled; those in the other group were handled but not tickled. Finally, the rats were returned to the set-up with the sounds and the lever, but now they were played a sound that was halfway between the two on which they had been trained. Would they then take the optimistic point of view and press the lever or be pessimists and not press it?

The results showed that the tickled rats pushed the lever significantly more often than the non-tickled group. This was seen as evidence that tickling and laughter induce optimism in rats, though other explanations are also possible. It could be, for example, that the tickled rats placed greater trust in the experimenters while the handled rats distrusted them. Further research and rat-tickling are clearly needed on this matter.

393. Why do kangaroo rats not come out on moonlit nights?

According to the 'moonlight avoidance theory', small mammals do not come out at night to forage for food when the Moon is bright. This seems to make sense: the darker it is, the less likely they are to be spotted by predators. In fact, it made so much sense that nobody bothered to test it until recently, when the results showed that matters are not so simple.

A study in 2013 in the Great Basin Desert in the USA revealed that most small mammals were just as active on bright moonlit nights as at other times. The only mammal that seemed to subscribe to the moonlight avoidance theory was the kangaroo rat, a giant rodent that hops around on two legs.

One theory is that kangaroo rats, being bigger than other rodents, generally beat the others to any food that's going. They therefore have the luxury of being able to stay at home on moonlit nights while the others, having run out of food, have to go out anyway, whatever the risk. Another suggestion is that the predators of small mammals are themselves preyed on by larger animals, so they too avoid bright nights to avoid being spotted, which makes it safe for the small mammals to come out after all.

Studies in other places such as New Mexico, however, have suggested that kangaroo rats come out more frequently on moonlit nights than on dark ones. Evidently the effect of moonlight on rodents' behaviour is much more complicated than had been thought and depends on many more factors than just the lighting.

See also ANIMALS 18; HUMOUR 245; MAMMALS 283; PANGOLINS 356; SEX 410; WALRUSES 486

RELIGION

394. What happened to the Ark of the Covenant?

According to the Book of Exodus, God told Moses to build the Ark of the Covenant to hold the two tablets on which were inscribed the Ten Commandments. The Ark and its powers are then frequently mentioned in the Old Testament until King Josiah of Judah (in 2 Chronicles 35) orders the caretakers of the Ark to return it to the temple in Jerusalem.

After that, the picture is confused. In the New Testament, Paul, in his Letter to the Hebrews, mentions that as well as the Ten Commandments, the Ark also contained Aaron's rod, a jar of manna, and the first Torah scroll, written by Moses. The Ark is also mentioned in Revelation as being in heaven, but since Moses' ark was meant to be a copy of one in heaven, the one mentioned in Revelation may be the original rather than Moses' copy.

According to the non-canonical Book of Maccabees, the prophet Jeremiah, after being warned by God of the Babylonian invasion, buried the Ark in a cave on Mount Nebo near the east bank of the River Jordan, where it would remain until God gathered his people together again. More recent accounts have placed the Ark in France, the USA, Rome, Egypt (including one version that had it in the tomb of Tutankhamun), the UK or Ireland.

The most detailed claim comes from the Lemba people of South Africa and Zimbabwe, who have said that their ancestors carried the Ark south. Arabic sources have maintained that it was first taken to Yemen, where the Lemba found it and brought it to Africa. According to Lemba oral traditions, the Ark self-destructed on arrival in their homeland and their priests constructed a new one from a piece of the original.

The interesting thing is that a German missionary found this alleged replica in the 1940s. It was taken to a museum in Harare, where it was carbon-dated to around 1350, which was about the time of the end of the Great Zimbabwe civilization.

395. Who was the Cretan Snake Goddess?

When the British archaeologist Arthur Evans discovered the Minoan civilization of Crete in 1903, he unearthed the first examples of ceramic Snake Goddess figurines. Several more were found later, all depicting a bare-breasted woman holding a snake in each hand, usually wearing a crown and having an owl on her head.

The figurines date back to around 1600 BC and stand out in a culture that appears to have produced very little art or sculpture. There is no other evidence of a snake goddess in Minoan beliefs, and while several other cultures had snake goddesses, nothing is known that would relate them to the Minoan version. Snakes were often used as a symbol of rebirth because of their habit of shedding their skins, and it has been suggested that the figurines represented some sort of Earth goddess, but there is no evidence that the Minoans worshipped such a goddess.

See also ANIMALS 19; ASTRONOMY 30; CHINA 101; CHRISTIANITY 106; GOLD 219; INCAS 247; JESUS CHRIST 259–63; PHILOSOPHY 364–5; SCIENCE 405; TURKEY 457; UNIVERSE 464

RIDDLES

396. What is the answer to Bishop Samuel Wilberforce's riddle?

Samuel Wilberforce, bishop of Oxford, is now best remembered for three reasons: his fervent opposition to Charles Darwin; the nickname

'Soapy Sam' given to him by Benjamin Disraeli, who described his manner as 'unctuous, oleaginous, saponaceous'; and the riddle that was found among his papers after he died in 1873:

Sweetest of sound, in orchestra heard,
Yet in orchestra never have been,
Bird in light plumage, yet less like a bird,
Nothing in nature has ever been seen,
On earth I expire, in water I die,
Yet I run, swim and fly,
If I cannot be guessed by a boy or a man,
A girl or a woman I certainly can!

A number of possible solutions, including 'whale' and 'mermaid', have been proposed, but none fits the description well enough for all to agree on what Wilberforce intended, so the riddle is generally considered still unsolved. Perhaps the most likely suggestion is 'a siren'.

RUSSIA

397. What created the Patomskiy crater in Siberia?

In 1949 the Russian geologist Vadim Kolpakov, exploring a region of Siberia near Irkutsk, discovered a massive convex cone made of limestone with a huge crater in its top and a rounded hill in the crater. Its appearance resembled a huge bird's nest with an egg in it, which is why the local people call it the 'Eagle's Nest'.

The cone is 80 metres tall with a diameter of 150 metres at its widest, and the depth of the inner circle crater is around 10 metres; it is thought to be about 250 years old, but that figure could be well out. More than sixty years after its discovery we still do not know what caused it. The obvious explanation is a meteorite impact, but no meteorite fragments have ever been found. Other theories include the following:

(i) It was caused by a secret nuclear test – which is unlikely as radiation levels are normal.

(ii) It is an ancient slag heap – unlikely as there is no evidence of a sizeable population ever having been in the region.

(iii) It could have been caused by a volcanic eruption – only there are no known volcanoes nearby.

(iv) It may have been built by aliens – which is a solution for some people to anything out of the ordinary.

As well as the mystery over its origin, the crater changes shape, rising and falling periodically, and trees near it are said to grow particularly fast, which also has not been explained.

See also CATS 92; GOLD 218

SALAMANDERS

398. How do adult salamanders regrow their limbs?

If an adult salamander loses a limb or even its tail, it can grow a new one. Salamanders are the only vertebrates that can regrow limbs in such a manner. In recent years, a great deal of research has gone into trying to discover what makes them so special, but we are not quite there yet.

When a human embryo is developing in the womb, its stem cells develop into specific types of cell for the various parts of the body. Soon after birth, however, we lose the ability to create all-purpose cells which can be sent to the region of any missing part and grow into whatever is necessary. Essentially that is what the salamander does and it is a very complex procedure. Not only must the animal send a supply of all-purpose cells to the affected area, but when they get there, they must recognize where they are in order to know what to grow into.

Recently something called the ERK pathway was discovered to play a vital role in this process. The ERK pathway acts as a communications highway between a cell's surface and the nucleus, which contains the cell's genetic material. Not only is the ERK pathway not fully active in adult mammals, but if it is turned off in salamanders, they lose the ability to regenerate limbs.

How salamanders keep the pathway turned on while we humans cannot must be a key question in accounting for their regeneration ability.

SALMON

399. How do salmon find their way back to their place of birth to spawn?

After being born in a river, salmon may swim to the open sea and spend two or three years there before returning to their original home to spawn. How they manage to find their way back has long been a puzzle. In 2013 a study at Oregon State University showed that the Earth's magnetic field may have something to do with it.

Their study involved looking at fifty-six years of fisheries' data monitoring sockeye salmon returning to the Fraser River in British Columbia. To reach the river, they must choose which way to go around Vancouver Island. Whether they chose the northern or the southern route was found to correlate with changes in the Earth's magnetic field. What was probably happening, the researchers concluded, was that some sort of map of the magnetic field was imprinted on the salmon on their outward journey and they were selecting the route that most closely resembled it. At what distance from their goal the geomagnetic data are useful, however, is unclear, and it is thought likely that the salmon also use the Sun as a compass, as well as tracking waves breaking on the beach with infrasound and using smell.

See also BEARS 41

SALT

400. Can we predict El Niño from sea-salt levels?

Every few years, the usual climate patterns of the western Pacific Ocean are thrown off balance by the phenomenon known as El Niño. In a normal year the trade winds blow westward, pushing warm surface water near Australia and New Guinea towards the western Pacific. The build-up of this warm water forces nutrient-rich cold waters to rise up from the deeper ocean off the west coast of South America. This colder nutrient-rich water fosters the growth of the fish population, much to the joy of the South American economy.

In an El Niño year, however, the trade winds weaken, warm waters are not pushed westward, cold water is not forced to the surface, and the fish stay away. Also, the warmer waters may add to the problems of the region by leading to heavy rain.

Forecasting when El Niño is going to strike is not an easy task. All we know is that it happens every three to seven years. The salinity of ocean water, however, is known to play an important part in determining its capacity to store and transport heat. Greater salinity results in an increase in ocean density, which affects the circulation of the waters. Since 2010 the NASA Aquarius satellite observatory has been monitoring ocean salinity from space to see how salt levels might be used to predict El Niño events.

SATURN

401. Why is there a hexagonal cloud pattern around the north pole of Saturn?

In 1981–2 the Voyager spacecraft sent back pictures of a hexagonal cloud pattern around the north pole of Saturn. In 2006 the Cassini mission confirmed that it was still there. The sides of the hexagon measure about 13,800 kilometres (8,600 miles), and it rotates with a period of 10 hours 39 minutes 24 seconds, which is the same as the period of the radio emissions from Saturn's interior.

The only hint at what might cause this regular geometric pattern is some research showing that regular polygons may appear in areas of turbulent flow between two fluids rotating at different speeds. The atmospheric winds of Saturn and the planet's rotation may create the conditions for such a pattern.

402. What is responsible for the anomalous surface temperatures on Saturn's moon Mimas?

William Herschel discovered Saturn's moon Mimas in 1789, and it was long thought to be a small and uninteresting piece of celestial rock and ice. In 2010, however, measurements from the Cassini spacecraft indicated that the temperatures on the surface of Mimas were very strangely distributed. As on Earth, temperatures at various places might have been expected to correlate with how much light was received from the Sun, but a very different pattern was observed.

A wide difference in thermal conductivity across the surface could account for the unexpected pattern, leading to some surface regions being heated directly by the Sun, while at others the solar heat soaks into the surface. The coldest regions are around the huge crater known as Herschel, but whether the crater has something to do with the temperature differential is not known.

See also ASTRONOMY 30; SOLAR SYSTEM 441

SCIENCE

403. Who built the Antikythera mechanism?

At the end of 1900 Greek divers found the wreck of an ancient ship off the coast of the island of Antikythera. Further investigations of the wreck revealed fragments of a clockwork mechanism made of at least thirty bronze gears, of which the largest was about fourteen centimetres in diameter and originally had 223 teeth.

After reconstruction, the Antikythera mechanism, as it was dubbed, was found to be a device for calculating the positions of the Sun and Moon, the cycles of the Olympic Games, and perhaps even the locations of the planets. The complexity and astonishing accuracy of its calculations have led to its being described as 'the world's first analog computer'.

According to recent estimates, the device dates back to 205 BC, but it seems reasonable to assume that its construction must have evolved from less complex instruments. Remarkably, however, nothing quite like it has ever been found. After the ship carrying it sank, it seems that the relevant technology was lost, and it was a long time before the Greeks rediscovered the ideas behind it.

404. Is science methodical?

Those who practise science take great pride in the scientific method: we form hypotheses, make predictions based on these hypotheses, then perform experiments to see if the predictions are correct. This scientific method dates back to Descartes, who established its framework in 1619 and later wrote that its essence was

> *never to accept anything for true which I did not clearly know to be such; that is to say, carefully to avoid precipitancy and prejudice, and to compromise nothing more in my judgment than what was presented to my mind so clearly and distinctly as to exclude all ground of methodic doubt.*

The great twentieth-century philosopher Karl Popper pointed out the cracks in this framework. A hypothesis, he said, is only worth considering if it is falsifiable. You form a hypothesis, make a prediction, test the prediction, and if it doesn't work, then you reject the hypothesis. So you can never actually prove that anything is right, you can only prove it wrong. When the experiment conforms to the prediction, it may increase your belief that the hypothesis is correct, but you can never be sure.

Even worse, the hypothesis-prediction-testing procedure may seem methodical, but there are no rules, or set procedure, or algorithm for coming up with hypotheses in the first place. So perhaps there's no real 'method' behind science at all.

405. Can science, pseudo-science and non-science be distinguished?

When is a science not a science? Closely connected to the previous question is what Karl Popper called the 'demarcation problem': what distinguishes a science from a pseudo-science or a non-science? Why is chemistry a science when alchemy wasn't? In what way does astronomy differ from astrology? Alchemists and chemists both performed experiments and built up theories based on their results; astrologers and astronomers both observed the motion of celestial bodies and looked for their effects.

In Popper's view the crucial difference was falsification: scientists formulate a hypothesis and design experiments which will test whether the hypothesis makes incorrect predictions; pseudo-scientists only perform experiments designed to verify their theories. Alchemy and astrology survived for so long because they were formulated in a way that was so vague as not to allow them to be disproved.

Popper's rival Thomas Kuhn, however, pointed out that a historical approach showed that this wasn't how scientists behaved at all. Far from following Popper's rules, they were liable to ignore falsifying data unless the evidence was overwhelming. Kuhn proposed that the essential ingredient of science is puzzle-solving. 'Normal science', as he called it, consists in solving puzzles posed by the existing theory. Only very rarely, after the theory had been found to create too many anomalies, did scientists turn to Popper's falsification methods.

Later writers on the philosophy of science have suggested that both Popper and Kuhn were too limited in their views and that there is no universal rule for what constitutes a science or where the boundaries are to be drawn between science, pseudo-science and non-science. So the scientific status of homeopathy, psychoanalysis, parapsychology and perhaps even religion may still depend on whom you are talking to.

SEX

406. Is there a gay gene?

In 1990 research was published purporting to show a small difference in the brain between gay and straight men. In 1993 it was widely reported that a gay gene had been discovered. Actually even the scientist responsible for the research never claimed to have found a gene for homosexuality. It was only a linkage between a small stretch of DNA on the X chromosome and homosexuality in males, but such an idea was too complex for the press to report.

In 2005 researchers at the University of Illinois identified several stretches of DNA on other chromosomes that occurred more often in gay men. They concluded that there is no single gay gene but that 'sexual orientation is a complex trait'.

In 2014 a study – claimed to be the biggest ever – of 409 pairs of gay brothers identified five genetic markers pointing to homosexuality, but stressed that other factors, both genetic and environmental, played a part in determining sexual orientation. Again, the study identifies only regions on chromosomes rather than specific genes. As one of the lead authors said: 'until somebody finds a gene, we don't know.'

The issue is further complicated by various studies showing that men with older brothers are more likely to be gay. There is also the question of gay women, for whom no genetic markers have been identified.

407. Who invented condoms?

The early history of condoms is shrouded in mystery. Some claim that a cave painting in France dating back 12,000 to 15,000 years depicts condom use, but that is disputed. People in ancient Egypt, Rome and Greece are all known to have practised birth control, but only female methods are well documented. There are some references to men taking responsibility for contraception, but these are short on detail and it is unclear whether they suggest condom use or simply coitus interruptus. Egyptian and Greek men are known to have worn very sparse loincloths, doing little more than covering the penis, but whether they kept these on during sex is arguable.

According to one legend dating back to the second century AD, King Minos of Crete was the victim of a curse that made his semen contain scorpions and snakes. He is said to have used a goat's bladder to keep his sexual partners safe, but that was probably as a female pessary rather than a male condom.

After the fall of the Roman empire, there seems to be no reference to contraception in Europe until the Middle Ages, when a few references appear about soaking the penis in tar or soaking it in onion juice to lessen the chance of conception.

The first clear reference to a condom appears in a treatise on syphilis, *De morbo Gallico*, written by Gabriele Falloppio (after whom the

Fallopian tube is named), which was published in 1564. His condoms were linen sheaths soaked in a chemical solution, left to dry, then attached to the penis with a ribbon. Falloppio claimed they were his own invention. Even then, however, the condom was seen as a device to guard against syphilis rather than contraception. The first definite reference to condoms being used to prevent pregnancy did not appear until 1655.

408. Why do females have orgasms?

The biological function of the male orgasm is easy to explain: men need to spread their seed to have a chance of procreating. Why females have orgasms, however, is less easy to explain. There are essentially three theories:

(i) It's part of the pair-bonding process: a good orgasm helps females select a suitable mate and bonds the male and female together to ensure that an offspring has two parents.

(ii) Female orgasms involve uterine contractions that help suck sperm into the uterus.

(iii) Female orgasms actually serve no functional purpose but are an evolutionary by-product of male orgasm. The erectile and nervous tissue necessary for female orgasm is effectively the same as the sperm delivery system in men and is no more use than male nipples, which are a similar evolutionary by-product.

Which of these is correct is hotly disputed.

409. Do poor and hungry men prefer women with bigger breasts?

Two interesting studies on men's preferences in female breast size were reported in 2013. The first study was conducted on men of varying socioeconomic status in Malaysia. The men were shown figures of women with varying breast size and the results revealed that the lower the economic status of the subject, the bigger the breasts he preferred. The second study showed the same female figures to men in Britain, but this time the difference between the subjects was that one group had recently been fed while the others had not eaten for some time.

The results this time showed that hungry men like bigger breasts.

The researchers suggested that the results showed that men's attractiveness ratings were influenced by resource security: poor and hungry men see larger breasts as a source of security.

Earlier research, however, had suggested that preference for larger female breasts was associated with tendencies to be sexist, to objectify women and to be hostile towards women. So an alternative explanation of the Malaysian result could be that men who are lower on a socioeconomic scale are more likely to be sexist.

410. Do aphrodisiacs work?

Scientific studies on the effects of items claimed as aphrodisiacs are almost unanimous in their view that they do not have a significant physiological effect to support the claims. They also agree that even if such items did have a genuine effect, it would be far less than the psychological results given by a placebo effect.

Cucumbers and bananas, sometimes touted as aphrodisiacs, probably owe their reputation to their similarity in shape to a penis. Avocados even take their name from an Aztec word for testicles. Chillies and Spanish fly may irritate the urinary tract, which may feel like sexual arousal.

More promisingly, in 2005 researchers in Miami and Naples announced to the American Chemical Society the results of a study of oysters and other bivalve molluscs. This included the discovery of two amino acids which had previously been found to trigger the production of the sex hormones testosterone in male rats and progesterone in female rats.

However, the research on the rats involved injecting the amino acids directly into their bloodstream, and it is not known if humans eating them would have a similar effect. The quantities involved are also so small that we would expect to have to eat a lot of oysters to have any noticeable effect. So perhaps Casanova's recommendation of fifty oysters for breakfast had some sense to it after all.

See also ANIMALS 17, 19; BABOONS 40; BEES 45; BIOLOGY 62; BONES 72; CHEESE 94; CHOCOLATE 105; DINOSAURS 137; FISH 190; INTELLIGENCE 254; MONKEYS 318; MUSIC 329; SQUID 447

SEX DIFFERENCES

411. Are women better than men at multitasking?

There has long been a popular belief that women are better than men at multitasking, but is this really true or has it arisen simply because women are more often seen to be responsible for doing more than one thing at the same time? Until recently, very little research had been done on this. Indeed, the word 'multitask' was first seen only in 1965, when it was used not of humans but of computers. In 2013, however, a study appeared which was reported to show that women are indeed better at multitasking than men, though that statement was heavily qualified.

The word 'multitasking' can be used in either of two senses: doing two or more things at the same time, or dealing with multiple demands while not necessarily having to do more than one at any given moment. The research supported the notion that women are better than men at the second type but not the first. They concluded: 'More research on this question is urgently needed, before we can draw stronger conclusions and before we can differentiate between different explanations.'

Four years earlier, in 2009, a study in China had also reported that women were better at multitasking but warned that their tests might not reflect real-life multitasking. They also advised that further research was required. A Swedish study in 2013, however, found that men actually outperformed women at handling multiple tasks simultaneously, with the performance gap being correlated to the female menstrual cycle.

Meanwhile, a study in France in 2009 reported that the structure of our brains' frontal lobes stops us from doing more than two things at the same time anyway, while a study in the USA in 2014 reported that only 2 per cent of people can truly multitask, in the sense of doing two things at the same time without it affecting performance at either of them.

412. Is there an innate difference between male and female brains?

Opinions on this question differ dramatically, and each side can advance strong arguments in support of its cause.

On the one hand, it is known that hormones have a strong effect on brain development. Boy babies are exposed to much higher levels of testosterone in the womb than girl babies, which may lead to greater analytic skills but lower social skills. On the other hand, differences between males and females are not consistent across cultures, which would suggest they are culturally influenced rather than innate. Also, maps of the neural connections in women's brains display a very different pattern from those in men's, but that distinction only begins to appear several years after birth, which is another argument for environment and conditioning rather than innate differences. A classic experiment in support of the innateness side, however, involved offering Barbary macaque monkeys the choice between dolls or toy trucks. The girls took the dolls; the boys favoured the trucks.

I once asked some psychologist friends, all of whom had young children, whether their personal experiences as parents supported or clashed with their academic views on this question. They all laughed and said that while their academic view was that boys' and girls' brains are innately the same, their own experience confirmed an innate difference. One mother of a boy and a girl, who had resolutely tried to bring them up unisex, said that when they went into the garden and found a stick, the boy used it as a weapon while the girl cuddled it. 'There is no doubt', said another, 'there is a gun receptor on the Y chromosome.'

The evidence seems to suggest that we may start with small innate differences, which are then exaggerated hugely by culture and upbringing.

SHAKESPEARE

413. Why did Shakespeare use the word 'all' less frequently than his contemporaries?

A study in 2013 of word frequencies in the plays of William Shakespeare, Thomas Middleton, Ben Jonson and John Fletcher revealed that Shakespeare used the word 'all' significantly less frequently than his contemporaries, but he used 'will' as a noun more frequently than the others.

Jonson was the writer who most often used the word 'any'; Fletcher had a fondness for 'have'; while Middleton liked 'master', 'gentleman' and 'widow' more than the other writers.

Middleton's city comedies may account for his extensive use of his favourites, but why Shakespeare kept away from the word 'all' is difficult to explain.

414. Did William Shakespeare love his wife?

We know very little about the relationship between Shakespeare and Anne Hathaway. They married when he was eighteen and she was twenty-six; they had their first child, Susanna, six months later; she stayed living in Stratford while he went to work as a playwright in London; and when he died, he left her his second-best bed. The rest of their life together – or apart – raises far more questions than answers.

Presumably it was Anne's pregnancy which led to the hurried marriage, but was it so hurried that a registrar got her name wrong when the banns were announced? One record in the Episcopal Register names the woman to marry Shakespeare as Anne Whateley. Was this another woman whom Shakespeare really wanted to marry before Ms Hathaway told him she was pregnant, or was it just a mistake? It has even been suggested that Anne Hathaway was a widow who had previously married a man named Whateley.

When Shakespeare, after about seven years' marriage to Anne, went to London, did she come to visit? How often did he return to Stratford to see her? Was it a separation or just a necessary business arrangement?

And was that 'second-best bed' line in his will just an innocent bequest or a piece of posthumous rudeness? It has been suggested that a wife would have been entitled to a sizeable portion of the estate, so the bed could have been just an extra loving touch. The bulk of the estate mentioned in the will, which must have included the best bed, went to his daughter.

415. How much of *Cardenio* did Shakespeare write?

In May 1613 Shakespeare's theatre company, The King's Men, performed a set of six plays at court including one called *The History of Cardenio*, based on a section in Cervantez' *Don Quixote*, which had first been translated into English in 1612. The company performed the same play later the same year for the ambassador of the Duke of Savoy, but it seems not to have been published at the time and all manuscripts of it have been lost.

In 1653 *Cardenio* was registered for publication and the authors were given as William Shakespeare and John Fletcher, which is very plausible as they had worked together before, notably on the play *Henry VIII*. If the play had survived, no doubt scholars would still be arguing about which parts were by Shakespeare and which by Fletcher. Instead, all we are left with is a trail of clues which have further complicated the matter.

In 1727 the playwright and Shakespearean editor Lewis Theobold announced that he had found the missing *Cardenio* manuscript and improved it to produce his own play *The Double Falsehood*. The manuscript Theobold claimed to have found is said to have been left in the Covent Garden Playhouse in London, which burnt down in 1808. There is no record of anyone else ever seeing the manuscript.

To confuse the issue still further, a play called *The Second Maiden's*

Tragedy, dating from 1611 and known only in manuscript, has also been claimed to have strong connections with *Cardenio*. The manuscript bears no author's name, but it also takes its theme from *Don Quixote* and is generally thought to have been written by Thomas Middleton. In 1994, however, a handwriting expert identified the calligraphy as Shakespeare's hand.

We are left with a play by Theobold allegedly based on a manuscript by Fletcher and Shakespeare, which may itself have had its origin in a play by Middleton copied out by the Bard. Extensive computer analyses have been performed to try to identify the parts of all this that are genuine Shakespeare, but how much credence can be placed on the results is unclear.

See also MURDER 323; THEATRE 453

SHARKS

416. How long do great white sharks live?

Telling the age of sharks is notoriously difficult. Attempts have been made by counting growth bands in their vertebrae, but it is not even known if these bands are deposited annually. Sharks in captivity are also known to have a considerably shorter lifespan than in the wild, so little useful information on longevity is gained from studying them. Tracking sharks for long periods has also proved difficult as they cover such large areas, though this has improved a little with the use of satellite data and GPS tracking.

Until very recently, estimates for the lifespan of great white sharks varied between just under thirty years and about forty. In 2013, however, a new technique involving radiocarbon dating indicated that great whites might live much longer than had been thought.

The new method is based on comparing radiocarbon values in the vertebrae of sharks with chronologies documenting the marine uptake of a radioactive carbon isotope produced by atmospheric testing of thermonuclear devices. Measurements on four male and four female sharks from the north-west Atlantic produced estimates of forty years of age for the largest female and seventy years for the largest male. If those figures are correct, some male sharks might be expected to reach the age of 100 or more.

SHEEP

417. Do sheep put on weight when they die?

In 1901 Dr Duncan MacDougal of Massachusetts conducted a bizarre experiment to determine the weight of a human soul. His idea was to weigh six patients just before and after the moment of death. The difference would be the weight of the soul, which had departed the body at the moment of death. In charge of a ward for terminally ill tuberculosis patients, he recognized when they were only two hours from death, then moved their beds onto an industrial scale.

Dr MacDougal discounted five of the six experiments because of 'technical difficulties', but the other patient, who was the first of the series, was found to have lost three-quarters of an ounce at the moment of death. MacDougal therefore proudly announced that three-quarters of an ounce was the weight of the human soul. He later performed the same experiment on dogs, for which he detected no weight loss. He took that as evidence supporting the belief that dogs have no souls.

In 2001 Lewis Hollander of Redmond, Oregon, repeated MacDougal's experiment, not on humans and dogs but on sheep and a goat. He reported that:

Twelve animals (one ram, seven ewes, three lambs and one goat)
were studied... At the moment of death an unexplained weight gain
transient of 18 to 780 grams for 1 to 6 seconds was observed with
seven adult sheep but not with the lambs or goat.

In other words, sheep gain weight when they die, but lose it again within a few seconds. Three possible explanations suggest themselves:
(i) Sheep's souls have a negative weight.
(ii) The cessation of, or change in, biomechanical processes at the moment of death may result in a small change in recorded weight.
(iii) Both MacDougal's and Hollander's experimental set-ups were insufficiently precise to measure what they claimed to.

The film *21 Grams*, directed by Alejandro González Iñárritu and made in 2003, was inspired by MacDougal's experiment. The title is the metric equivalent of his three-quarters of an ounce.

See also BIOLOGY 61; CAMELS 83; CANNIBALISM 88; DISEASE 144–5

SHELLFISH

418. Do crayfish worry?

Until 2014 crayfish were seen as ancient and simple creatures incapable of experiencing emotions. Then an experiment was reported that seemed to show there might be much more to them.

First, some crayfish were subjected to electric shocks for about twenty minutes to induce stress. Then they were placed in a cross-shaped tank in which two arms of the cross were brightly lit and two dark. The crayfish were seen to avoid the well-lit areas and instead stay in the dark.

Other crayfish that had not been given the electric shocks explored all areas of the cross-shaped tank, both light and dark. However, when these crayfish were injected with serotonin, they started behaving like the others, staying out of the lit areas. Serotonin is a neurotransmitter associated with anxiety in humans and the stressed crayfish were found to be producing it naturally. When they were treated with drugs used to treat anxiety in humans, their apparent fear of the well-lit areas disappeared.

The experiment does not show that crayfish get worried, but it certainly indicates that their responses to stress have many similarities with those of humans.

SHIPS

419. What happened to Captain Gray of the SS *Great Britain*?

In 1872 the captain of the most celebrated ship in the British merchant fleet disappeared. John Gray had been captain of the SS *Great Britain* for eighteen years. Six feet tall and weighing nearly seventeen stone, he was a huge man, very popular with his passengers and enjoying a reputation and record no other captain could match. While Brunel's ship was under his command, it took some 13,000 people from Britain to start a new life in Australia, as well as transporting a large number of convicts there.

On the night of 25 November 1872, while the ship was returning to Liverpool from Melbourne, Gray vanished. He had retired to his cabin early, complaining of pains in his bowels, which nobody took seriously as he had a reputation for being a bit of a hypochondriac. A steward checked on him later and found him writing a letter and, in the steward's words, 'as sensible as ever'. The next morning his cabin was found to be empty and Gray could not be discovered anywhere on board. The only clue was an open transom window in the lower saloon at the stern of the ship, which another steward had screwed shut the previous night.

The manner of his disappearance suggested suicide, but no good reasons to support that explanation have ever been given.

420. What happened to Sir Cloudesley Shovell?

Admiral of the fleet Sir Cloudesley Shovell (1650–1707) was one of the most successful ship's captains in a long career in the English navy and became a favourite of Queen Anne for his heroic victories.

In 1707, after an attack on Toulon which had ended in the French scuttling their own fleet, Shovell's ship HMS *Association* hit the rocks near the Scilly Isles and sank in only three or four minutes. None of the 800 men on board survived. Shovell's body was later found at Porthellick Cove in the Scillies, some seven miles from where the wreck took place, near the bodies of his two stepsons, suggesting that they had escaped from the *Association* in a lifeboat, but the manner of his death has become a subject of much debate and various legends.

According to one story, he reached the shore barely alive and was murdered by a woman for the emerald ring he was wearing. In 1709, two years after the disaster, it was reported that Shovell's body had first been found by two women, stripped of his shirt and with his emerald ring missing. Some thirty years later, a woman, on her deathbed, was reported to have confessed to a clergyman to having killed the admiral. She is said to have produced the ring, but there is no evidence of that. Another story – for which no evidence has ever been produced – was that a sailor on *Association* warned Shovell that they were off course and the admiral had him hanged for inciting mutiny.

Whatever happened to Sir Cloudesley Shovell, it had one good and lasting effect: a large prize was offered by the British government for a reliable method of calculating longitude, and it resulted in improvements in navigation that must have saved thousands.

421. Did poor communication sink the *Mary Rose*?

On 19 July 1545 Henry VIII's flagship the *Mary Rose* sank in the Solent. The only eyewitness account of the sinking reported that she was executing a tight turn when she was caught by a gust of wind, but various theories about contributory factors have been put forward.

The French claimed she had been hit by their cannon, but when the ship was finally raised in 1982, there was no evidence of that. Overloading, with soldiers or guns, has been suggested, but the ship had crossed the Channel successfully, so why should she sink in the comparatively calm Solent? A more likely explanation is that water rushed in through the open gun-ports on one side of the ship, an idea that has often been associated with possible human error by the captain. In 2008, however, a new theory emerged from a Canadian criminologist.

Lynne Bell had examined bones and teeth from human remains of the *Mary Rose* crew and was surprised to find that the evidence suggested that many of them were not British but may have been from Spain. 'The reason the *Mary Rose* sank', she said, 'is because there was very poor communication between the crew because you have this really large foreign contingent.' It wasn't so much a careless crew failing to close the gun-ports in the heat of battle as a foreign crew failing to understand their captain's order to do so.

422. What happened to the crew of *Kaz II*?

On 18 April 2007 a helicopter pilot flying over Australia's Great Barrier Reef spotted a catamaran apparently drifting and out of control. He reported it and the maritime authorities reached the boat, called *Kaz II*, and boarded it on 20 April. What they found was mystifying: everything about the boat seemed normal but there was no sign of the three-man crew. Food was set on a table, a computer was on, the engine was running, all the life jackets were in place and untouched, and all the emergency systems were in good working condition. The only sign of anything untoward was a big rip in one of the sails. A video camera was also found with footage of the crew close to the time they disappeared. The men looked relaxed and nothing out of the ordinary was recorded.

At a hearing to determine what had happened to the men, the state coroner said that the men must be presumed to have died but said that he 'cannot be so definitive about the circumstances in which the deaths occurred'. In his opinion, the most likely scenario was that one of the men had fallen overboard trying to deal with a problem with the fishing lure and the other two perished trying to save him.

No explanation was offered for what caused the rip in the sail, why nobody put on a life jacket or called for help over the radio, how it all happened when they were about to sit down for a meal, and why the engine was turned on. All three men were experienced and cautious sailors, and no plausible explanation of what happened to them has ever been given.

See also DOLPHINS 157; MEXICO 312; MICE 313; PREHISTORY 381; SCIENCE 403

SLEEP

423. Can birds sleep while they fly?

When birds are observed in their nests or at ground level, we can see that they sleep, but some birds remain on the wing for days or weeks or even longer. Can they sleep while they are flying? Birds, like mammals – as we mentioned when discussing ostriches and platypuses (→ 375) – exhibit two types of sleep: slow-wave sleep (SWS) and rapid eye movement (REM) sleep. The first of these may occur in both hemispheres of the brain at the same time, or in just one hemisphere. While each of a mammal's eyes is connected to both halves of the brain, a bird's left eye connects to its right brain and its right eye to its left brain. So a bird can, in theory, keep one eye open watching the sky while the other eye sleeps. REM sleep, however, can only occur in both halves of the brain at the same time and is usually accompanied by a loss of muscle tone, making it unlikely that this type of sleep is compatible with flying at all.

Until recently it was supposed that birds on the wing obtained enough rest from slow-wave sleep, alternating halves of the brain until they reached their destination, then recovering with an extensive REM sleep. In 2013, however, alpine swifts were tracked on a long migratory flight to Africa and thereafter, and it was found that they remained in the air for 200 days without touching down. Since their main diet is airborne insects, of which there are far more in Africa than in their northern summer residences, all the food they need is in the air. How they survive for 200 days without proper sleep will only be understood when electroencephalogram recording devices are developed that can monitor the birds' brains over long periods and long distances.

424. When did sleep begin in animal evolution?

From an evolutionary perspective, it is not easy to see why we, and all other mammals, sleep. There is no doubt that our bodies perform a number of essential recuperative functions while we sleep, such as repair of cells, consolidation of memories and restoration of energy, but why these functions demand a cessation of conscious activity is unknown.

While we sleep, the risk from predators and from being unaware of our surroundings would seem to be a great survival threat. Even some primitive organisms are known to exhibit circadian rhythms that make them alternate between periods of activity and periods of rest, and it seems likely that sleep evolved from these rest periods.

Mammalian sleep, to judge from electroencephalogram (EEG) readings, is far more complex than the sleep-like states of reptiles and fishes, but it is still difficult to see the evolutionary advantages of a period of total loss of consciousness or to tell whether early mammals exhibited our type of sleep or whether it developed much later. Perhaps sleep, as we know it, only arose when the mammalian brain had evolved sufficiently for it to design safe sleeping places.

425. Do centipedes sleep?

In 2014 the genome of a species of centipede was sequenced for the first time. *Strigamia maritima* is a venomous and carnivorous centipede found on the coast of the Moray Firth in Scotland, and is a representative of a group that evolved over half a billion years ago. Its genome indicates that it has no genes related to vision and must have lost its eyes at least 200 million years ago. It also has no genes relating to the circadian clock, which regulates an animal's sleep.

Since they live underground, these centipedes have no need for light receptors or eyes: this may explain the lack of a circadian clock, which usually relies on light input to tell day from night. But how the centipede sleeps, and indeed if it sleeps at all without a circadian clock to tell it when to do so, remain open questions.

426. Why does sleep deprivation provoke epileptic seizures?

A link between epilepsy and sleep deprivation has been suspected for well over 2,000 years. Around 400 BC Hippocrates advised sufferers from epilepsy to 'spend the day awake and the night asleep. If this habit be disturbed, it is not so good... worst of all when he sleeps neither night nor day.'

Over the past fifty years a great deal of research has been done on the subject, but we still cannot claim to understand the nature of the link. Some epileptics seem to have seizures predominantly while asleep or at the point of falling asleep or waking. Some people have had their only epileptic seizure when sleep-deprived. In others, the occurrence of seizures seems to have no connection with their sleep cycle.

Since sleep deprivation is also usually caused by a disorder, it could be that the same disorder is responsible for triggering the seizure directly, rather than the seizure being caused by the sleep deprivation. Sleep certainly results in changed electrical activity in the brain, and changed electrical activity is strongly associated with epileptic seizures, but the precise connection between the two is still unknown.

427. Do women need more sleep than men?

Over the past few years many pieces have appeared in both academic journals and the popular press claiming to compare the amount men sleep and the amount women sleep. Some say that men sleep more; others say that women sleep more. The *United Kingdom 2000 Time Use Survey* reported that women sleep longer, particularly in the 30–60 age group. A survey in the USA in 2005, however, reported that women do sleep longer than men but complain more about their sleep quality. Other reports say that women spend longer in bed, but take longer to get to sleep, and when they do, the sleep is more disturbed, all of which results in them actually sleeping less than men. More recently, there have been claims that women need more sleep than men, whether they get it or not.

The vast majority of all this is anecdotal, or at best speculative, but a clear suggestion of a possible difference in quality of male and female sleep came in a study of physiological stress in 2013. Based on research at the University of California, it measured blood levels of C-reactive protein (CRP), which is known to rise in response to inflammation. The research showed that the strongest single factor correlating with an increase in CRP for women was their taking longer than half an hour to fall asleep at night. The conclusion was that women are not only more likely than men to suffer from insomnia, but also more likely to suffer the effects of physiological stress associated with it.

428. What is the function of REM sleep?

We have already discussed rapid eye movement (REM) sleep briefly in the context of platypuses (→ 375) and birds (→ 423), but the real function of REM sleep is still a puzzle. Shortly after it was first identified in 1953, REM sleep was thought to be strongly associated with dreaming. Subjects woken up when they began the characteristic rapid eye fluttering tended to report strong memories of dreams they had been having. Later, the dreaming–REM connection was found to be weaker as non-REM dreaming was also found to exist. REM sleep, however, still seems to be accompanied by more vivid and lifelike dreams.

Adults spend 20 to 25 per cent of their sleeping time in REM sleep; the figure is higher in infants. We have four or five sleep cycles a night, each with a few minutes of REM sleep. People with depression have less REM sleep than others; we are more likely to snore during REM sleep; the activity of the brain's neurons is more intense, but the body stops releasing the neurotransmitters that are responsible for stimulating our motor neurons and our muscles become paralysed.

Even with such physiological effects identified, however, we cannot really claim to understand what the function of REM sleep is. One theory is that REM sleep is the period during which our brains consolidate memories. Another idea is that it is when our brains repair themselves and build the neural connections that are essential for conceptual thought and creativity. This may help explain why infants have longer periods of REM sleep as their brains grow and develop.

Because our brains are so active during REM sleep, it is sometimes called 'paradoxical sleep', but we need to know much more before all its paradoxes are resolved.

429. Why do some animals sleep longer than others?

Giant armadillos sleep for around eighteen hours a day. Some species of bats sleep for almost twenty hours. Lions sleep for nearly fourteen hours, humans and rabbits both sleep around eight hours, but cows get by on four hours and horses manage on less than three. So what is responsible for these wide variations?

The size of an animal, the amount of time it spends eating, its brain size as a percentage of body size, its metabolic rate and its risk from predators have all been suggested as factors determining how much sleep it gets. The time spent in short naps rather than one long sleep may also play a role. Some studies have suggested that an animal's evolutionary past may play a highly significant part, but we have too little evidence of the sleeping patterns of long-extinct animals to be sure.

See also BIOLOGY 59; BRAINS 79; DREAMS 160–1; HYPNOSIS 246; LEMURS 272; MEDICINE 300; PHILOSOPHY 359; PLATYPUSES 375

SLOTHS

430. From which ground sloth species did three-toed sloths evolve?

Until around 10,000 years ago, giant sloths roamed South America. The fossil record has now revealed over 100 genera of giant sloths since the first skeleton was discovered in 1796. Now the only species that remain are the two-toed *Choloepus* and the three-toed *Bradypus*.

A detailed analysis of the bones of ancient and modern sloths has indicated that *Choloepus* is allied with extinct members of the family Megalonychidae, but where *Bradypus* came from is far more difficult to say. The results of the analysis suggested that the split between the two varieties of modern sloth may date back 40 million years, with *Choloepus* evolving from known species of giant sloth, with whom *Bradypus* probably had an unknown common ancestor even further back. The habit of hanging upside down in rainforest canopies, which the much larger ground sloths were of course too big to do, would then have evolved independently in each species.

431. How fast could a giant ground sloth run?

Modern sloths, as their name suggests, are very slow at moving around on the ground. Their front and hind legs have evolved to make them perfectly designed for hanging upside down from branches in the forest canopy and when necessary scampering along in the same upside-down position. At ground level the best they can do is drag themselves along slowly with their front claws, but that was not always the case.

The giant ground sloth was about the size of an elephant and is thought to have walked around rather like a bear, either on all fours or on its hind legs. Having little or nothing to run away from, it seems to have been built more for stability than speed, with thick bones in its short hind legs and its thick tail giving it a low centre of gravity. Its front legs were long and strong for both weight-bearing and stretching to help it strip vegetation from high branches of trees.

The giant sloth's large claws would have meant that it had to turn its feet inwards to walk, and while some examples of fossil footprints confirm that they sometimes walked bipedally, the prints are not far enough apart to suggest that they were running. What speed these animals did or could move at remains unknown.

432. Why do sloths have orange patches on their backs?

One of the many projects at the Sloth Sanctuary of Costa Rica is to try to discover why male three-toed sloths have evolved bright yellow or orange patches on their backs. The patch, known as a speculum, begins to develop around the age of three as the sloth reaches sexual maturity. The patch is divided by a central black stripe and other black markings that are unique to each sloth. Unlike the rest of the sloth's fur, the orange patch has no algae growing in it, and it has a different texture from its other hair. It is also covered with an oily secretion which, when rubbed off, takes the yellow or orange pigment with it.

Whether the patch has some significance in mate selection is unknown, but with the rest of the animal so well camouflaged against the rainforest background, it seems very odd to display a bright patch of orange.

433. Why do three-toed sloths poo on the ground?

Three-toed sloths climb down from their trees once a week to urinate and defecate on the ground, then slowly climb back up again. Some two-toed sloths do the same, but others don't bother to make the energy-consuming climb but just let their bodily waste fall downwards through the tree.

In 2014 a link was established between a sloth's lavatorial habits and its nutrition. Sloth fur is covered in algae and moths. When the sloth relieved itself on the ground, moths were found to lay eggs in its poo, and when the eggs hatched, the newborn moths would hop back into the sloth's fur. Sloths' stomachs were also found to contain samples of nutritional algae which they had presumably licked from their fur. The tree-climbing habit gave the three-toed sloths a higher concentration of moths than their two-toed, poo-where-you-hang cousins; more moths correlated with a greater concentration of nitrogen, and more nitrogen meant more algae to lick.

On the other hand, climbing down a tree represents an immense expenditure of energy for the sloth. Whether it represents a greater expenditure of energy to climb a tree with only two toes is unknown, but that could, perhaps, tip the balance and be the reason why *Choloepus* stays hanging in the canopy while *Bradypus* makes the long trip down on poo-days.

434. How do sloths communicate?

We know very little about how sloths communicate with one another or how often they do it. Generally they are very solitary creatures; some mutual grooming has been observed, but only between mothers and infants. Although they are usually silent, sloths sometimes emit sounds. An infant separated from its mother will emit a loud bleat which may last around a minute. A defensive hiss has also been noted, though their distress call is low-pitched, which ties in with a finding that the sloth's ear picks up low-frequency sounds best.

Little research seems to have been done into the range of sloth sounds or what they may mean, but these animals must have some sort of communication. In 2012 a male sloth named Leander arrived in London from Germany in the hope that he would mate with London Zoo's resident female Marilyn. In 2013 zoo-keepers announced with some astonishment that Marilyn was pregnant. Not only had the keepers not known that they had mated, but they did not even think the pair had acknowledged each other's existence.

See also AVOCADOS 37

SMELL

435. Why do we like some smells and not others?

It is undeniable that people's reactions to smells differ. Some people may quite enjoy a smell that others find repulsive. Even the smell that a skunk emits in defence is liked by some people.

People's abilities to detect certain smells also differ and such traits are determined genetically, but until recently our smell preferences were widely thought to be formed through culture and experience. In 2014, however, research at Duke University, North Carolina, indicated that our personal smell preferences depend on some extremely fine tuning of our amino acids. Around 400 genes are known that code for smells, and the difference of a single amino acid on a single gene can lead to a difference in our smell perception. By comparing the scent receptors of different people and seeing their reactions to a variety of odour molecules, the researchers found that the receptors of any two individuals differ by about 30 per cent.

The conclusion is that we are born with the potential specifically to like or dislike particular smells. What we don't know is how our personal smell preference profile emerges in the first place, and what the connection is between the sensory perception of a smell and the emotional appreciation of it.

436. How does the smell of a queen bee influence the behaviour of others in the hive?

A queen bee emits a substance known as queen mandibular pheromone (QMP), which is a cocktail of pheromones that have different effects on members of the hive. About a week after hatching, the queen goes on a mating flight during which she passes through colonies of drones (though we do not know how she finds them) where her QMP attracts them to fly after her. Back in the hive, they queue up politely awaiting their turn to mate with her, then drop off her and die shortly after. Once mating has been completed, the QMP starts performing its second main function, which is to suppress the reproductive systems of the workers in the hive, thereby ensuring that the queen is the only reproductive female.

Identification of the chemicals in QMP has allowed it to be synthesized, and when the synthetic version is sprayed in the hive, it has been seen to achieve the same effects, even when the queen is absent. Precisely how the chemicals achieve their results is unknown.

See also ANATOMY 4; ASPARAGUS 26; BRAINS 75; CATS 90; CHEMICALS 95; COFFEE 110; DOGS 149; EBOLA 165; FOOD 195; GENETICS 210; NOSES 342, 345; OCTOPUSES 347; POLAR BEARS 377; SALMON 399

SNAILS

437. Are left-handed snails better off than right-handed snails?

Most snails in South-east Asia are right-handed. That is to say, their shells coil in a clockwise direction. This can make life difficult for left-handed snails, for mating between left-handed and right-handed snails is very difficult, if not impossible. There is, however, one big potential advantage conveyed by left-handedness for a snail, which was found by examining the teeth of a group of snakes known as pareatids.

Being quite partial to an occasional mouthful of snail, these snakes have evolved in a manner that is best suited to extract a snail from a right-handed shell. Their tooth arrangements and hunting strategies both find southpaw snails trickier. Research has confirmed that there are, in fact, higher proportions of left-handed snails in regions with the highest populations of pareatid snakes.

What gave rise to the preponderance of right-handed snails in the first place, however, is not known. Nor is it known how long it will take for specialist left-handed-snail-eating snakes to evolve.

438. Does chocolate improve the memory of snails?

In 2012 researchers at the University of Calgary performed an interesting experiment on two groups of snails. The snails in one group were put in ordinary pond water; those in the other group were placed in pond water to which the flavonoid epicatechin, which is present in chocolate, had been added.

The snails then underwent thirty-minute training sessions to teach them to keep their breathing tubes closed in deoxygenated water. Snails usually breathe through their skins, but when oxygen levels are low, they stick their breathing tubes above the surface of the water to increase the oxygen supply. For this experiment, the researchers tapped the snail's breathing tube if the snail tried to open it above the water. The snails therefore quickly learnt to keep their breathing tubes shut.

The next day the snails were put back in the deoxygenated water to see if they remembered the lesson. In general, the snails that had been in normal pond water did not remember the lesson but stuck their breathing tubes out of the water to breath, but the snails in the epicatechin-spiked water kept their breathing tubes closed.

Later experiments concluded that chocolate does not improve memory in humans, but the result on snails has been neither confirmed nor contradicted.

SNAKES

439. Are snakes right-handed?

Talking of handedness in creatures that have no hands may sound strange, but research published in 1999 suggested that garter snakes are not totally symmetric and may prefer one side of their body to the other.

Male snakes possess one testis, one hemipenis and one kidney on each side of its body and these are not symmetric. In particular, the right hemipenis and testis are both larger than their counterparts on the left. When garter snakes mate, only one hemipenis enters the female and the males tend to alternate between them. There are advantages in using the right, however, particularly at the conclusion of mating, when the male deposits a gelatinous 'mating plug' that prevents, or at least delays, the female from mating with any other snake. It may therefore be of evolutionary advantage for the male to prefer his right side as it would give a better chance of procreation.

At high body temperatures the male was also found to prefer using the right hemipenis when mating, which the researchers suggest may have something to do with the ability to make 'subtle postural adjustments'. They conclude, however, that their inferences are speculative:

> We have no direct evidence to show that a larger hemipenis... is actually a more effective copulatory device than a smaller unit. The nonrandom patterns in hemipenis usage suggest that the asymmetry is not a trivial one, however, and further work to clarify these issues would be of great interest.

See also BIRDS 64; PANGOLINS 356; PREHISTORY 382; PSYCHOLOGY 386; RELIGION 395; SEX 407; SNAILS 437

SOCRATES

440. Was Plato's account of Socrates' death honest?

When the Greek philosopher Socrates was found guilty both of corrupting the minds of the youth of Athens and of not believing in the gods of the state, he was condemned to death by drinking hemlock. His pupil Plato, in his dialogue *Phaedo*, gives a touching account of Socrates' willingness to take the poison and accept his death, but there has long been argument over whether this account was factual or a fictional romanticization of what happened.

After Socrates had taken the poison, Plato tells of a numbness slowly creeping over him from the feet upwards, with the philosopher remaining calm and lucid until it reached his heart and killed him. This has long been criticized, however, as it is not how hemlock works at all. Hemlock is a neurotoxin which attacks the central nervous system and leads to a very gruesome and nasty end. Defenders of Plato, on the other hand, argue that the effects of hemlock were well known in ancient Greece and it would have made no sense for Plato to tell anything other than the truth. Furthermore, the word 'hemlock' may then have been used for a wide variety of drugs.

Experts from the world of medicine have generally been critical of Plato's account, while experts on the Greek language have sprung to his defence. We shall probably never know the truth.

SOLAR SYSTEM

441. Why does the minor planet Chariklo have rings?

Until 2013 the only bodies in the Solar System known to have ring systems were the large planets Saturn, Jupiter, Uranus and Neptune. Then a fifth ring system was found around the minor planet Chariklo, which orbits the Sun between Saturn and Uranus. Chariklo has an estimated diameter of about 250 km, which had been thought far too small to support a ring system. The rings consist of two bright, narrow bands about 7 and 3 km wide, separated by a distance of about 9 km.

They orbit Chariklo at a distance of about 400 km, but what they are, how they got there and how long they are likely to stay there have all yet to be ascertained.

Since the gravitational pull of Chariklo is thought to be too weak to hold the rings in place for more than a few million years, either they are very young or they are held in place by so-called 'shepherd moons', which have not yet been discovered. The likeliest cause of such rings is that they are debris from a collision, but whether it was something colliding with Chariklo, or with an unknown moon of Chariklo which possibly no longer exists, is unknown.

In 2015 it was announced that Chiron, an even smaller minor planet, is also suspected of having a ring system.

442. Why is there a rapid fall-off in astronomical objects in the Kuiper Belt after a certain distance?

After Pluto was discovered in 1930, orbiting the Sun at a greater distance than any of the previously discovered planets, astronomers began to speculate about what else might be out there. In 1951 the Netherlands-born US astronomer Gerard Kuiper suggested the existence of a disc of objects in the outer regions of the Solar System. Many of his assumptions were later shown to be incorrect, but when such a region of small bodies was later confirmed, it was given the name Kuiper Belt. Consisting mainly of comets, it is thought to contain more than 100,000 objects greater than 100 km in diameter in a region between 30,000 and 50,000 astronomical units (AU) from the Sun. Since one AU is the distance from the Earth to the Sun, that is a very long way out.

Over 1,000 large Kuiper Belt objects have now been discovered, but once we get beyond 50 AU from the Sun, the number suddenly falls off. This distance is known as the Kuiper Cliff, and none of the theories of how the Kuiper Belt was formed accounts for it. The rapid decline is known not to be caused by observational bias. The most likely suggestions are that material at that distance was too scattered to form large objects, or that something happened to remove or destroy such objects as were formed. The only other suggestion is that the gravitational pull of an undiscovered massive object has rid the region of material.

443. Did the Earth collide with a planet known as Theia in the early Solar System?

The fact that the Moon's orbit around the Earth always keeps the same side facing us supports the view that the Earth and the Moon were once a single body. This theory goes on to suggest that the Earth collided with an astronomical body the size of Mars about 4.5 billion years ago, which was very early in the life of the Solar System. That hypothetical body has been given the name Theia, after the Greek Titan who gave birth to the Moon goddess Selene.

The impact, if it happened, is supposed to have destroyed Theia, one part of which merged with the Earth, another with part of the Earth which broke away to form the Moon, and another that spun off into space. While some comparisons between the composition of the Earth and the Moon support the suggestion that they were once together, other measurements are difficult to reconcile with the 'giant impact hypothesis', as it is known.

A major problem in assessing the truth of the hypothesis is that the same findings have often been interpreted either in support or in opposition to it. Differences in Moon rocks and Earth composition are cited by some as evidence that they were never the same body, while others see it as evidence that Theia contributed the un-Earthly parts of the Moon. Equally, similarities between the Earth and the Moon may be seen either as evidence that they were once together or as evidence of an absence of any contribution by Theia.

444. What is the probability that the Sun will rise tomorrow?

In the eighteenth century, the French mathematician Pierre-Simon Laplace raised this question as an early example of applied probability theory. His approach to the problem was to apply his 'rule of succession', which was a way of modifying one's initial expectations after subsequent observations. If we have seen one sunrise, we may be open-minded about whether the Sun will rise again tomorrow, but when it continues rising day after day, we become more certain that it will rise tomorrow. Taking a creationist reading of the Bible, which put the age of the Earth at 6,000 years, Laplace calculated that we had had about 6,000 x 365 = 2,190,000 sunrises, so he estimated the chance of the Sun rising tomorrow as 2,190,001/2,190,002 = 0.9999995.

With our modern scientific knowledge, however, we might insist on a different means of calculating. We could, for example, ask what would stop the Sun rising. Since what we see as sunrise is caused simply by the Earth's rotation on its axis, the only reasons the Sun wouldn't rise would be the Sun blowing up or the Earth ceasing to rotate. The latter could only happen if something very large collided with the Earth before morning, which we think is not going to happen. But we may have missed something. What are the chances that something very large slipped past the Hubble telescope without our noticing? What are the chances that our entire theory of astronomy since Newton is all hopelessly wrong and the Sun is going to explode before tomorrow? Is our faith in the development of scientific knowledge subject to the same rule of succession as Laplace's probability calculations?

Working out the probability of the Sun rising tomorrow is not as easy as it may seem.

See also COMETS 113; ENERGY 174; INTELLIGENCE 253; MARS 285; MILKY WAY 315–17; VENUS 479

SPIDERS

445. How do spiders find their way home at night?

The male Namib Desert spider goes for long walks at night searching for females and always finds its way home. How it navigates, however, is unclear. Research in 2003 showed that they can wander long distances in erratic paths over featureless dune surfaces, then walk back in a straight line to their burrows.

Further research in 2007 showed that they do not use their sense of smell to find their way home, but computer-tracking in 2012 reported that they make learning walks on exiting their burrows. By making stereotyped movements in an unfamiliar area, they seem to learn the appearance of their home. But we still don't know how they tell one patch of sand from another or how they unerringly navigate their way home from a distance.

See also CHIMPANZEES 98; MERCURY 303

SPORT

446. How do we decide how to catch a ball?

How does a fielder in cricket or baseball decide how to run in order to catch a ball? Several researchers have attempted to answer this question by tracking the movements of sportsmen trying to make a catch. Their experiments have reached a surprising conclusion: what sportsmen do is run at a speed and along a path that keeps the acceleration of the tangent of the angle of elevation of gaze to the ball equal to zero.

This strategy will not tell the fielder where or when the ball will land, or send him on an optimal trajectory to intercept it, but it will take him on a path that ensures that he runs through the place where the ball is at catching height at the moment when the ball arrives there. Specifically, what the fielder does is wait about half a second watching the ball, then start to run, accelerating until the acceleration of the tangent of the angle of elevation of gaze to the ball is equal to zero – in other words, until the rate of change of the tangent of the angle is constant. Only in the final moments will the fielder change strategy, but he will then be in the right position to catch the ball.

This is all very surprising, because most of the subjects in the experiment would probably not know their tangent from their cosine, let alone know how to measure its rate of change. Clearly, when we run to catch a ball, our brains are making complex calculations, but they are not telling us what they are.

See also DOGS 154; TENNIS 451

SQUID

447. How do squid get pregnant?

Well, a girl squid finds a boy squid whom she really likes, and then... it all gets a bit complicated, because squid sex is one of the most mysterious things in the animal world. One thing that makes it unusual is that the female does not have a vagina. Another is that the male's penis does not touch the female. Instead, the penis extrudes needle-like structures called spermatophores into its own body. It then reaches in with one of its arms, called a hectocotylus, to retrieve the spermatophores which it places on or inside the female's body. The spermatophores then ejaculate, leaving a sticky substance called spermatangium on the female skin. Sometimes, the spermatangium seems to burrow its way into the skin.

What happens next is up to the female squid, for she keeps the spermatangia in special receptacles until she is ready to fertilize an egg. She may even store the spermatangia of a number of different males, then select which she wants to use. However, the sperm in a spermatangium must first migrate to parts called spermathecae before it can be used to fertilize an egg.

Nobody knows how the female chooses which of her stored sperm to use for fertilization, or how she gets it to the egg, or whether she uses the spermatangia or the spermathecae. The fact is that no female squid has ever been observed at the task of sperm-picking or sperm-moving, so it is even possible that the sperm makes its own way to the egg.

See also WHALES 490

SQUIRRELS

448. Why do squirrels approach rattlesnakes?

In California the greatest threat to ground squirrels is posed by rattlesnakes. So why, when a squirrel sees a rattlesnake, does it walk straight towards it and hold its tail high?

Observations of squirrel–snake interactions show that rattlesnakes are often deterred from striking a squirrel when it performs its tail-flagging display. It is also liable to leave the area and try its luck elsewhere. It could be that the rattlesnake has learnt that its chances of catching a squirrel are far greater if the squirrel has not seen it, so the display may be taken as meaning 'I know you're there and I'm ready to run away if you come a step closer'. The tail-flagging may also serve as a warning signal to other squirrels, which may be what persuades the rattlesnake to try somewhere else. All the same, walking up to your greatest enemy and waving your tail still seems a rather dangerous policy.

SUICIDE

449. Did Jeremiah Clarke toss a coin before committing suicide?

Jeremiah Clarke (1674–1707) was organist at the Chapel Royal and one of England's leading composers. He is most famous for his 'Prince of Denmark's March', commonly known as the 'Trumpet Voluntary'. He is also well known for an often-repeated story about his suicide in 1707.

The tale, as recounted by the eighteenth-century musical historians Sir John Hawkins and Dr Richard Burney, tells of Clarke 'falling into a hopeless passion for a lady of high position' who was 'so far above his own social station as to remain forever unattainable'. As a result, he fell into a state of melancholy and resolved to kill himself. After riding to a field where he saw a pond, he is said to have been quite unable to decide whether to hang himself or drown himself, so he tossed a coin. The coin landed on its side in the mud, so he went home and shot himself.

Clarke definitely shot himself at his home, but the indecision and coin-tossing may be a romantic embellishment of the story. According to a contemporary account, he apparently spent the day very 'Chearful and Merry' at home, where he was visited by his father and friends and was 'Playing on his Musick for a considerable time'. After his father left, however, he went to his room and later the fatal shot was heard.

See also BIOLOGY 57; SHIPS 419; TERMITES 452

TECHNOLOGY

450. How did the ancient Egyptians put their obelisks up?

The Egyptian obelisks represent one of the major technological feats of the ancient world. From 2300 to 1300 BC they erected around a hundred of these massive monuments. From a square base, they were made with a single piece of stone, tapering upwards to the top which was usually surmounted with a small pyramid shape. Some were over 30 metres (100 ft) high and weighed almost 500 tons. Unfinished or fallen obelisks of over 1,000 tons have also been discovered. The standing obelisks were not embedded in the ground, but simply stood on their bases, and some are still standing after 4,000 years.

Various theories have been suggested concerning how these structures were erected. Some have suggested that elephants may have been used, which is very unlikely as elephants were not known in Egypt at the time, and cow-power has also been proposed, but it is generally thought that humans must have done most of the pulling.

In the 1990s attempts were made, for a US TV series, to emulate the ancient Egyptians by erecting a 25-ton obelisk using only technology available to the ancient world. The first two attempts, in 1994 and 1999, ended in failure. The third attempt involved dragging the obelisk up a gravel-and-stone ramp. In the middle of the ramp a pit was dug and filled with dry sand. By pulling on ropes tied to the obelisk, it was dragged into the pit and lifted, then the sand in the pit was slowly removed.

Modern technology was used for some of the process, but experiments convinced the late twentieth-century obelisk-erectors that it could have been done using manpower alone. That, however, was only a 25-ton obelisk. The Lateran Obelisk, now in Rome but originally erected at the Temple of Karnak, weighs 455 tons. Even with the almost unlimited manpower available to the Egyptian pharaohs, putting that up cannot have been easy.

See also COMPUTERS 116; HUMAN EVOLUTION 235; METEOROLOGY 308; SCIENCE 403; WINE 494

TENNIS

451. Are left-handers innately better than right-handers at tennis?

It has often been claimed that there are disproportionately many left-handers at the top of world tennis. One recent report even claimed that 40 per cent of top tennis players are left-handed, compared with only 12 per cent of the general population. If that is true (and some statistical surveys have challenged the finding), there are two plausible explanations: either lefties are at an advantage because righties are less used to playing against them, or being left-handed somehow conveys an innate advantage.

Rafael Nadal, a great left-handed champion, was quoted in 2012 as dismissing the innate advantage theory:

The thing that everybody say, 'Well, you have your forehand against the backhand of the righty'... But the righty have the forehand against the backhand of the lefty. The outside slice, outside serve against the backhand, the righty have the same on the deuce. Seriously, the only thing is probably you play less times against lefties than righties. That's the only advantage.

In 2006, however, a study in Australia reported that left-handers are faster at conveying information between the two halves of the brain. On a task involving matching letters displayed to the left and right visual fields and thus involving both hemispheres in detecting a match, left-handers were on average 43 milliseconds faster than right-handers. That may not sound much, but a tennis ball served at 100 mph can travel six feet in forty-three milliseconds.

TERMITES

452. How do exploding suicide termites synthesize toxic crystals?

By far the best suicide bombers in the insect world are *Neocapritermes taracua* termites. Older members of this species have been found to carry a backpack of toxic chemical crystals of two types. These older termites are sent into battle, and when they are attacked by members of another species, their backpack explodes, the two types of stored crystals mix, the termite's body wall ruptures, and a chemical reaction is created that results in the enemy termites being sprayed with a toxic mess.

How the crystals are synthesized and how the two-component explosive defensive system evolved in this species are both unknown.

See also ANTS 21; BEES 47

THEATRE

453. Who was the first English professional actress?

Until 1660 the acting profession was considered unseemly for a woman to enter and it was illegal for women to appear on the stage. Who was the first to do so, however, is unclear and there are several claimants to the title.

The first recorded instance of women on stage in England was in 1629, when a troupe of French players, male and female, gave performances at Blackfriars. Their names are not known, but they were not well received. According to a letter written to the bishop of London, the French actresses were 'hissed, hooted, and pippin-pelted from the stage', and the writer said he 'did not think they would soon be ready to try the same again'.

In May 1656 a respectable married English woman referred to only as 'Mrs Coleman' appeared in the first performance of *The Siege of Rhodes* by Sir William Davenant in a private theatre at Sir William's home, Rutland House, in the City of London. Despite the fact that it was a private theatre, it was played to a paying audience, so Mrs Coleman has some claim to be considered England's first professional actress.

That title, however, is most commonly given to Margaret Hughes, who is thought to have appeared as Desdemona in a performance of *The Moor of Venice* (a reworking of Shakespeare's *Othello*), given by The King's Company on 8 December 1660. Margaret Hughes went on to great stage success as well as being famous as the mistress of the English Civil War general and later Restoration admiral, Prince Rupert of the Rhine.

It is not totally clear, though, that Margaret Hughes did indeed play the part of Desdemona on the first night of that play on 8 December, as The King's Company had two other actresses who also appeared in that role during the run. Anne Marshall certainly appeared as Desdemona in some of the performances, while Katherine Corey has also been suggested as a possible casting for the first-night Desdemona. Many commentators, however, have rather ungallantly suggested that Corey's lack of physical beauty would have made her unsuitable for the role.

See also CARROLL 89; SHAKESPEARE 415; USA 482

TIME

454. Does time slow down during a frightening event?

An experiment in 2007 attempted to investigate whether there is any scientific basis for the belief that time slows down when you are frightened. To create the frightening event, subjects were dropped from a Suspended Catch Air Device (SCAD) at an amusement park. After falling backwards 30 metres (100 ft), they landed safely in a net.

Two measurements were taken of possible time dilation. The simpler one was to ask them how long they thought the fall had taken and to compare their answers with their estimates of the time other subjects' falls had lasted when they saw them on video. The second measure involved a device strapped to their wrists while they fell. This displayed a dot-matrix image which alternated between showing the number 4 and its reverse image (with the dots forming the 4 now unlit and the others lit). The speed of alternation was gradually increased until the viewer could not distinguish between the two images, which now appeared as a continuously lit screen. The cut-off alternating speed at which that happened was compared with the cut-off previously found before the subject went on the SCAD.

The results were inconclusive. On the one hand, subjects judged their own falls as lasting on average 36 per cent longer than other people's, which would support the hypothesis of time slowing down. On the other hand, the alternating displays in the flashing screen merged together at exactly the same rate of alternation during the fall as earlier.

The researchers concluded that 'subjective time is not a single entity that speeds or slows, but instead is composed of separable subcomponents'. In other words, in some ways time seems to slow down, but in other ways it doesn't.

See also BIG BANG 55; BIOLOGY 59; COSMOLOGY 123, 126

TREASURE

455. Is there a Money Pit on Oak Island?

Just a couple of hundred metres from the shore of Nova Scotia in Canada lies Oak Island, the site of a mystery dating back more than 200 years. The story began in 1795, when eighteen-year-old Daniel McGinnis saw lights coming from the island and, when he went to investigate, found a circular depression in an area cleared of trees. There was also a block and tackle attached to a tree branch that overhung the depression. With the help of friends, he excavated the area to a depth of nine metres and reported finding a wooden platform every three metres. There was also talk of them finding a large flat stone covered with inscriptions, which some say mentioned a £2 million treasure buried below.

The pit subsequently flooded. Later attempts at excavation over the next 150 years reached depths of over fifty metres but revealed only enough evidence to fuel all sorts of rumours. Among these are suggestions that the pit may have been used by the pirates Captain Kidd or Blackbeard to bury their plundered treasure, or French gold, or Marie Antoinette's jewels, or even the Holy Grail. There are even tales of evidence of chests at a great depth along with human remains, but what the pit was originally used for, and whether any of it is still there, remain an enigma.

See also CODES 107, 109; GOLD 218–19

TROY

456. Was the myth of the Trojan War based on fact?

Homer's *Iliad* is perhaps the greatest of all early works of literature. It is thought to be the culmination of a long period of story-telling transmitted orally. Its theme of a struggle between men and gods is the stuff of myth, but was the story based on real events?

Until the 1870s Homer's tale was generally seen as pure fiction, but Heinrich Schliemann's archaeological excavations at Hisarlik in Turkey were then seen as evidence that the city of Troy might actually have existed. We now know that there were at least three Trojan wars and that Troy was destroyed at least twice between 1300 and 1000 BC. We know that the kingdoms of the Mycenaeans and the Hittites were expanding during that period, and Troy may have been caught between them. We know there was a great palace at Mycenae, which could have been the model for Agamemnon's kingdom.

From having no evidence at all to support the claim that the *Iliad* was based on a real war, we now have almost too many possible scenarios to choose from. While many of the archaeological remains support the view that the stories may have been based on historical events, however, nothing has ever been found that can clearly be identified as identical with Homer's account.

TURKEY

457. Why and by whom were the stone circles at Göbekli Tepe built?

Six thousand years before Stonehenge was built, long before the Egyptian pyramids or any signs of approaching civilization, thousands of years before the wheel was even invented, stone age man constructed the amazing stone circles at Göbekli Tepe in Turkey. These consist of dozens of massive limestone pillars, cleanly carved and decorated with sculptures of gazelles, snakes, scorpions, foxes and other animals. The pillars are arranged in circles, each pillar fitting neatly into a slot carved into the rock beneath it.

The stone circles were discovered in 1994, since when excavations have revealed more and more pillars, with geological surveys indicating that hundreds more remain underground. When they were made, people are thought to have lived in small communities living in huts, yet the scale of Göbekli Tepe is massive and must have required large numbers of people for its construction.

No signs of living accommodation have been found nearby, however, and there is no evidence of any source of drinking water closer than three miles away. How they dragged the stones there, without domesticated beasts of burden or even the wheel, is a mystery. The entire site is massively bigger than any other man-made construction known on Earth at the time, and the level of co-operation required to build it is far beyond anything known to exist in human groups so long ago.

The meticulousness and sheer size of the stone circles at Göbekli Tepe suggest that it was some sort of temple, perhaps the world's first, which in turn suggests that religion may have been the driving force behind the development of civilization. But how small nomadic groups came together to share the common vision behind the construction remains unexplained.

See also TROY 456

TURTLES

458. Are roads bad for turtles?

Campaigns have been run at various places in North America to help turtles cross roads. One study even reported that some drivers swerve their vehicles in order to run over a turtle. Yet in 2014 a survey in Canada came to the paradoxical conclusion that, despite all the figures for turtle road-kill, roads may not be bad for turtles after all.

The study was based on analysis of the figures for the sizes of painted turtle populations at twenty ponds in eastern Ontario. Ten of the sites were selected as close as possible to high-traffic roads while the other ten were as far away as possible from such roads. The researchers reported:

> There was no significant effect of roads on painted turtle relative abundance. Furthermore, our data do not support other predictions of the road mortality hypothesis; we observed neither a higher relative frequency of males to females at Road sites than at No Road sites, nor a lower average body size of turtles at Road than at No Road sites.

They suggest that although roads can cause substantial turtle mortality, other factors may act in the opposite direction. Many types of turtle predator, for example, may tend to avoid roads, thus making the near-road locations safer. They stress, however, that the findings should not be extrapolated to other species of turtle.

See also BIRDS 64

TYRANNOSAURUSES

459. How big was a newborn tyrannosaurus?

Our knowledge of tyrannosauruses is greatly hampered by the extreme rarity of their young in the fossil record. Furthermore, no tyrannosaurus eggs have ever been discovered. As if that weren't bad enough, there is the confusion caused by *Nanotyrannus lancensis*. For a long time fossils of *Nanotyrannus* were thought to be examples of young tyrannosauruses, but in 2010 close examination of the skull of a *Nanotyrannus* identified clear differences, suggesting that it was a different species.

So now, quite apart from the problems of assessing the ages at which tyrannosaurus fossils died, in many cases we cannot even be sure that the fossils previously classified as young tyrannosauruses were members of the species at all.

460. What did tyrannosauruses do with their arms?

Even a tyrannosaurus would probably admit that for the huge size of the creature, its arms were ridiculously short. What it used those arms for continues to be a matter of debate. One suggestion is that it used its arms to hold its mate during love-making. Another idea is that the arms were used to hold prey. A third suggestion is that their main function was to provide lift to help the tyrannosaurus stand from a seated position – though we have no evidence that tyrannosauruses made a habit of sitting down.

Studies on the shape of the bones and possible muscle layout may help with this question, but perhaps the most likely answer is that the forelimbs were as near useless as made no difference.

461. How long did tyrannosauruses live?

In the early years of dinosaur study, it was thought that dinosaurs must have been long-lived creatures, some estimates of their lifespan even suggesting 100 to 200 years. Such guesses were based on the general rule that large reptiles live longer than small ones and on a comparison between tyrannosauruses and modern crocodiles.

In the 1980s, however, growth lines were found in some dinosaur bones which allowed far more precise estimates to be made from their skeletons of the number of years these creatures had lived. Conclusions were also drawn about the growth rates of tyrannosauruses by comparing the sizes of animals that had died at different ages. One result of all this was a drastic reassessment of a tyrannosaurus's lifespan down from about 100 years to something closer to thirty.

The trouble is that we have no way of comparing the size of a tyrannosaurus at one age with the size of the same animal some years later. The conclusions about growth rates have been reached by comparing one animal with another and assuming they would have been about the same size at the same age. We simply do not have enough specimens of tyrannosauruses to know how valid that assumption is.

See also DINOSAURS 137

UNITED KINGDOM

462. Who wore the Allerton Cope?

In 1858, at the bottom of a chest in Chapel Allerton Church in Somerset, was found an exquisite piece of medieval embroidery now known as the Allerton Cope. The embroidery portrays the Assumption of the Virgin Mary, with the details of cherubs' tiny faces beautifully worked around it. The fabric of the cope and the silver threads of the embroidery mark it as an object that must have been highly valued, but its history is completely obscure.

The cope (which is a word for a mantle worn by a priest or other churchman) has been dated to around the end of the fifteenth century, and one suggestion is that it was given to Chapel Allerton Church by John Gunthorpe, dean of Wells Cathedral from 1472 to 1498. Why it should have been given to such a relatively insignificant church, however, is a mystery. Chapel Allerton was not even important enough to be dignified with the name of a saint. However, Gunthorpe had purchased the parish of Chapel Allerton shortly before his death. It is possible that his cope found its way there and was later hidden in the chest at the time of the Dissolution of the Monasteries.

Yet that did not happen until some forty years after Gunthorpe died, and there is no known mention of the cope at Allerton during that period.

See also ANIMALS 18; AUTISM 36; CANCER 86; CHAPLIN 93; DEATH 131; DISEASE 145; FASHION 188; PSYCHOLOGY 384; RELIGION 394; SLEEP 427

UNIVERSE

463. Is the universe unstable?

One of the things that the discovery of the Higgs boson has done is to increase our belief that the universe may be unstable. According to the Standard Model of particle physics which led to the prediction of the existence of the Higgs boson, the vacuum occupied by the universe is not empty but full of particles and antiparticles that pop into existence and annihilate each other in tiny moments of time. As long as they do it quickly enough, this constant creation and annihilation does not contradict any laws of physics. The question is whether this mayhem-rich vacuum is stable.

According to our understanding of the Standard Model, the necessary condition for vacuum stability is that our universe exists at a minimum of potential energy. A good guide to whether that is the case is given by the masses of two fundamental particles, the Higgs boson and the top quark. Current estimates of those masses suggest that it is too close to call. Both appear to be very close to the limit required for the universe to be stable. So it could be that a random quantum fluctuation might lead to a vacuum bubble sweeping through space and destroying the universe – in which case the Sun will not rise tomorrow (→ 444). But even if that is the case, it will probably not happen for several billion years.

464. Did the universe have a beginning?

Our current view of the beginning of the universe dates it back to about 13.8 billion years ago when it all started with a Big Bang. Specifically, it was a massive explosion of energy from a single point which has fuelled the expansion of the universe ever since. The figure of 13.8 billion years comes from calculations of the separation of galaxies. Tracing their movements, we can not only predict where they will go in the future but we can work out where they have come from, and the figures seem to show that they were all in the same place 13.8 billion years ago.

And this is where the mathematics breaks down. Going back to the moment of the Big Bang, we reach a singularity: all the energy in the universe is in the same place, time itself stops, and all the laws of physics stop working. There are several ways round this problem:

(i) Religion: in the beginning God created... That's what we've always said. We're glad you scientists at last agree with us. And His 'Let there be light' is just your Big Bang.

(ii) Multiversal: that Big Bang stuff only applies to our three-dimensional universe. There were probably plenty of other universes before ours came along. String theory says we're probably just a slice of a ten- or eleven-dimensional universe anyway, so what's the problem?

(iii) No boundary: just like the surface of the Earth, space–time itself is finite in extent but has no boundary. The universe had a beginning, but its beginning was determined by the laws of physics. The singularity is not a problem.

(iv) Actually, we've got it slightly wrong and everything wasn't quite at the same place at the same time. If we trace the galaxies back properly, they just miss each other. There never was a singularity.

465. Can we experimentally obtain evidence of higher spacial dimensions?

Superstring theory says there are ten space–time dimensions. It originated from the more fundamental M-theory, which was based on eleven dimensions. If the extra dimensions that these theories require exist, they must be hidden from us by some physical mechanism. One suggestion is that the extra dimensions may be 'curled up' at such tiny scales that they are effectively invisible. If there is no measurable effect of these extra dimensions, how can we ever test whether they exist?

In the early years of string theory, this posed a philosophical problem. If it made no testable predictions, the theory failed Karl Popper's condition of falsifiability ($\rightarrow$ 404), which it had to satisfy in order to qualify as worthy of consideration as a scientific hypothesis. More recently, however, superstring theory has appeared to be the most likely candidate to produce a Grand Unified Theory to explain all the fundamental forces of physics. The problem with this has always been the weakness of gravity compared with the other forces, but if our gravity is viewed as a pale, three-dimensional component of a ten- or eleven-dimensional force, it could explain why it is so weak in our slice of the universe. The extra dimensions could then be revealed by variations in gravity within the part of the universe we can test.

This idea has been around for more than a decade now, but we still have not found any real evidence for further dimensions. But it may not be out of the question.

466. Do we live in a cyclic universe?

The universe is not only expanding, but that expansion is accelerating. We do not know what causes that acceleration, so we do not know how long it will continue, but it has made the old picture of a cyclic universe less likely. In that scenario, the expansion continued until it ran out of energy, after which it would start shrinking as gravity drew all the matter closer together. In the end, just as at the Big Bang, it would finish in a Big Scrunch. This gave rise to a cyclic universe theory, with all the matter, now sucked up into one massive black hole, exploding outwards again in another Big Bang, with the cycle of Bangs and Scrunches endlessly repeating.

One problem with this idea was that it seemed to contradict the second law of thermodynamics, which demands a continuous increase in entropy or disorder. As the universe gets more and more disordered, it cannot get back to the state of perfect order that existed at the Big Bang.

More recently, amended theories of a cyclic universe have appeared with all the matter in the universe spreading ever more thinly and decaying until everything is energy. When that happens – according to whose theory you read – there will be either another Big Bang, or a huge series of Big Bangs, each creating its own universe. In either case, the time taken for each cycle will be in the region of a trillion years.

467. Is the rapid expansion in the early universe related to its current expansion?

In the tiniest fraction of a second after the Big Bang, the universe is thought to have expanded at an unbelievably fast rate, probably faster than the speed of light. One proposal for the mechanism fuelling this is a hypothetical field called the 'inflaton field', caused by as yet undiscovered particles called 'inflatons'. The inflaton field created a form of dark energy which was the driving force behind the early expansion. Subsequent changes in the inflation rate may have been caused by the interaction of this inflaton field with gravity and the residual momentum from the Big Bang.

The dark energy which has been credited with the current acceleration in expansion could be the same energy field that fuelled the original expansion.

See also ASTRONOMY 27; BIG BANG 54–6; BLACK HOLES 71; COSMOLOGY 118–19, 121, 123–4, 126; ENERGY 173–4; EVOLUTION 181; FUNDAMENTAL PARTICLES 205; GRAVITY 222; INTELLIGENCE 253; MILKY WAY 315; OUTER SPACE 350; PHILOSOPHY 365; PHYSICS 370; QUASARS 390–1

USA

468. What caused the Great Chicago Fire of 1871?

On Sunday 8 October 1871 a fire started in the barn of Patrick and Catherine O'Leary in Chicago. By the time the fire was put out a day and a half later, it had destroyed property valued at $192 million, left 100,000 people homeless, and 300 others had lost their lives. A long inquiry was held into the cause of the fire, but it eventually reported that 'whether it originated from a spark blown from a chimney on that windy night, or was set on fire by human agency, we are unable to determine'.

According to a popular nineteenth-century belief, the fire was caused by Mrs O'Leary's cow knocking over a lantern, but there is no more evidence for this than countless other suggestions explored at the Inquest. Might the fire have been caused by a man named Regan, who had been visiting the O'Learys that evening, whose peg leg could have slipped on the floor of the barn and caused him to drop his pipe? Might he have tripped over the feet of his companion Daniel Sullivan? We shall probably never know, but the cow story is as good as any other.

469. How big is the Lost Sea in Tennessee?

In 1905 a thirteen-year-old boy named Ben Sands discovered an underground lake in Sweetwater, Tennessee, after crawling through a muddy opening 90 metres (300 ft) underground. He was amazed to find himself in a huge cave half-filled with water. When he went back with his father some time later, the entrance to the lake had become hidden and it was some years before it was rediscovered and proper explorations of the lake began.

In 1974–5 a survey reported depths of over 30 metres in the lake, which in one cavern occupied an area 240 metres long and 67 metres across. A later exploration added another 460 metres to the length of various passages from the lake. Its full extent is still unknown, though it is already classed as the world's second-biggest non-glacial underground lake, after Dragon's Breath Cave in Namibia.

470. Where did all the Confederate gold go?

As the American Civil War was nearing its end in 1865, a large amount of gold held by the Confederates went missing. Originally it was probably taken away by train from New Orleans. Some say the train was robbed and the gold hidden by a variety of plantation owners; others say it was taken by a group of deserters from both sides who divided it up.

There is hardly an area of the USA where some legend or other does not say the gold is buried. Its value is also unknown, with estimates varying between about $500,000 and $2 million at today's prices.

471. Why does the city of Taos in New Mexico hum?

The town of Taos in New Mexico has, since the 1990s, been famed for its hum. When this hum of unknown origin was first researched, around 2 per cent of the town's inhabitants claimed to have heard it. Sensitive devices were set up in the homes of several hearers but nothing unusual was detected. Secret government mind-control experiments, underground UFO bases, hippies and an assortment of paranormal phenomena were suspected of causing the hum, but further investigations suggested that there might be more than one sort of hum, as some called it a 'whir' and others a 'buzz', as well as the usual 'hum' description.

Whether there really is a hum at all must be open to doubt, in which case the question is how the rumour started in the first place.

472. Is the stovepipe hat in the Abraham Lincoln Presidential Library and Museum authentic?

Two American institutions possess items that claim to be stovepipe hats worn by Abraham Lincoln. There is no doubt about the hat at the Smithsonian: it is the size 7⅛ hat Lincoln put on to go to Ford's Theatre on the night he was assassinated. After he was shot, the hat was found on the floor beside his chair and was taken to the War Department. With permission from Lincoln's widow Mary, the department gave the hat to the Patent Office, which in 1867 transferred it to the Smithsonian Institution.

There is some dispute about the other hat, however, which may be seen at the Abraham Lincoln Presidential Library and Museum in Springfield, Illinois. Lincoln is said to have given it to William Waller, a farmer and political supporter in Jackson County, Illinois, whose family kept it for decades. It was later sold to a collector and donated to the library.

In 2013, however, a member of the board that oversees the library was quoted as saying, 'I think we have a credibility gap with this hat', and the Illinois State Police were asked to conduct DNA testing of the hat to see if Abraham Lincoln ever really wore it. The hat size is also 7⅛, and like the Smithsonian hat, it also carries the mark of Lincoln's usual hat-maker. The trouble is that there is no clear evidence, other than the Waller family's assertions, that the hat really was Lincoln's.

The Lincoln Library curator has described the proposal to DNA-test the hat as 'even worse than a bad idea' and ridiculed the suggestion that it be vacuumed for traces of Lincoln's dandruff.

473. Did Benjamin Franklin ever make tofu?

The United States owed a great deal to Benjamin Franklin in its early years. Lightning rods, rocking chairs and bifocal spectacles were all his

USA

idea, and he is also credited with the introduction of tofu. The earliest-known mention of tofu by an American is in a letter written by Benjamin Franklin, who was in London, to John Bartram in Philadelphia dated 11 January 1770. The letter included a sample of soya beans, and with them what he called 'Father Navarrete's account of the universal use of a cheese made of them in China'.

This 'cheese', he said, so much aroused his curiosity that he took steps to find out how it was made, and he went on to describe the procedure to Bartram. The method involved adding 'some runnings of salt' to water, then adding the soya beans 'to turn it to curds'. And the curds, Franklin said, 'are what the Tau-fu is made of'.

Whether Franklin took the recipe on trust, however, or made his own tofu with it before passing it on to Bartram, is not known.

474. Which speech did Lincoln deliver at Gettysburg?

Seven score and twelve years before this book was written, Abraham Lincoln brought forth, in Gettysburg, Pennsylvania, one of the greatest speeches ever uttered. There are, however, five known copies of the speech in Lincoln's handwriting, each with a slightly different text, and nobody knows which was the one delivered by Lincoln.

Two of the copies are thought to have been written before the speech was made and three were written as responses to people who asked him for copies later. The text of the speech on the walls of the Lincoln Memorial in Washington is taken from the copy Lincoln gave to Colonel Alexander Bliss for use as a fundraiser for soldiers. It is the only copy signed and dated by Lincoln. This is, however, the last copy Lincoln is known to have made, so it cannot be the one he read from at the time. Perhaps the best candidate for that description is the copy he gave to White House assistant John Hay, which is thought to be the second draft of the speech as it includes some handwritten changes by Lincoln.

He could, however, have made some spontaneous changes while delivering the speech, so the versions written afterwards may be more accurate accounts of what he actually said. They all differ only by a few unimportant words, but it is sad there is no definitive version of such a momentous speech.

475. Did Pocahontas save John Smith?

The story of the young Native American girl Pocahontas intervening to save the life of the pioneer settler John Smith has become one of the great American legends, but what really happened?

The essence of the story is that John Smith, a leader of the settlement in Jamestown, Virginia, was captured with two others by a group of Native Americans led by a chief called Powhatan. Two of them were later killed, but Smith was allowed to live until Powhatan decided that the moment for his execution had arrived. When Powhatan was about to cudgel him to death, however, the chief's daughter Pocahontas came between them and put her head on Smith's. This brave act of humanity and benevolence led to peace breaking out between the settlers and the natives.

That's the story, but the only corroboration for it comes in Smith's own account written some seventeen years after the event. He had already given two other accounts without mentioning it at all. There are three theories:

(i)   It happened exactly as Smith said.
(ii) It was actually an elaborate ritual for pardoning Smith and letting him live with the tribe, but Smith totally misunderstood what was going on.
(iii) It was a self-serving invention by Smith to enhance his reputation and identify himself with a girl who had now become a prominent woman.

The first version is the one the Disney organization chose to believe, and even then they turned Pocahontas from a ten-year-old into a young lady to make a better romance of it all.

476. Did Betsy Ross sew the first American flag?

The story goes that, one day in 1776, George Washington and two others from a congressional committee called on Mrs Betsy Ross, an upholsterer and seamstress, to ask for her help sewing a flag. Washington took a sketch from his pocket showing thirteen red and white stripes and thirteen stars representing the thirteen colonies and soon-to-be states. When asked if she could do it, Ross replied, 'I do not know, but I will try.' Her only immediate suggestion, which the men agreed to, was to change the stars from six-pointed to five-pointed.

But did any of this really happen? The evidence for it is so scanty as to be almost non-existent. The earliest-known account of the story dates from more than 100 years later when Betsy Ross's grandson William Canby said he'd heard it from Betsy herself. Canby said that Washington was a family friend who had often visited Betsy's shop.

There is, however, no written evidence of any business between Washington and Ross, nor do congressional records contain any reference to a committee in 1776 going out to make a flag. Congress passed a law about the flag on 14 June 1777, which mentioned thirteen red and white stripes and thirteen white stars on a blue field, but there is no evidence of a flag committee a year earlier.

On the other hand, one of the men accompanying Washington in the story is named as George Ross, who was the uncle of Betsy's husband. Also, in May 1777, records suggest that Betsy was paid for making flags for the Pennsylvania State Navy. Still, that is a long way from making the first one for George Washington a year earlier, especially as Washington was not a member of Congress at the time but commander-in-chief of the Continental Army.

477. Did George Washington cut down his father's cherry tree?

The uplifting tale of the young George Washington admitting to cutting down his father's cherry tree was something all Americans were brought up on in the nineteenth century at least. The story was first related in print by Mason Locke Weems (1759–1825), an itinerant preacher known as 'Parson Weems', in his bestseller *The Life of Washington*, which went through dozens of editions after its first publication in 1800.

The tale, as he wrote it, was that the six-year-old George Washington had received a present of a hatchet which he gleefully tested in his garden. When his father returned, he found the bark of his favourite cherry tree had been hacked away and asked who had 'barked' (not cut down) the tree. The young George then replied, 'I can't tell a lie, Pa; you know I can't tell a lie. I did cut it with my hatchet.' 'Run to my arms, you dearest boy,' cried his father in transports, 'run to my arms; glad am I,

George, that you killed my tree; for you have paid me for it a thousand fold. Such an act of heroism in my son is more worth than a thousand trees, though blossomed with silver, and their fruits of purest gold.'

Weems said that he had been told the story by 'an aged lady who was a distant relative [of Washington]', but much suspicion later grew that he had made it all up. In 1896 future president Woodrow Wilson, in his own biography of Washington, described it as a fabrication, saying, 'Of its factual truth there is no evidence whatsoever.' Other writers called it 'idle quip and irreverent jest', 'pernicious drivel' or a 'slush of plagiarism and piety'.

In 1912, however, US historian Carl Anthony came across a long-forgotten earthenware mug, made in Germany no later than 1790, which shows a young man standing beside a fallen tree along with a large hatchet; it is marked by the date 1776 and the initials 'G.W.'. It seems that the story was around at least a decade before Weems used it, so perhaps he did not make it up after all.

See also FASHION 188; FRANCE 202; IOWA 257; MURDER 325; NORTH DAKOTA 341

VANUATU

478. What is the explanation of the headless bodies buried in Vanuatu?

Between 2003 and 2009 archaeologists on the Pacific islands of Vanuatu, about 1,750 kilometres east of Australia, excavated an extra-ordinary ancient cemetery. In all, they dug up seventy or seventy-one skeletons, all of which had their skulls missing. Two of the bodies were buried with three skulls each, though none of the heads belonged to the body.

The bodies are thought to have been placed in their graves about 3,000 years ago and are believed to have been buried with their heads. Only after the flesh rotted away were the heads removed. A number of ritualistic procedures seem to have been enacted during the burials, but the rituals appear to have differed at different levels of the burial site. The only common feature was that all the heads were removed.

Nothing seems to be known about what all this signified, where the people came from or anything else about their culture.

VENUS

479. Are there any live volcanoes on Venus?

Of all the planets in the Solar System, Venus has by far the most volcanoes. Over 1,600 major volcanoes or volcanic features have been identified, and estimates of the number of smaller volcanoes vary between around 100,000 and 1 million. While Venus is much the same size as Earth, its surface temperature is much higher, its atmosphere is very different, and its air pressure is much higher. It also seems to have no plate tectonics, which is what causes most earthquakes and volcanic eruptions on Earth. All of these features could greatly influence the frequency and types of volcanic activity.

One big question, however, is whether any of the Venusian volcanoes are still active. No volcanic activity has ever been recorded, but we have so little data about what is going on there that it is impossible to rule it out.

480. Why are the winds on Venus getting stronger?

The atmosphere on Venus is very dense and rich in carbon dioxide, which leads to the planet being covered by a blanket of yellowish cloud. Tracking the movement of this cloud has revealed extremely powerful high-altitude winds around 70 kilometres above the planet's surface.

These winds have been observed and measured both by spacecraft and directly from Earth, but the latest observations from the Venus Express have revealed some surprising features. After cloud movements had been monitored for ten Venusian years, wind speeds were found to change according to the time of day and latitude, but the most remarkable finding was that overall these super-hurricane-force winds have been speeding up.

What is driving these strange atmospheric patterns is completely unknown.

See also MERCURY 304

VIKINGS

481. Where exactly was Erik the Red's Vinland?

The discovery and exploration of North America by the Vikings Leif Eriksson and Erik the Red were written about in two Icelandic sagas, the *Greenlanders' Saga*, written around 1200, and *Erik the Red's Saga*, which appeared about fifty years later. Both sagas are thought to form part of the oral history of the Icelanders dating back some 200 years before the sagas were written down.

According to the *Greenlanders' Saga*, North America was first sighted by Bjarni Herjolfsson, who was blown off course on his way from

Iceland to Greenland in 985 or 986. He did not go ashore, but Leif Eriksson decided to follow up on his sightings. With a crew of thirty-five, Eriksson landed first at a place that he called Helluland, the 'Land of Flat Stone'; then went to 'Markland' ('Forest Land'); then landed on an unnamed island; and finally, in autumn 1001, reached Vinland, which means either the 'land of the vine' or the 'land of the pastures'.

All the sagas tell us about the location of Vinland is that Eriksson reached it by following a river that led to a lake and that the mouth of the river was on the west of a large peninsula pointing north. A number of places in North America have staked their claims to have been part of Eriksson's Vinland. There are mysterious symbols on a rock at Dighton, Massachusetts, that may be Norse carvings; there is a tower in Rhode Island that may be the remains of a Norse church; there are depressions at Cape Cod which could mark where Eriksson left his ship. Or was it at L'Anse aux Meadows on the north-eastern tip of Newfoundland, where remains of a Norse settlement were found in the 1960s? None of these places offer more than a tantalizing glimpse of where the true discoverers of America may have been.

See also DEATH 132

VOLCANOES

482. Where was the volcano whose eruption killed thousands in London around 1258?

In 1258 a volcanic eruption wiped out a third of the population of London and we have no idea where the volcano was. That was the conclusion reached from what began as an ordinary archaeological investigation in 2012 on the site of the ancient St Mary Spital church in

East London. The archaeologists knew that the church had a cemetery, so they were not surprised to unearth a number of skeletons, but the more they dug, the more skeletons appeared, until they numbered over 10,000. With more of the cemetery inaccessible under the nearby market, the total number of bodies was estimated at 18,500, which was more than a third of the total population of medieval London.

Carbon dating indicated that the skeletons dated from around 1250, which was too early for them to have been victims of the Black Death or the Plague, but investigations of chronicles of the period gave strong clues to what had happened. They spoke of a failure of crops, 'unendurable cold' and a winter that never abated. It was the sort of cataclysm that can only be caused by a massive volcanic eruption, spewing out sulphurous clouds that block out the Sun. Other references do indeed mention a massive volcanic eruption, but where it happened is unknown. The most likely culprits are thought to have been El Chichón in Mexico, Quilotoa in Ecuador or the Samalas volcano in Indonesia, but really it could have been anywhere on Earth.

483. Did the same volcano trigger the onset of the Little Ice Age?

Throughout the Middle Ages, the world climate went through a period known as the Little Ice Age. Some put its start at around 1650, others say 1350, but the most recent evidence suggests that what triggered it was a series of major volcanic eruptions between 1250 and 1300. Radiocarbon dating of dead plant matter in the Arctic indicates that something happened in this period that killed off vast numbers of plants, probably by freezing. Measurements of Icelandic glaciers also indicate that the ice grew quickly in thickness by a large amount at the same time.

The massive eruptions of the volcanoes in Ecuador, Mexico and Indonesia mentioned above (→ 482) all occurred in the late 1250s, as did the disastrous deaths in London in 1258. All these things could be linked.

See also EARTH 164; GEOLOGY 212; MAYANS 293; VENUS 479

WAITRESSES

484. Why do blonde waitresses get bigger tips?

There seems to be no doubt about it: a number of studies have reported that blonde waitresses get bigger tips than brunettes. Whether a change in hair colour is effected by dyeing the hair or by wearing a wig, blondes' tips are on average about 8 per cent higher. One study reported that blondes get higher tips even if their dark roots are showing.

While they all agree on the results, however, a number of different explanations have been offered. The obvious suggestion is that it ties in with other research showing that men give higher attractiveness ratings to women if their hair is blonde. Some of the tipping research also suggests that the higher tips received by blondes are mostly due to the behaviour of male customers.

Another possibility, however, is linked to a finding that blonde women are perceived as less intelligent than brunettes. This perceived stupidity may lead to a lower expectation of good service, so the blonde waitress has only to perform at an average level to exceed expectations and earn a larger tip.

Finally, it could be that having blonde hair changes the behaviour of the waitress, perhaps by increasing her confidence, or perhaps by increasing her flirtatiousness with customers.

See also FOOD 194

WALES

485. What happened to Owain Glyndŵr after 1412?

Owain Glyndŵr was the last native Welshman to hold the title Prince of Wales. In 1400 he instigated the Welsh Revolt against the rule of Henry IV of England. Initially very successful, the uprising gained control of large areas of Wales, but the superior resources of the English eventually drove Glyndŵr out of his strongholds. In 1409 he fled and avoided capture. The last documented sighting of him was in 1412.

Glyndŵr was twice offered a pardon from the new king Henry V of England, but ignored them. Despite large rewards offered for his capture, he was never betrayed to the English. Various theories have emerged concerning where he may have hidden after 1412, but no convincing evidence has ever been found to support them. His death was reported by a former follower to have occurred in 1415, but there is no corroboration of that either.

WALRUSES

486. Why do walruses have such large penis bones?

Humans and hyenas are in a very small minority of mammals that do not have a penis bone. This bone, also known as a baculum, is present in dogs, cats, bats, rats, mice, bears, weasels, lions, sea lions, chimpanzees and gorillas, among others. It is located in the tip of the penis and ranges in size from only a few millimetres in gorillas and mice to around eight centimetres in large dogs. And the largest of all is the sixty-centimetre-long baculum of the walrus.

Why does the walrus have such a long one? The function of the bone is unclear. Presumably it helps the male maintain an erection and it may help move the penis inside the female. It may also have a role to play in directing the male's ejaculate, but humans seem to have survived perfectly well without bacula, so why the walrus has evolved such a long one is a puzzle.

See also BONES 72

WATER

487. Why does warm water freeze more quickly than cold water?

In the fourth century BC, Aristotle noticed that hot water may freeze more quickly than cold water. In the seventeenth century, Francis Bacon and René Descartes also noticed it. The first scientific investigation of the phenomenon, however, did not happen until the 1960s, when a Tanzanian student named Erasto Mpemba was making ice-cream in a cookery class and noticed that a warm mix of ingredients froze faster than a cold one.

This 'Mpemba effect' was then confirmed in some properly conducted scientific experiments. In fact not all the experiments confirmed it, but nobody could explain what the difference was between the successful and unsuccessful versions. Suggestions have included:

- evaporation, which is an endothermic reaction, taking heat away from water;
- insulation, caused by the formation of frost on the top of the lower-temperature water;
- convection currents in the warmer water causing more rapid cooling;
- dissolved solids and gases in the water having different effects on freezing at different temperatures.

The latest idea is based on the possible energy released by a loosening of the hydrogen bonds in the water molecules, but there is still no general agreement on which explanation is correct.

488. How much water is in the Earth's interior?

Most of what we know about the interior of the Earth comes from the investigation of seismic waves caused by earthquakes. By monitoring the waves at the surface and detecting their speed at various depths, conclusions may be drawn about the nature of the material they pass through. In 2014 a study of over 500 earthquakes by 2,000 seismometers revealed a massive ocean about 700 kilometres below the Earth's surface containing around three times as much water as all the seas and oceans we can see.

This finding throws new light on the question of where the Earth's oceans came from and how they have stayed the same size for millions of years. The investigation, however, only relates to water beneath the United States. It could extend all the way round the planet occupying a region between the upper and lower parts of the Earth's mantle. The total amount of water down there could easily be enough to submerge the planet if it were on the surface.

489. Can water remember?

In 1988 the French immunologist Jacques Benveniste published a paper that was immediately seized on by homeopaths as complete justification of their views. The core of Benveniste's claims was that when something is dissolved in water, then diluted so many times that not even a single molecule of the original substance is present, the water still retains a 'memory' of its having been there. Specifically, his claim was that the configuration of the molecules of water is 'biologically active' in a way that makes it change when something is dissolved in it and retain that change after dilution.

Benveniste's paper aroused intense debate, ranging from huge support from believers in homeopathy to utter condemnation by those who criticized it as pseudo-science at its worst. Attempts to repeat Benveniste's experiments, however, were generally unsuccessful and the topic of 'water memory' fell under a cloud until the debate was reignited by research conducted by the Nobel Prize-winning virologist Luc Montagnier in 2010.

Montagnier's claim was that bacterial DNA dissolved in water created electromagnetic signals from which the entire DNA sequence could be obtained. Again the results were viewed with exultation by homeopaths and incredulity by most of the scientific community. Montagnier himself, however, went no further than suggesting that his result indicated that water may contain an information storage-and-retrieval property and that one 'cannot extrapolate it to the products used in homeopathy'. Attempts to replicate Montagnier's experiments, however, have not been successful.

See also ANIMALS 16; BIRDS 64; DINOSAURS 137; FROGS 203; GLOBAL WARMING 216; INVENTIONS 255; LEMURS 272; MARS 285; METEOROLOGY 309–10; PHYSICS 369; RIDDLES 396; SALT 400; USA 469

WHALES

490. How do sperm whales catch squid?

Every year, sperm whales eat half a million tons of squid, but how they manage to catch them is a bit of a mystery. Squid are faster and much more manoeuvrable than whales, so how the larger, lumbering creatures catch them so frequently and apparently so easily is a puzzle.

One old theory was that the whales stunned the squid with a sudden burst of sonar clicks, but research has shown that squid seem impervious to such whale sounds, even when played at very high volume through loudspeakers. Another idea is that the whales tend to catch the squid at great depths where the coldness of the water may make them sluggish, while yet another idea is that the squid may be lured into the whale's mouth by the pale pigmentation of its interior.

Whales have been seen vacuuming up squid from a few feet away with a powerful sucking action, but even so, one might expect the squid to see the whale coming and get out of the way.

491. Why has the song pitch of blue whales been getting lower?

From the northern Pacific to the Southern Ocean, the song of male blue whales, which is believed to play a role in their searching for mates, has been deepening. Scientists who have monitored whale song for over forty years have reported that their voices have deepened by some 30 per cent over that period.

One theory is that it is a result of competition in mate selection. Female blue whales are known to prefer larger males. A deep voice may indicate a bigger whale, which would convey a survival benefit to deeper-voiced males.

Another idea is that it may be the result of a recovery in the population of blue whales following bans on hunting them. That would result in their being less sparsely distributed, so the males would expect to find females a shorter distance away and would not need to sing so loudly. Since it is easier for whales to sing loud at higher frequencies, the need to sing high would therefore have diminished.

492. Why are whales so big?

The blue whale is the biggest animal that has ever existed. Bigger than the biggest dinosaur and thirty times as heavy as an elephant – indeed, a whale's tongue alone can weigh as much as an elephant – whales are enormous, but it's not easy to see why.

From an evolutionary standpoint, being large is not always an advantage. It may help in battles against competitors, but larger animals need more food to stay alive. When resources become scarce, it is the bigger animals that die out, as was the case with the several varieties of megafauna that became extinct around 10,000 years ago (→ AVOCADOS 37).

How whales have become so large is easier to explain than why they have done so: Arctic krill, which have formed the main part of the diet of many whale species, have long been plentiful, and whales can take huge mouthfuls of them. Floating at sea also requires far less energy than lumbering around on land. A creature the size of a whale would simply be too big to survive out of water: its legs would be unable to support its bulk.

All the same, once a creature has reached a size that enables it to dominate potential predators, the evolutionary advantages of growing even bigger seem to be outweighed by the disadvantages.

See also DOLPHINS 155; RIDDLES 396

WILD BOAR

493. Why do wild boar scatter their acorns?

When animals hoard their food, the threat of its being stolen by others of their species gives them essentially two options: larder-hoarding or scatter-hoarding. The first of these involves hiding all the food together in one cache, the second involves having a number of smaller caches. Wild boar like to scatter-hoard their acorns, but it is not clear that this is the best strategy.

In 2014 an experiment was conducted in which researchers buried a fixed number of acorns over a fixed number of patches within a fixed area, varying cache size and cache depth. They then recorded how successful wild boar were at finding and pilfering acorns from the various caches. As expected, they found that the time wild boar needed to stumble across the first cache and steal the acorns was shortest for scatter-hoarding, but the time needed to pilfer all the caches was slightly longer for scatter-hoarding than for larder-hoarding. Overall the rate of pilferage did not differ between scatter-hoarding and larder-hoarding.

The question of why the wild boar bother to scatter-hoard, which takes longer and involves greater expenditure of energy than larder-hoarding, is therefore still open.

WINE

494. Are screw-caps good for red wine?

Cork or screw-cap? The question of how best to seal a wine-bottle has aroused intense debate over the past couple of decades. A common view is that screw-tops are fine for most white wines, but many say that good red wines that need long ageing in the bottle require corks. But is this just the view of wine snobs, or is such a belief justified?

It all comes down to the question of how airtight one wants the bottle to be. On the one hand, there is a need to prevent air from entering the bottle and spoiling the wine; on the other hand, a small amount of oxygen may help the wine develop. The cork was long seen as the perfect way to keep the wine safe from degradation while letting enough oxygen seep through to improve it over the years. Screw-caps, however, are completely resistant to the mould that sometimes affects corks.

In the early years of screw-cap bottles, the seal was seen as too absolute to allow wines to age. More recently, types of screw-cap have been developed which allow the wine to be exposed to a small amount of oxygen to aid the ageing process. This technology, however, is too recent to be able to judge whether such screw-caps allow the wine to mature as well as corks.

It is also worth mentioning that whatever the quality of the wine, the sound made by a cork being pulled is unlikely ever to be matched by that of a screw-top being opened.

See also BRAINS 75; CHOCOLATE 104; FOOD 196; MESOPOTAMIA 305

WITCHES

495. Where were the Salem witches buried after their executions?

In 1692, in the town of Salem, Massachusetts, over 200 people, mostly women, were arrested on suspicion of witchcraft. The resulting trials later the same year ended in the execution of nineteen of them by hanging. But where the hangings took place and where the victims were buried is unknown. According to court records, the hangings took place at 'Gallows Hill'. There is a location in Salem now known by that name, but there are some good reasons for doubting that it is the right place. For one thing, the hill is too steep for the cart supposedly going to fetch the bodies to have made its way up to the supposed point of the hangings; and for another, the son of one of the victims was said to have rowed a boat to the base of the hill after the burials to exhume his mother and give her a proper Christian burial. Yet there is not, and never has been, a waterway leading to the present Gallows Hill. Other smaller hills in the area have been suggested as the location of the original Gallows Hill, but without any convincing evidence.

All the court records tell us is that the bodies were buried in an unmarked, shallow grave because of their association with the Devil. Their unstated desire to keep the precise location a secret has been successful up to the present day.

496. Why did the women in Salem behave like witches?

The arrests, trials and hangings at Salem were the culmination of a witchcraft hysteria that began with some decidedly odd behaviour from three girls, Abigail Williams, Betty Parris and Ann Putnam Jr. Their various antics included hallucinations, shouting out in church, having fits, making strange sounds, and feeling as if they were being pricked and poked. When physicians could find no cause for this, it was put down to the work of Satan and the girls were encouraged to reveal who was controlling them.

One of those accused was a slave girl called Tituba. She confessed to seeing the Devil, who appeared to her 'sometimes like a hog and sometimes like a great dog'. She also confessed that a conspiracy of witches existed in Salem, and the arrests began. But what made the three girls behave the way they did in the first place? There are several theories:

(i) Mental illness causing hysteria and delusions – though for that to have affected three girls simultaneously is unlikely.

(ii) Puritanism: it may all have been a reaction to the strict Puritan lifestyle. The restrictions imposed on the girls may have caused them to behave in the way they did, then blame it on possession by the Devil.

(iii) Ergot poisoning: ergot of rye is a plant disease causing a poisonous fungus which can bring on convulsive fits, muscle spasms, nausea, vomiting and hallucination.

(iv) It may all have been a plot by the girls' parents to have their own enemies denounced as witches.

WORDS

497. What does the 'drawn' in 'hanged, drawn and quartered' refer to?

From 1351 until it was finally removed from the statute book in 1870, the crime of high treason under English law could carry a penalty of being hanged, drawn and quartered. Specifically, the full sentence was:

That you be drawn on a hurdle to the place of execution where you shall be hanged by the neck and being alive cut down, your privy members shall be cut off and your bowels taken out and burned before you, your head severed from your body and your body divided into four quarters to be disposed of at the King's pleasure.

This has led to a long-running dispute over the function of the word 'drawn' in the phrase 'hanged, drawn and quartered'. As the word is used in the description above, 'drawn' means 'dragged along behind a horse', but that punishment is surely 'drawn, hanged and quartered'.

Because the words, in the phrase as it is usually seen, are ordered as they are, some take 'drawn' to refer to the drawing out of the intestines or disembowelment. The confusion is well expressed by the *Oxford English Dictionary*, which says:

in many cases of executions it is uncertain whether this [evisceration], or sense 4 [To drag... to the place of execution], is meant. The presumption is that where drawn is mentioned after hanged, the sense is [evisceration].

498. Is 'Huh?' a word?

What is the difference between a word and a grunt? Those who study linguistics attempt to differentiate between the two by defining 'word' as 'a lexical, conventionalised form that has to be learnt'. One cannot, for example, know that 'word' means a word without having learnt it; it is just a convention among English-speakers that that's what it means. 'Ow!', on the other hand, is just an involuntary expression of pain whose meaning is clear without having been learnt. So where does this leave 'Huh?'?

In 2013 researchers in the Netherlands examined the use of 'Huh?' as a 'repair initiator' – a comment indicating a problem in hearing or comprehension inviting the speaker to repeat or explain – in ten unrelated languages, in all of which recognizable versions of 'Huh?' are used with similar meanings. They say that its use 'is so common as to be practically universal, and yet calibrated to specific language systems such that it qualifies as a word'.

This leaves two possibilities: 'Huh?' is similar across languages because it is an innate grunt; or the similarity is a result of convergent evolution. In other words, we say 'Huh?' the world over because we all ran up against the same problem in similar conditions, as communication evolved, when it came to indicating a need for clarification. Some, however, may view the argument in favour of this latter explanation with a strong 'Huh?'.

See also SHAKESPEARE 413

WORMS

499. Is knowledge edible?

In the early 1960s a remarkable series of experiments was performed on flatworms to test a new theory of memory. The theory predicted that every new memory corresponded to a new molecule of RNA which could be reproduced and stored throughout the body. It was tested on planarians (a kind of flatworm) which were conditioned to behave in a certain way, then cut in half and allowed to regenerate, and then cut in half again and allowed to regenerate again; the result of all this was a worm none of which had been present for the original conditioning. Remarkably, it still seemed to retain knowledge of what it had learnt. More remarkably still, later experiments seemed to confirm that if a worm was taught something, then minced and fed to another worm, the worm that ate it could ingest the knowledge. Sadly, the RNA theory of memory was then shown to be wrong, so the worm experiments were abandoned and other explanations were found to explain why knowledge had appeared to be edible.

In 2013, however, knowledge came back on the menu – for worms anyway – in experiments on stem cells at Tufts University, Massachusetts. The focus of this research was less on the mechanics of memory storage than on the way a worm can regenerate its head and brain when it has been cut in half. How does a cell know when and how to grow into a brain? The research did, however, confirm one finding from the work done half a century earlier: if you teach a worm something, then cut its brain off, it will remember what it learnt once the brain has grown back. In other words, the memory must be stored somehow in its ordinary cells rather than in the brain itself. Which raises again the question of whether a memory can be taken from the body of one creature and transplanted into another, possibly even by eating. Knowledge may be edible after all.

500. How old is the oldest flatworm?

Research at Nottingham University in 2012 was reported to have shown that the ability of worms to regenerate over and over again with no sign of ageing may indicate that they could live forever. After creating a colony of 20,000 worms from one original by successive division and regeneration, they reported that the evidence showed that the worms could be immortal.

If this is correct, it would suggest that we cannot hope to tell the age of a flatworm: it can regenerate over and over again and stay just as young as it was at the start. It follows that we cannot know how old the oldest flatworm is.

See also ANIMALS 19; BIOLOGY 63; LONGEVITY 279

ZEBRAS

501. Why do zebras have stripes?

When I was at school long, long ago, everyone knew why zebras had stripes: obviously it was for camouflage in the long grass. Actually that theory had been dismissed even in Darwin's time. There was simply not enough long grass around for it to be credible. Darwin himself had suggested that the beautiful stripes might be for mate selection, while Alfred Russel Wallace suggested that the stripes acted as a defence against predators. 'In twilight,' he wrote, '[zebras] are not at all conspicuous, the stripes of white and black so merging together into a grey tint it is difficult to see them at a little distance.'

Recently, two more theories have emerged. In 2014 a report was published showing that the amount of striping on zebras in different parts of Africa correlated with the prevalence of biting flies. The stripes, the researchers concluded, are there to confuse the flies. In 2015, however, another study appeared suggesting that the stripes had a valuable function helping the zebra keep cool in the African heat. The definition of the stripes on a zebra's back did not correlate with the number of tsetse flies at all, but with temperature and rainfall. Light and dark stripes heat up at different rates, and this may generate cooling currents of air across the zebra's skin.

Whether these currents really occur, however, has yet to be experimentally tested, so for the time being we just have to accept that the question of why zebras have stripes is just another thing that nobody knows.

ACKNOWLEDGEMENTS

Finding another 501 questions that nobody knows the answers to would have been impossible without the help and tolerance of all the people I have pestered to tell me their expert ignorance and those who have steered me towards unexpected troves of ignorance. I cannot name you all, partly for reasons of space, but also because I have forgotten many of your names, but my forgetfulness does not diminish my gratitude.

Of those whose names I can remember, I am particularly grateful to Prof Charles Spence for telling me about the joys of eating with one's fingers, and to my work experience student Kazio Bakowski for revealing his unexpected knowledge of Romanian gold.

My work has also been considerably eased by the increasing availability of several scientific journals on the Internet, of which I should give special mention to PLoS ONE (www.plosone.org) and Animal Behaviour (available online at: http://www.sciencedirect.com/science/journal/00033472), which have been an endless source of the latest findings and the latest areas in which we realize that further research is needed.

Most of all, though, I am indebted to all at Atlantic Books for having confidence in me to come up with another *501 Things That Nobody Knows*, particularly to James Nightingale for being so understanding when, as usual, I was late with the manuscript. Many thanks also to my editor, Ben Dupré, for his meticulous work in correcting my errors and suggesting areas where improvements were needed. Any mistakes that remain, however, are all my own work.

BIBLIOGRAPHY

This is just a selection of references that may be useful and interesting as sources of further information on the topics discussed. The references are ordered according to the number of the question in the preceding material.

7. Blackburn, K., Schirillo, J. (2012), 'Emotive hemispheric differences measured in real-life portraits using pupil diameter and subjective aesthetic preferences', *Experimental Brain Research*

15, 16. Mora, C. et al. (2011), 'How many species are there on Earth and in the ocean?', *PLoS Biology*

19. Bagemihl, Bruce (1999), *Biological Exuberance: Animal Homosexuality and Natural Diversity*, St Martin's Press

21. Hölldobler, B. and Wilson, E. (1994), *Journey to the Ants: A Story of Scientific Exploration*, Harvard University Press

26. Lison, M. et al. (1980), 'A polymorphism of the ability to smell urinary metabolites of asparagus', *British Medical Journal*

28. Acedo, L. (2014), 'The flyby anomaly: a case for strong gravitomagnetism?', *Advances in Space Research*

40. Crockford, C., Wittig, R. M., Seyfarth, R. M. and Cheney, D. L. (2007), 'Baboons eavesdrop to deduce mating opportunities', *Animal Behaviour*

41. Clapham, M., Nevin, O. T., Ramsey, A. D. and Rosell, F. (2013), 'The function of strategic tree selectivity in the chemical signalling of brown bears', *Animal Behaviour*

41. Clapham, M., Nevin, O. T., Ramsey, A. D. and Rosell, F., 'Food availability affects the scent marking frequencies of wild brown bears', in preparation for submission to *Animal Ecology*

43. Gross, H. J. et al. (2009), 'Number-based visual generalisation in the honeybee', *PLoS ONE*

44. Preece, K. and Beekman, M. (2014), 'Honeybee waggle dance error: adaption or constraint? Unravelling the c omplex dance language of honeybees', *Animal Behaviour*

45. Ruhul Amin, Kyi Kyi Than, Yong Jung Kwon (2009), 'Copulation duration of bumblebee Bombus terrestris (Hymenoptera: Apidae): impacts on polyandry and colony parameters', *Journal of Asian-Pacific Entomology*

68. Kiera, L. M. and Drummond, H. (2014), 'Extrapair behaviour reveals flexible female choosiness and mixed support for classic good genes in blue-footed boobies', *Animal Behaviour*

69. Heinig, A. et al. (2014), 'Male mate preferences in mutual mate choice: finches modulate their songs across and within male–female interactions', *Animal Behaviour*

72. Gilbert, S. F., 'Congenital human baculum deficiency: the generative bone of Genesis 2:21–23', *American Journal of Medical Genetics*

78. Rogers, L. J. (2000), 'Evolution of hemispheric specialization: advantages and disadvantages', *Brain and Language*

86. Parkin, M. et al. (2011), 'The fraction of cancer attributable to lifestyle and environmental factors in the UK in 2010', *British Journal of Cancer*

94. Ropars, J. K. et al. (2012), 'Sex in cheese: evidence for sexuality in the fungus *Penicillium roqueforti*', *PloS ONE*

98. Wilson, M. L. et al. (2014), 'Lethal aggression in *Pan* is better explained by adaptive strategies than human impacts', *Nature*

104. Messerli, F. H. (2012), 'Chocolate consumption, cognitive function, and Nobel Laureates', *New England Journal of Medicine*

104. Maurage, P., Heeren, A. and Pesenti, M. (2013), 'Does chocolate consumption really boost Nobel award chances? The peril of over-interpreting correlations in health studies', *Journal of Nutrition*

110. Wilson, P. S., (2014), 'Coffee roasting acoustics', *Journal of the Acoustical Society of America*

128. Costello, R. A. and Symes, L. B. (2014), 'Effects of anthropogenic noise on male signalling behaviour and female phonotaxis in Oecanthus tree crickets', *Animal Behaviour*

130. Platt, S. G. et al. (2013), 'Frugivory and seed dispersal by crocodilians: an overlooked form of saurochory?', *Journal of Zoology*

139. Bos, K. I. et al. (2014), 'Pre-Columbian mycobacterial genomes reveal seals as a source of New World human tuberculosis, *Nature*

147. Anglin, R. E., Samaan, Z. et al. (2013), 'Vitamin D deficiency and depression in adults: systematic review and meta-analysis', *British Journal of Psychiatry*

148. Tiira, K. et al. (2012), 'Environmental effects on compulsive tail chasing in dogs', *PLoS ONE*

149. Takaoka, A. et al. (2014), 'Do dogs follow behavioral cues from an unreliable human?', *Animal Cognition*

151. Marshall-Pescinia, S. et al. (2011), 'Social eavesdropping in the domestic dog', *Animal Behaviour*

151. Nitzschnera, M. et al. (2014), 'Side matters: potential mechanisms underlying dogs' performance in a social eavesdropping paradigm', *Animal Behaviour*

152. Ratcliffe, V. F. et al. (2014), 'Cross-modal discrimination of human gender by domestic dogs', *Animal Behaviour*

154. Shaffer, D. et al. (2004), 'How dogs navigate to catch frisbees', *Psychological Science*

171. Foerder, P. (2011), 'Insightful problem solving in an Asian elephant', *PLoS ONE*

171. Nissani, M. (2006), 'Do Asian elephants (*Elephas maximus*) apply causal reasoning to tool-use tasks?', *Journal of Experimental Psychology*

180. Sander, P. M. et al. (2011), 'Biology of the sauropod dinosaurs: the evolution of gigantism', *Biological Reviews*

186. Stokkan, K.-A. et al. (2013), 'Shifting mirrors: adaptive changes in retinal reflections to winter darkness in Arctic reindeer', *Proceedings of the Royal Society B*

189. Muntz, W. R. A. and Cronly-Dillon, J. R. (1966), 'Colour discrimination in goldfish, *Animal Behaviour*

190. Long, J. A. et al. (2015), 'Copulation in antiarch placoderms and the origin of gnathostome internal fertilization', *Nature*

193. Spence, C. and Piqueras-Fiszman, B. (2014), *The Perfect Meal*, Wiley

199. Kranjec, A. et al. (2010), 'A sinister bias for calling fouls in soccer', *PLoS ONE*

208. Glass, B. D., Maddox, W. T. and Love, B. C. (2013), 'Real-time strategy game training: emergence of a cognitive flexibility trait', *PLoS ONE*

210. Dias, B. G. and Ressler, K. J. (2013), 'Parental olfactory experience influences behaviour and neural structure in subsequent generations', *Nature*

211. Gierman, H. J. et al. (2014), 'Whole-genome sequencing of the world's oldest people', *PLoS ONE*

216. Deutsch, C. et al. (2014), 'Centennial changes in North Pacific anoxia linked to tropical trade winds', *Science*

225. Zipser, B. et al. (2013), 'Dimensions of animal personalities in guinea pigs', *Ethology*

236. Raspopovic, J. et al. (2014), 'Digit patterning is controlled by a Bmp-Sox9-Wnt Turing network modulated by morphogen gradients', *Science*

241. Gómez-Robles, A. et al. (2013), 'No known hominin species matches the expected dental morphology of the last common ancestor of Neanderthals and modern humans', *Proceedings of the National Academy of Sciences*

251. Kastak, C. R. et al. (2001), 'Equivalence classification by California sea lions using class-specific reinforcers', *Journal of the Experimental Analysis of Behavior*

265. Janis, C. M. et al. (2014), 'Locomotion in extinct giant kangaroos: were sthenurines hop-less monsters?', *PLoS ONE*

274. Balme, G. A. and Hunter, L. T. B. (2013), 'Why leopards commit infanticide', *Animal Behaviour*

296. Sansone, R. A. and Sansone, L. A. (2008), 'Pain, pain, go away: antidepressants and pain management', *Psychiatry*

301. Madden, J. R. et al. (2009), 'Why do meerkat pups stop begging?', *Animal Behaviour*

307. Francis, J. A. and Vavrus, S. J. (2012), 'Evidence linking Arctic amplification to extreme weather in mid-latitudes', *Geophysical Research Letters*

311. Screen, J. A. and Simmonds, I. (2014), 'Amplified mid-latitude planetary waves favour particular regional weather extremes', *Nature Climate Change*

313. Gabriel, S. I. et al. (2011), 'Of Mice and "Convicts": origin of the Australian house mouse, *Mus musculus*', *PloS ONE*

314. Walsh, P. T. et al. (2013), 'Faecal avoidance and selective foraging: do wild mice have the luxury to avoid faeces?', *Animal Behaviour*

319. Wheeler, B. C. (2009), 'Monkeys crying wolf? Tufted capuchin monkeys use anti-predator calls to usurp resources from conspecifics', *Proceedings of the Royal Society B*

322. Balababova, S. et al. (1992), 'First identification of drugs in Egyptian mummies', *Naturwissenschaften*

327. Lai, K.-M. et al. (2011), 'Propagation of respiratory aerosols by the vuvuzela', *PLoS ONE*

343. Andrade, C. and Srihari, B. S. (2001), 'A preliminary survey of rhinotillexomania in an adolescent sample', *Journal of Clinical Psychiatry*

347. Tricarico, E. et al. (2011), 'I know my neighbour: individual recognition in *Octopus vulgaris*', *PLoS ONE*

349. Mumm, C. A. S and Knörnschild, M. (2014), 'The vocal repertoire of adult and neonate giant otters', *PLoS ONE*

374. Furlan, E. et al. (2012), 'Is body size variation in the platypus (*Ornithorhynchus anatinus*) associated with environmental variables?', *Australian Journal of Zoology*

375. Lesku, J. A. et al. (2011), 'Ostriches sleep like platypuses', *PloS ONE*

376. Schlicht, E. J. et al. (2010), 'Human wagering behavior depends on opponents' faces', *PLoS ONE*

377. Owen, M. A. et al. (2015), 'An experimental investigation of chemical communication in the polar bear', *Journal of Zoology*

378. Sonne, C. et al. (2015), 'Penile density and globally used chemicals in Canadian and Greenland polar bears', *Environmental Research*

379. Sakai, M. et al. (2011), 'Do porpoises choose their associates? A new method for analyzing social relationships among cetaceans', *PLoS ONE*

385. Symmonds, M. et al. (2010), 'Metabolic state alters economic decision making under risk in humans', *PLoS ONE*

385. de Ridder, D. et al. (2014), 'Always gamble on an empty stomach: hunger is associated with advantageous decision making', *PLoS ONE*

392. Rygula, R. et al. (2012), 'Laughing rats are optimistic', *PLoS ONE*

406. Sanders, A. R. et al. (2014), 'Genome-wide scan demonstrates significant linkage for male sexual orientation', *Psychological Medicine*

409. Swami, V. and Tovee, M. J. (2013), 'Resource security impacts men's female breast size preferences', *PLoS ONE*

411. Stoet, G. (2013), 'Are women better than men at multi-tasking?', *BMC Psychology*

417. Hollander Jr, L. E. (2001), 'Unexpected weight gain transients at the moment of death', *Journal of Scientific Exploration*

418. Fossat, P. et al. (2014), 'Anxiety-like behavior in crayfish is controlled by serotonin', *Science*

423. Rattenborg, N. C. (2006), 'Do birds sleep in flight?', *Naturwissenschaften*

433. Pauli, J. N. (2014), 'A syndrome of mutualism reinforces the lifestyle of a sloth', *Proceedings of the Royal Society B*

437. Hoso, M. et al. (2010), 'A speciation gene for left–right reversal in snails results in anti-predator adaptation', *Nature Communications*

438. Fruson, L. et al. (2012), 'A flavonol present in cocoa enhances snail memory', *Journal of Experimental Biology*

439. Shine, R. et al. (1999), 'Are snakes right-handed? Asymmetry in hemipenis size and usage in gartersnakes', *Behavioral Ecology*

440. Bloch, E. (2001), 'Hemlock poisoning and the death of Socrates: did Plato tell the truth?', *Journal of the International Plato Society*

445. Nørgaard, T. et al. (2012), 'Nocturnal homing: learning walks in a wandering spider?', *PLoS ONE*

446. McLeod, P. and Dienes, Z. (1996), 'Do fielders know where to go to catch the ball, or only how to get there?', *Journal of Experimental Psychology*

454. Stetson, C. et al. (2007), 'Does time really slow down during a frightening event?', *PLoS ONE*

458. Dorland, A. et al. (2014), 'Do roads reduce painted turtle (*Chrysemys picta*) populations?', *PLoS ONE*

484. Jiang, C. and Galm, M. (2014), 'The economic benefit of being blonde: a study of waitress tip earnings based on their hair color', *Journal of Behavioral Studies in Business*

493. Suselbeek, L. et al. (2014), 'Scatter hoarding and cache pilferage by superior competitors: an experiment with wild boar, *Sus scrofa*', *Animal Behaviour*

498. Dingemanse, M. et al. (2013), 'Is "Huh?" a universal word? Conversational infrastructure and the convergent evolution of linguistic items', *PLoS ONE*

499. Ziegler, R. A. (1963), 'Is knowledge edible? A study of conditioned responses in *Planaria*', *Worm Runner's Digest*

499. Shomrat, T. and Levin, M. (2013), 'An automated training paradigm reveals long-term memory in planaria and its persistence through head regeneration', *Journal of Experimental Biology*

501. Caro, T. et al. (2014), 'The function of zebra stripes', *Nature Communications*

501. Larison, B. et al. (2015), 'How the zebra got its stripes: a problem with too many solutions', *Royal Society Open Science*

INDEX

Entries are followed by item numbers

Abraham 83

actresses 453

acupuncture 294

addiction 58, 209, 299

Aesop 1

aggression 20, 98, 326, 386

albatross 19

Alcatraz 129

Alchemy 2, 201, 280, 372, 405

alcohol 3, 31, 58, 87

Alexander the Great 168

Alexandria 168

Alfred the Great 176

Allerton Cope 462

Alzheimer's disease 143

Amomongo 220

amygdala 74

anatomy 4–7, 78, 103, 162, 237, 269

Andromeda 315–7

Anne Boleyn 230

angiosperm 179

ant 20–1

antidepressants 296

Antikythera mechanism 403

antimatter 56, 205

aphrodisiac 105, 410

appendix 6

Arbuthnot, J. 26

archaeopteryx 64

Aristotle 1, 487

Ark of the Covenant 394

armadillo 37, 429

arsenic 337

Arthur, King 333

Arthur I, Duke of Brittany 323

asparagus 26

Asperger's syndrome 298

asteroid 48, 64, 111, 181, 212

asthma 153, 295

astronauts 73, 195

Atilla 31–2

Austen, Jane 33–4

Austen-Leigh, J. E. 33

Australia 35, 43–4, 69, 156, 240, 265, 313, 374, 400, 419, 422, 451

Autism 36, 298

avocado 37, 410

Aztecs 8, 9, 38–9, 105, 410

Babcock, M. A. 31

baboons 40

Bacon, Francis 487

bacteria 4, 63, 178, 198, 295, 344, 489

baculum 72, 378, 486

Baghdad 305

Baiae 258

Bagemihl, B. 19

Baltic Sea 381

baseball 154, 446

basketball 77

Basque 383

bat 165, 167, 429, 486

ears 4, 103, 162

Earth 21, 30, 48, 117, 120, 163–4, 181, 212, 216, 253, 286, 304, 308, 399, 443–4, 488,

earthquake 48, 293, 479, 488

Eastwood, C. 129

eavesdropping 40, 151

Ebola 165–7

echolocation 157

Ecuador 482–3

Edward II 134

Edward VII 188

Egypt 83, 168, 255, 322, 382, 394, 407, 450

Einstein, A. 54, 122, 126, 169–70, 172–3, 223, 292, 317, 362–3

El Niño 400

Eleanor of Aquitaine 187

elephant 37, 171, 242, 450, 492

energy 27, 54–6, 71, 117, 120–2, 124, 126, 172–4, 309, 370–2, 390, 463–4, 466–7, 487

epilepsy 426

Eriksson, Leif 481

Esther, Book of 50

Euler, Leonard 287, 289, 291

Eusebius 106

Everest, Mount 321

evolution 4, 6, 19, 78, 178–84, 190, 210, 221, 234–43, 253, 268–9, 271, 274, 283, 320, 329, 354–5, 358, 386, 408, 424, 492

execution 131, 159, 219, 224, 475, 495, 497

eyes 84, 133, 160, 185–7, 239, 423, 425

face 7, 25, 74, 351, 376

Fawcett, P. 82

FBI 93, 129

fear 148, 210, 418

feathers 64, 180, 183, 354

Fermat, Pierre de 289

Fermi, Enrico 253

Fersen, count Axel von 202

fertility 3, 87

Feynman, Richard 369–70

finch 66, 69

fine-structure constant 370

fingers 194, 236, 239, 343, 344

firearms 326

fish 78, 143, 155–6, 189–91, 282, 399, 400

flavanols 104

Fletcher, John 413, 415

flies 15, 143, 243, 501

fleas 15, 148

Florida 157, 192

flowers 179

fly-by anomaly 28

Flynn effect 249

football 199–200

foreign accent syndrome 384

France 67, 134–5, 187, 201–2, 323, 394, 407

Frank, Anne 339

Franklin, B. 26, 473

free will 77, 365, 387

French Revolution 202, 224, 330

friendly numbers 290

frisbee 154

frog 203, 329, 345

Fulcanelli 2,

Gainsborough, T. 24

galaxies 27, 54, 56, 118–9, 121, 124, 173–4, 253, 315–6, 350, 390, 464

garlic 95

Gell-Mann, Murray 206

A NOTE ABOUT THE AUTHOR

William Hartston graduated in mathematics at Cambridge but never completed his PhD in number theory because he spent too much time playing chess. This did, however, lead to his winning the British Chess Championship in 1973 and 1975 and writing a number of chess books and newspaper chess columns.

When William and mathematics amicably separated, he worked for several years as an industrial psychologist specializing in the construction and interpretation of personality tests. After ten years writing a wide variety of columns for the *Independent*, he moved to the *Daily Express*, where he has been writing the Beachcomber column of surreal humour since 1998. In addition to writing about chess, he has written books on useless information, numbers, dates and bizarre academic research, including sexology.

Recently, his skills at sitting on a sofa watching television have been appreciated by viewers of the TV programme *Gogglebox*, but he has still not decided what he wants to be when he grows up.